Power, Resistance, and Literacy

Writing for Social Justice

A volume in
Critical Constructions: Studies on Education and Society

Series Editor:
Curry Stephenson Malott, *Queens College/CUNY*

Critical Constructions:
Studies on Education and Society

Curry Stephenson Malott, Series Editor

*Parental Choice? A Critical Reconsideration of
Choice and the Debate about Choice* (2010)
by P. L Thomas

*Critical Pedagogy in the Twenty-First Century:
A New Generation of Scholars* (2011)
edited by Curry Stephenson Malott and
Bradley Porfilio

*Power, Resistance, and Literacy:
Writing for Social Justice* (2011)
by Julie A. Gorlewski

Power, Resistance, and Literacy

Writing for Social Justice

by

Julie A. Gorlewski
State University of New York at New Paltz

INFORMATION AGE PUBLISHING, INC.
Charlotte, NC • www.infoagepub.com

Library of Congress Cataloging-in-Publication Data

ISBNs: 978-1-61735-405-2 (PB)
       978-1-61735-406-9 (HC)
       978-1-61735-407-6 (E-book)

Printed in the United States of America

Dedication

For Joshi, for kindness

Praise for *Power, Resistance and Literacy: Writing for Social Justice:*

Engaging ethnographic investigation of the experiences and practices of writing instruction over a full year in a White working class high school located in a first ring suburb, Julie Gorlewski uncovers the processes through which even well intended teachers reproduce social class. Arguing that neoliberalism and the new capitalism have all but silenced the collective discourse of the White working class with regard to their labor power, Gorlewski suggests that young people must reconstruct their identities in a society saturated by the rhetoric of equality yet surrounded by schools that reproduce dominant social relations. A model of the ways in which sociocultural and sociostructural work can be linked, Gorlewski both ethnographically "makes the familiar strange" while simultaneously offering far ranging yet concrete ideas about the teaching and learning of writing. *Power, Resistance and Literacy: Writing for Social Justice* is a "must read" for all those interested in the reshaping of social class; youth identity; and the ever widening range of theoretical and practical issues that confront teachers and students as they engage the teaching and learning of writing in these new times.

Lois Weis
State University of New York Distinguished Professor
Author of *Class Reunion: The Remaking of the White Working Class*

CONTENTS

ACKNOWLEDGMENTS

No composition is comprised of one voice. My gratitude to all those whose shared voices are reflected in the construction of this work is beyond words, but here words must suffice. First, I am profoundly grateful to have had the privilege of working with Lois Weis, who perfects the balance between evaluation and encouragement. She embodies a level of pedagogy and scholarship that I will always strive to emulate. Thanks are also due to Greg Dimitriadis, whose insights contributed immensely to this work as well as to my thinking about its further applications. Suzanne Miller provided essential perspectives into theoretical considerations and pushed me to think deeply about the implications of policy in real classrooms. In addition, I am thankful for the participation of Robert Stevenson, whose assistance in the early phases of this project was significant. Finally, I am greatly indebted to Curry Malott for his confidence in and time spent on this project, as well as to Ira Shor; his inspiration and vision has created the possibility for a book such as this one to be written.

This work would not have been possible without the people at Pontiac High. I sincerely appreciate the efforts of administrators, teachers, and support staff who offered encouragement, collaboration, and material assistance throughout this project. While there are many, many people who should be named here, I am especially grateful to Gail, who has been steadfast in her energy and perspective. Pontiac High's students, whose presence sustained my purpose, also deserve recognition. Teacher and student participants were invaluable in the completion of the project, and I am particularly grateful for their generosity of spirit. Their words are the soul of this work.

Thank you to my dear friends: Tricia, Ellen, John and Rich who provide physical, psychological and emotional sustenance; Diane and Tim, whose lives exemplify enduring passion and commitment; Kate and Tom, consummate educators; and the Depew girls, who have not given up on me yet!

I am enormously grateful to my remarkable family, from whom I learned to question assumptions and for whom explanations are never necessary. Thanks especially to my parents, Dawn and Jim Ryan, genuine models of what is most important in life. My children, Jeffrey, Jacob, Jonathan, and Jennie Lee, keep me grounded in the present. Each is a constant source of surprise and delight. My admiration and love for them are limitless. Devotion to my grandchildren, Noah, Adison, Benjamin, and Joshua, forces me to consider the future and challenges me to find hope there. And to my husband, David, whose belief makes all things possible: thank you for the hours, days, months, and years—yesterday, today, and tomorrow. I love you.

FOREWORD

Ira Shor

Julie Gorlewski has written an outstanding critical ethnography. Her close study of one high school reveals painfully reduced conditions for teaching and learning due to invasive testing regimes. Her classroom observations at "Pontiac High," described as a "white working-class first-ring suburban high school," generate compelling insights into the predicaments of public education in this age of runaway testing:

> Students in public schools serving poor and working-class students are inundated by the effects of high-stakes examinations. Teachers are demoralized and deprofessionalized, and students [given]substandard curricular and pedagogical experiences. These effects are clearly articulated by students and teachers in a working-class high school that provided the setting for the investigation.

Such is the distressing outcome of NO CHILD LEFT BEHIND (NCLB), the signature education reform of the Bush Administration passed in 2001 with major support from Democrats in Congress. This destructive bipartisan education policy continued despite the 2008 election of Barack Obama, who promised "audacity" and "change." Obama's Secretary of Education Arne Duncan has been doggedly pursuing his enhanced version of NCLB renamed RACE TO THE TOP. Duncan, who brought a strident corporate outlook to the Department of Education, would do well to read soon this book by Julie Gorlewski to find out just how mistaken he and President Obama are in their business-model education goals. Julie's line of research on what happens when testing displaces teaching and when rote memorization displaces understanding is persuasive: "In this study, data analysis indicates that dialogic pedagogical interactions are a rare phenomenon. In general, students(and student writers)repeat the words and ideas of authorities(teachers and texts)." Mere repetition of prescribed information is hardly education but rather is ritual mimicry on command.

In this regard, Gorlewski opens Chapter 4 with a telling quote: "High-stakes testing often harms students' daily experience of learning, displaces more thoughtful and creative curriculum, diminishes the emotional well-being of educators and children, and unfairly damages the life-chances of members of vulnerable groups."(NCTE, 2007) She uncovers at Pontiac what could be called "minimalist education"—the result of high-stakes testing reducing learning to low-scale items. At Pontiac, English teacher June Summers in Chapter 6 calls this minimalism "Reuse, recycle, regurgitate." Against this narrow and silencing process, another vision of schooling is asserted by Gorlewski, a "social constructivist" and "sociocultural" one, where teaching and learning are student-centered, where dialogic inquiry is the base strategy, where broad subject matters of concern to students drive the syllabus, where unrestricted literacy in writing-rich classrooms is the norm, and where sequentially-designed projects which draw students into deeper understandings is the expectation. As Gorlewski suggests, opposing narrow behavioral methods with rich learning goals requires repositioning students "as participants in learning, constructors of knowledge and meaning in which their own experiences figure prominently." These alternative ideals for pedagogy are especially developed in Chapter 7 and Chapter 8, which explore dialogics as key to enfranchising students as stakeholders generally in the learning process and specifically in the writing class.

Gorlewski uses well Foucault's notion that power is not a commodity or possession but rather is a relationship, a process, and an activity that circulates in social structures and disciplinary lattices. Foucault insisted that dominant power relations not only produce compliance but also resistance. Student encounters with behaviorist schooling, teacher-talk and high-stakes testing provoke resistance to knowledge-making and literate practice, Gorlewski argues. How can critical alternatives deal with this conditioned withdrawal of students from academic learning? Gorlewski proposes "resistance literacy" where "first, students can be provided with increased controls over their own choices vis-à-vis literacy to minimize their desire to resist school and schooling in ways that inhibit potential empowerment. Second, educators can capitalize on resistance that does emerge to develop instructional activities that build on the critique and critical thinking that resistance expresses. That is, tap into resistance as a means of engaging students. She proceeds to unpack these alternatives and the class-based obstacles to their realization. All in all, then, Julie Gorlewski has composed a study of schooling which brings critical theory and practice productively together, from which all educators can derive compelling lessons on what needs to be done in this troubled nation to stop public education from being run off a cliff.

Ira Shor
City University of New York Graduate Center
March, 2011

PREFACE

DO THE FISH SEE THE WATER?

Public schools in the United States today are engulfed in the effects of national and state reform initiatives. Annual tests, publicized rankings, and increased accountability coupled with decreasing resources have contributed to the construction of a culture in which existing power relations are reinforced—and opportunities to hear voices of resistance and dissent are diminished. The dominant, pervasive nature of these reforms absorbs tremendous amounts of energy from education systems, requiring time, effort, and attention that is necessarily subtracted from other endeavors. Since 1999, when mandated high-stakes tests were introduced in New York State, concentration on the administration and scoring of assessments, and analyzing data connected to them, has come to seem a natural and normal part of public schooling—part of the everyday culture of the educational experience of teachers and students. What's more, every school year brings to the profession new teachers—products of a public education system themselves—whose only experiences of schooling involve mandated high-stakes standardized assessments. They may complain about various aspects of the assessments, but they are unlikely to question their existence or—like the fish with respect to the water in which they are immersed—perceive larger, sociocultural effects of standardized reform on themselves and their students. In fact, they may find it difficult to imagine a world without standards and assessments.

This is in no way meant as a criticism of public educators, who are swimming vigorously in an attempt to prevent their students—particularly those who attend schools in poor and working-class communities—from drowning. A significant consequence of increased top-down accountability is that educators are forced to put the requirements of reform ahead of the needs of their students. President George W. Bush introduced, with bipartisan support, the No Child Left Behind (NCLB) legislation which established a system of mandatory assessments, rankings, and reporting requirements. Although the disproportionately deleterious effects of standardized tests on marginalized populations have been well-documented, NCLB was adopted. Educators, forced into compliance, identified many flaws in the legislation and its implementation. When President Bush's term ended, educators hoped that a new national administration might signify a real (and less Orwellian) commitment to social justice. Unfortunately, we have been disappointed. In fact, President Obama's *Race to the Top* initiative has placed states in direct competition for precious, essential funding – creating winners and losers in a way that is rhetorically stark; a "race" evokes the image of many participants who are "left behind."

Participants in the system of public education are suffering the effects of standardized reform, effects that influence the daily interactions of teachers and students in ways that are almost invisible. Our water has become contaminated; but how can we resist our very environment?

ETHNOGRAPHY: A LENS FOR INVESTIGATING

This book is based on a study which investigated students' and teachers' experiences and practices of writing instruction over the course of a school year. Critical ethnography, which explores the lived experiences of participants as they navigate social structures, provided the foundation for the study. Because it seeks to "make the familiar strange" (Erickson, Florio, & Buschman, 1980), critical ethnography is an ideal means of understanding an environment in which participants are immersed. Methods included in-depth interviews, participant and nonparticipant observation, and document analysis. While a variety of factors affecting students and teachers experiences and practices of literacy emerged, the most significant by far involved high-stakes standardized testing.

By discussing the results of this study, this book will reveal how the role of current reform initiatives exacerbate social inequality by limiting the imaginative possibilities of poor and working-class students through their experiences of writing and literacy. Students in public schools serving poor and working-class students are inundated by the effects of high-stakes examinations. Teachers are demoralized and deprofessionalized, and students suffer substandard curricular and pedagogical experiences.

These effects are clearly articulated by students and teachers in the working-class high school that provided the setting for the investigation.

High-stakes mandated tests, which were further entrenched in the United States by NCLB and seem destined to be reinforced by the new administration's *Race to the Top* educational initiative, have intensified administrative support for alienating, commodifying approaches to writing and writing instruction. This is particularly problematic because experiences of writing connect directly to experiences of thinking and, therefore, identity construction. That is, students who are not exposed to empowering literacies develop identities that are disempowered and, therefore, incapable of challenging the status quo. Moreover, restricted experiences of literacies limit people's imaginative possibilities.

Also noteworthy is the effect of high-stakes testing regimes on the interrelations between students and teachers. Although the school in this study serves a predominantly white, working-class community that is similar to the ones in which the teachers were raised and educated, there is little sense of solidarity or collective agency among the two groups. Teachers resent being judged on the basis of students' performance on standardized assessments. They are deprofessionalized and their roles are oriented toward working-class norms as decision-making about what counts as knowledge and learning is situated in the state. Students feel alienated by content that is meaningless and test-based pedagogies that are disempowering.

SWIMMING UPSTREAM TOGETHER
COLLECTIVE RESISTANCE

While these findings are disturbing, critical theory provides a foundation for seeking hope. Because critical theory incorporates inquiry and dialogue, this theoretical framework opens a space where resistance—which Foucault (1983) asserts is an integral component of power relations—can be revealed and examined. In this case, the study exposed glimmers of resistance, spaces in the structure of schooling where students and teachers critique the system and suggest ways of subverting the negative effects of neoliberal reforms through dialogic, empowering, culturally responsive pedagogies.

Teachers in the school studied are experiencing deprofessionalization and, as they lose control and become alienated from their labor, are being re-socialized toward norms of working-class identity. While this may result in replication of power relations historically prevalent in working-class schools, it also reveals a space of praxis that offers the possibility for seeking solidarity. If teachers can seek to learn about and *from* the culture of their working-class students (with the intent of developing connections that foster a space for constructive resistance to destructive neoliberal reform), pedagogical and social progress might occur. The collective power of working-class resistance is latent in this new economy and the reconstruction of a white working-class identity that includes teachers and students as partners rather than adversaries is an exciting prospect.

Social institutions are powerful and self-sustaining. Experiences of students and teachers, however, reveal glimmers of resistance that illuminate spaces of praxis. To effect reform, all participants in the process of education must seek to explore and inhabit those spaces. Collective resistance, achieved through dialogic pedagogies that build on understandings of resistance and power through critical theory, can cultivate theoretical and material spaces of praxis that can enhance possibilities for social justice.

ORGANIZATION OF THE BOOK

To explore these ideas, this book is organized as follows:

Part I, Power, invokes Foucault's conception of resistance as an integral component of power. Since we know it exists, even in the most authoritative and hegemonic institutional structures, we can develop and use it to foster social justice, rather than allow it to remain marginalized in ways that perpetuate the status quo. Part I includes Chapters 1 through 5.

Chapter 1, titled "Introduction: From Neoliberalism to Dialogicality" explores the social, political, and economic effects of neoliberal philosophies on schools through standardized reform initiatives and discusses the connections among neoliberal philosophies, standards-based reform initiatives, and the mandated assessments that consistently accompany these reforms. Although state and federal reform strategies target students most in need of advocacy, the particulars of the reforms tend to exacerbate inequities, exposing students in poor and working-class schools to restricted curricula and test-based pedagogies that are associated with low achievement and limited life chances. In this chapter, I review research in the areas of high-stakes testing, learning, and literacy as well as the interrelations among discourse, power, and language; and, finally, I propose dialogicality as a means of ameliorating inequalities.

Chapter 2, "The Study," provides a description of the ethography, with particular emphasis the theoretical underpinnings of the research. These include connections among neoliberalism, class, and the economy. It also includes a discussion of data collection and analysis for this critical ethnographic study.

Chapter 3, "Social Class, Writing Instruction and Identity Construction" explores the complex interrelations between and among writing,

writing instruction, schooling, and identity. Teachers and students—like all human beings—influence and are influenced by the cultures they inhabit. Experiences of schooling and writing, therefore, have significant effects on the abilities of teachers to provide empowering experiences of writing for their students.

Chapter 4, "High-Stakes Testing: Social and Emotional Effects," examines the demoralization and anxiety connected with the high-stakes testing that dominates curriculum and instruction in schools. Teacher deprofessionalization is described in the voices of both teachers and students.

Chapter 5, "Restricted Literacies," explains that the types of writing privileged by examination-based instruction are not conducive to dialogic, transformational literacies. Instead, students repeat memorized formats and restate information provided in authoritative texts—both characteristics of domesticating writing instruction typical of working class schools (Finn, 1999) and consistent with a structuralist epistemology. The narrations of students and teachers at Pontiac High provide evidence that printcentric, linear literacies predominate. Personnel and practices at Pontiac High cling to a structuralist epistemology in which examinations drive curricula and instruction, leaving little space for the literacy culture that exists beyond the school walls.

Part II: Resistance

This section of the book will explore the possibilities of collective action as a means of transforming the experiences of schooling for students who attend public schools in poor and working-class communities.

Chapter 6 is titled "Teaching or Selling Out?" As an aspect of culture and an instrument of discourse, language reveals and reinscribes social class in ways that are invisible to those whose norms are dominant. Making these norms visible is an essential first step toward transformation and toward critical literacy. It will also reveal, through the words of teachers, the dilemmas facing educators who understand the negative effects of current reform policies.

Chapter 7, "Writing Instruction: What 'Is' and What 'Ought to be,' " explores narrations of students and teachers who are openly critical of the experiences of writing and writing instruction that are dominant in this school. This chapter situates these narrations in the context of current scholarship as well as juxtaposing them with sociocultural, dialogical approaches to learning.

Chapter 8, "Hints at Hope, Glimmers of Resistance," will reveal the narrations of students and teachers who condemn of the effects of neoliberal policies on their classroom practices. This chapter will delve into the glimmers of resistance narrated by teachers and students who critique that status quo represented by instruction that mirrors and is driven by high-stakes assessments. In addition, it will examine the possibilities of a sociocultural understanding of learning, in which teachers partner with students in the learning process.

Chapter 9, "Resistance Literacy: Two Approaches," is devoted to the implementation of critical, dialogic approaches to writing and literacies, approaches intended to interrupt the hegemonic influences that perpetuate social reproduction by capitalizing on the potential for collective agency among the students and teachers who populate and educate the working classes. This chapter will present practical examples of instructional activities in which students and teachers seek to uncover the assumptions of accepted, authoritative texts. These instructional activities are linked to critical theory and, therefore, merge the sociological and pedagogical aspects of the field of education.

Chapter 10 is titled "Looking Forward: Empowerment, Social Justice, and Collective Agency." This chapter will consider the implications of empowering students and teachers in working-class communities with respect to learning, literacies, knowledge, and thinking, as well as the possibilities of solidarity with respect to the achievement of social justice.

REFERENCES

Erickson, F., Florio, S., & Buschman, J. (1980). *Fieldwork in educational research* (Occasional Paper No. 36). East Lansing: Michigan State University, Institute for Research on Teaching.

Foucault, M. (1983). The subject and power. In H. L. Dreyfus & P. Rabinow (Eds.), *Michel Foucault: Beyond structuralism and hermeneutics*. Chicago, IL: University of Chicago.

PART I

POWER

CHAPTER 1

INTRODUCTION

From Neoliberalism to Dialogicality

This book is based on an ethnographic study, grounded in critical theory, which links aspects of social class, schooling, and identity through teachers' and students' experiences of writing instruction. Such complex linkages involve elements relating to the economy, politics, pedagogies, and literacies. Although intersections among these socially constructed concepts are inherent and ubiquitous, they may not be obvious. I will begin, therefore, by standing on the shoulders of scholarly giants, whose ideas help make explicit connections among neoliberalism, schooling, discourse, and dialogicality. It may seem questionable to make connections between neoliberal political philosophies and the experiences of writing in a working-class school. However, an understanding of the principles in which new capitalism and neoliberalism are based, as well as a critical consideration of the role of assessment technologies in the development and implementation of particular pedagogies, makes these associations visible.

NEOLIBERALISM AND CLASS IN THE NEW CAPITALISM

Shifts in the development and application of capitalism have had significant effects on the lives of people in the United States. Gee (2004) refers to old capitalism as "the sort of capitalism we associate with the great

Power, Resistance, and Literacy: Writing for Social Justice, pp. 3–18
Copyright © 2011 by Information Age Publishing
All rights of reproduction in any form reserved.

economic success after World War II" (p. 95). The old capitalism allowed working-class laborers to earn incomes that enabled them to purchase most of the commodities they produced (p. 95). Principles of efficiency epitomized by "Taylorism" (p. 95) required compliance from workers in completing repetitive tasks; thinking was not necessarily part of their occupations. As Gee notes, this mentality was paralleled in working-class schools which, at the time, prepared students for manufacturing jobs.

> In the old capitalism, knowledge and control was situated at the top (the bosses) not at the bottom (the workers).... This became, too, pretty much how knowledge was viewed in schools: knowledge was a system of expertise, owned by specialists and imposed top-down on students. (p. 95)

The highly competitive labor market in the new capitalism requires much more from its work force in terms of knowledge and expertise. According to Gee (2004), "new capitalist workplaces...require empowered employees who can think for themselves and who think of themselves as smart and creative people" (p. 102). People who do not develop the skills and dispositions necessary for success in the new capitalism may be relegated to jobs marked by low wages, minimal benefits, and instability. A key issue in this study involves whether and how principles of the new capitalism are manifest in public schools. In general, neoliberal philosophies enacted in the form of high-stakes tests undermine students and teachers' perceptions of themselves as autonomous, intelligent, creative intellectuals.

New capitalism is marked by diminishing government investment in public services intended to benefit the poor and working class (Beach Parks, Thein, & Lensmire, 2007). Gee (2004) contends that the New Capitalism is grounded in the philosophy of neoliberalism. He describes this philosophy as follows:

> According to the neoliberal philosophy, everything should be on a (free) market and people ought to get what (and only what) they can pay for (Hayek, 1996; Sowell, 1996; von Mises, 1997). If, for humane reasons, there has to be, within a given area, something "off market" (i.e., free or subsidized), then it must be "basics," otherwise it will encourage people to back away from the market and disrupt it. (p. 110)

To be successful in this era of new capitalism, workers must construct identities which can affiliate with "socially and economically distinctive types of knowledge, information, skills, experiences, and lifestyles" (Gee, 2004, p. 109). It is generally understood among scholars that schools— even excellent schools—cannot alone provide the experiences for young people to develop the cultural capital necessary to compete in the new economy. Schools that offer a curriculum oriented toward "the basics" will not provide students with the skills they need to be successful upon graduation. Academic language and skills are not sufficient for maintaining class status, much less for achieving upward mobility. Gee explains how neoliberalism and the new capitalism affect children who depend on public schooling.

> The great barrier today for many poor and minority children ... is that mastery of academic language and affiliation with school-based values is necessary for success in the new capitalist world, but now this is only a small part of the whole picture. At the same time, the recent standards, testing, and accountability regime has committed schools to supplying all children, especially poor children, with no more (and no less) than "the basics." (p. 109)

Workers in the new capitalism require more than basic academic literacy practices in order to thrive. However, the structuralist perspective dominant in this school privileges old literacies and canonical content over performance; therefore, students are not encouraged to develop competence at performing new literacies in school. Data analysis in this study reveals that New York State's standards-based reform initiative has, in fact, contributed to a focus on basic skills rather than tasks that require higher order cognitive engagement.

STATE REFORM AND HIGH-STAKES TESTS

In the mid-1990s, New York State anticipated the political movement that later engulfed public schools through the federal legislation titled No Child Left Behind (United States Department of Education, 2003). Portending developments enacted through this legislation, the state's education department implemented common, comprehensive learning standards meant to drive local district curricula. In addition, the state unveiled a plan to attach the standards to mandatory assessments for students, beginning in the area of English Language Arts (ELA).

Consequences for students and educators were significant and comprehensive. In addition to gauging individual student performance, tests at all levels were designed to measure schools' progress towards meeting the state's established standards and to rank schools according to student achievement. Scores and rankings were published and distributed by districts, the state education department, and media outlets; and schools with inadequate scores and unacceptable levels of improvement were threatened with the possibility of being designated as a "School Under Regents Review" (SURR). Identified SURR schools would be required to show rapid, significant improvement on standardized assessments or face state takeover (New York State Education Department, 1999; United States Department of Education, 2003).

Prior to this reform, taking classes that culminated in state examinations (called "Regents" exams) was optional for students in New York State public schools. In general, public school students planning to attend college elected to complete a more challenging curriculum and earn a "Regents" diploma by passing the required examinations in each of four core subject areas (mathematics, English language arts, social studies, and science) plus a foreign language. Students who did not choose to take Regents examinations could earn a local diploma by completing a less rigorous curriculum that was not tied to state examinations. New York State's reform effectively abolished the dual track system by removing the lower track and eliminating the possibility of earning a local diploma. Since 2001, students in New York State's public schools must score at least 65% on five Regents exams in order to earn a diploma. Because it removed the lower track, this development was introduced and continues to be promoted as "raising the bar" for disadvantaged students. It is clear, however, that mandated high-stakes examinations have disproportionately deleterious effects on students from backgrounds marked by poverty, as well as those who represent racial and ethnic minorities (Dorn, 2007; Gunzenhauser, 2006; Nichols & Berliner, 2007; Orfield & Kornhaber, 2001). Standardized assessments exhibit class bias (Finn, 1999; Giroux, 2003). Yet the fact that poor and working-class students tend to perform worse than middle-class students on standardized assessment is ultimately exploited as justification for what amounts to politically and educationally sanctioned social reproduction.

Since New York State's Regents assessments impact graduation, they fit the category of a "high-stakes" assessment, that is, one that affects promotion, commencement, or admission (Dorn, 2007; Nichols & Berliner, 2007). Although consequences of the state's standards-based reform have affected all those involved in the public education system, assessments were immediately high-stakes for students. In June 1999, passing the commencement level ELA examination (intended for students in Grade 11) became a graduation requirement for the high school graduating class of 2000. Examinations in other subject areas were phased in so that the graduating class of 2005 was required to pass five Regents examinations in order to earn a diploma.

Nationally, the trend is toward more standardized, assessment-based curricula (Apple, 1996). The federal No Child Left Behind (NCLB) legislation requires standardized testing from Grades 3-11; districts' federal funding is contingent on students' test scores. The Obama administration is advocating for the adoption of common core standards by all states, an action which portends a national curriculum and, very likely, assessments that are linked to it. Federal and state legislation that legitimates testing as the central measure of learning undermines the ability of educational institutions to inspire excellence and achieve social justice. These mandates and the associated consequences have significant effects on how students and teachers experience schooling.

HIGH-STAKES TESTS, LEARNING, AND LITERACY

Many scholars have argued that it is through evaluation that definitions of knowledge become realized. Bernstein (1973) explicates associations between and among curriculum, instruction, and assessment: "Curriculum defines what counts as valid knowledge, pedagogy defines what counts as a valid transmission of knowledge, and evaluation defines what counts as a valid realization of knowledge on the part of the taught" (p. 85). He notes the inextricable, recursive connections among curriculum, pedagogy, and evaluation. Bernstein's analysis illustrates the *constructed* nature of knowledge by illuminating the fact that curriculum, pedagogy, and evaluation *define* what counts as knowledge. "Knowledge" is not empirically determined; it is a result of many sets of decisions at many levels of educational systems. High-stakes standardized tests, however, situate what is defined as knowledge squarely in the authority of the state, rather than in local decisions of teachers and learners. Data analysis indicates that, in the working-class high school where the study took place, teachers and students have adopted the language of state assessments in constructing the curriculum and describing what counts as learning, achievement and effective writing.

A wealth of scholarship has shown that high-stakes examinations have a reductive effect on curriculum and instruction (Hillocks, 2002; Ketter & Pool, 2001; Neill & Gayler, 2001; Nelson, 2001; Nichols & Berliner, 2007; Popham, 2001). Neill and Gayler (2001) "conclude that states with high school graduation exams place more emphasis on testing throughout the system, and that this emphasis has a strong impact on curricula and instruction" (p. 111). Dorn (2007) and Nichols and Berliner (2007) demonstrate that high-stakes testing often results in a pedagogical orientation toward test-preparation, a narrowing of curriculum, and an instructional emphasis on lower-level cognitive tasks. In educational systems dominated by high-stakes assessment, curriculum is narrowed to represent only the knowledge and skills that will be assessed, and critical thinking is not emphasized because standardized examinations emphasize questions that measure low-level cognitive skills. Data analysis upholds these assertions and also indicates that high-stakes testing reinforces in teachers and students a sense of alienation from curricula.

Critics maintain that high-stakes assessments serve to perpetuate current class structures by maintaining skill gaps and controlling ideology, particularly beliefs in individualism, meritocracy, and what counts as knowledge (Dorn, 2003; Hillocks, 2002). Gunzenhauser (2006) extends this concept, asserting that high-stakes examinations redefine not just knowledge, but the identities of learners and teachers who are forced to perform according to their specifications. Popham states that: "In an evidence-oriented enterprise, those who control the evidence-gathering mechanisms control the entire enterprise" (as cited in Smith, 1986, p. 130). This is relevant in that the basis of assessment—which is the driving element of definitions of knowledge—has "progressed" from student/teacher, to school, to district, to state, to federal control.

Dorn (2007) and Nichols and Berliner (2007) describe teachers' experiences of deprofessionalization as a result of high-stakes testing. Teachers inundated by the rhetoric and results of high-stakes assessments lose autonomy in both symbolic and material terms. Relationships between students and teachers are affected because teachers' livelihoods are unfairly linked to student performance on standardized examinations and students perceive teachers as disempowered by state-assessments (Dorn, 2007; Nichols & Berliner, 2007). In addition, students and teachers suffer anxiety related to high-stakes tests. Data analysis demonstrates the prevalence of these perceptions among teachers and students who participated in the study.

Standardized curricula and the associated high-stakes examinations have also been shown to affect students' and teachers' experiences with and practices of writing. Hillocks (2002) examined high-stakes writing assessments in five states (including New York) and concluded that instruction based on these assessments undermined effective writing instruction as well as the development of critical literacy. Shor (1997) defines critical literacy as grounded in ongoing inquiry:

> critical literacy is language use that questions the social construction of the self. When we are critically literate, we examine our ongoing development, to reveal the subjective positions from which we make sense of the world and act in it. (Introduction, para. 4)

A conception of knowledge consistent with critical literacy would undermine the static, authoritative conception of knowledge promoted by high-stakes standardized assessments. Wiggins (1998) reinforces the negative effects of state assessments on what counts as good writing.

Many state writing assessments run the risk of undercutting good writing by scoring only for focus, organization, style, and mechanics without once asking judges to consider whether the writing is powerful, memorable, provocative, or moving (all impact-related criteria, and all at the heart of why people read what others write). (as cited in National Writing Project & Nagin, 2006, p. 78)

Analysis of data in this study revealed conclusions that are similar to those asserted by Hillocks (2002), Dorn (2007), and Nichols and Berliner (2007). In the working-class school studied, state assessments have a powerful reductive effect on writing. The effects are made visible in that writing assignments in each of the four core subject areas parallel state assessments in form and content, writing is assessed in accordance to state-published rubrics, and the expression and development of original or critical thought is discouraged.

DISCOURSE, POWER AND LANGUAGE

Discourse, power, and identity are inextricably interrelated. Apple (2003), drawing on Gramsci's conception of hegemony, discusses the intersections between hegemony and discourse. Apple states that

Hegemony is both discursive and political. It includes the power to establish "legitimate" definitions of social needs and authoritative definitions of social situations. It involves the power to define what counts as "legitimate" in areas of agreement and disagreement. And it points to the ability of dominant groups to shape what political agendas are made public and are to be discussed as "possible." (p. 6)

Discourse, according to Apple, is a facet of both hegemony and identity because hegemonic power is not static; it is a process which involves continuous reconstruction of identities and relationships within the existing (ever-evolving) social structure. Hegemony functions discursively because those in power employ discursive means in order to remain in power. They do this by creating ideological discourses that define common sense and legitimate social meanings. Lemke notes that "Discourse functions ideologically in society to support and legitimate the exercise of power, and to naturalize unjust social relations, making them seem the inevitable consequence of commonsense necessity" (Lemke, 1995, p. 20). Foucault defines discourses as:

ways of constituting knowledge, together with the social practices, forms of subjectivity and power relations which inhere in such knowledges and relations between them. Discourses are more than ways of thinking and producing meaning. They constitute the nature of the body, unconscious and conscious mind and emotional life of the subjects they seek to govern (as cited in Weedon, 1987, p. 108)

He further characterizes discourse as "a form of power that circulates in the social field and can attach to strategies of domination as well as those of resistance" (as cited in Diamond & Quinby, 1988, p. 185). Foucault (1993) describes how relations between power and discourse relate to the production of "discursive regimes" of knowledge. Discursive regimes consist of the sets of knowledges which emerge as permissible or desirable in specific social contexts. Such regimes function to "produce permissible modes of being and thinking while disqualifying and even making others impossible" (Escobar, 1995, p. 5). Gee (1997) explains how discourses operate in institutions like schools.

"Discourses" are characteristic (socially and culturally formed, but historically changing) ways of talking and writing about, as well as acting with and toward people and things (ways which are circulated and sustained within various texts, artifacts, images, social practices, and institutions, as well as in moment-to-moment social interactions) such that certain perspectives and states of affairs come to be taken as "normal" or "natural" and others come to be taken as "deviant" or "marginal" (e.g., what counts as a "normal" prisoner, hospital patient, or student, or a "normal" prison, hospital, or school, at a given time and place). (para. 14)

Discourses operate throughout societies, affecting identity construction and perpetuating power relations through everyday activities of cultural participants. Ways of being, thinking, and knowing are governed by discursive forces which are perceived as natural and normal—common sense—and can thus proceed unquestioned. Foucault conceives of social control as being regulated through the "regularization" of practices, discourse being a central facet through which control is maintained. Furthermore, because resistance is integral to power, discourse can serve as a site of both hegemonic reproduction and penetration/resistance. Competing discourses are constitutive of hegemonic relations and, therefore, constant in the construction and reconstruction of the state and its relationships to individuals and groups.

Gee (1996) works in the spaces opened by Willis (1977), Apple (1982, 1996), and Foucault, working in and through concepts of cultural politics and resistance to show how these notions relate to literacy. Asserting the relationship between schooling and the political realities of knowledge,

Apple (2003) states that "curriculum talk is power talk" (p. 7). Discourses serve to produce knowledge. In a broad sense, discourse produces official knowledge. Likewise, in a linguistic sense, individuals' consumption and production of discourses shape thinking, social interactions and learning. However, the influences of discourses are not predetermined, nor are they one-directional. The existence of ideologically-saturated discourses neither dismisses agency nor does it prohibit possibilities for change. Apple quotes Touraine (2001), who states: "We must resolutely reject all discourses that try to convince us that we are powerless. How long can we go on listening to and speaking a language that contradicts what we feel and even what we do?" (as cited in Apple, 2003, p. 17). Apple (1996) notes that "there is a close connection between how the state is structured and acts, and the formation of social movements and identities" (pp. 43-44). He further asserts that "who we are and how we think about our institutions are closely connected to who has the power to produce and circulate new ways of understanding our identities" (2001, p. 9). Apple, then, effectively sets the stage for the pervasive influence of ideology through cultural politics on schooling. Gee layers on to that assertion the influence of cultural politics in literacy practices.

Gee (1996) states that "any technology, including writing, is a cultural form, a social product whose shape and influence depend on prior political and ideological factors" (p. 58). He further notes that "reading and writing only make sense when studied in the context of social and cultural (and we can add historical, political, and economic) practices of which they are but a part" (Gee, 1997 para. 1). Gee, like Apple, perceives the cultural conflicts that emerge from discursive practices as necessary components of various, ideologically-rich social discourses (both in the larger social sense and the more narrow linguistic sense). Gee explains how even the derivation of the meanings of words encompasses conflict based on power relations, since discursive practices always involve a balance between seeking status and seeking solidarity: "Meanings, and the cultural models that compose them, are ultimately rooted in negotiation between different social practices with different interests. Power plays an important role in these negotiations" (p. 81). Gee notes that because literacy practices are rooted in social practices, mastery of dominant literacies is not inherently transformational. Literacy is purported to be a means of cognitive development, social mobility and success in society; however, the opposite often obtains.

Anyon (1981), in her landmark study of social class and school knowledge, demonstrated how experiences of schooling differ according to students' social class. Finn (1999), focusing on literacy in schooling, reached similar conclusions. Referring to a set of studies about the effect of literacy on poor and working-class people, Gee (1996) states that:

In all these societies, literacy served as a socializing tool for the poor, was seen as a possible threat if misused by the poor (for an analysis of their oppression and to make demands for power), and served as a technology for the continued selection of members of one class for the best positions in the society. (p. 59)

Willis (1977) showed how working-class students constructed oppositional identities that resulted in their own continued economic repression. Apple (1982) describes the process: "Their rejection of so much of the content and form of day to day educational life bears on the almost unconscious realization that, as a class, schooling will not enable them to go much further than they already are" (Apple, as cited in MacLeod, 1995. p. 19). Furthermore, in a recent book, Gee (2004) discusses schooling and social class construction within the new capitalism, which is marked by increased commodification and entrepreneurialism coupled with intense competition. In this environment, obtaining basic skills such as those traditionally understood as "academic" is not sufficient for socioeconomic success:

Security in the new capitalism, such as it is, is rooted not in jobs and wages, but in what I will call one's "portfolio." By one's portfolio I mean the skills, achievements, and previous experiences that a person owns and that he or she can arrange and rearrange to sell him or herself for new opportunities in changed times. (Gee, 2004, p. 97)

Class distinctions are also affected by one's experiences of literacies through schooling:

Class means something different in the new capitalism than it did in the old. In the old capitalism there was a broad and massive "middle class" defined by one's ability to consume standardized commodities. In the new capitalism class is defined by the nature of one's portfolio, the sorts of experiences, skills, and achievements one has accrued (which one shares, by and large, with the "right" sort of people) and one's ability to manage these in a shape-shifting way. One's portfolio surely correlates with one's parents' income (though by no means perfectly), but what matters is the portfolio and the way in which it is viewed and managed. If you have no portfolio or don't view yourself in portfolio terms, then you are at risk in the new capitalism. (Gee, 2004, p. 106)

Gee (2004) argues that public schooling, with its increased pressures to standardize instruction and assessment, does not provide portfolio-building experiences for students. While acquisition of academic literacies is important, it is no longer sufficient, and students whose pedagogical experiences are limited to traditional schooling will be disadvantaged in terms of social class mobility.

Language is a key aspect of discourse. As Giroux (1992) states: "Language makes possible both the subject positions that people use to negotiate their sense of self and the ideologies and social practices that give meaning and legitimacy to institutions that form the basis of a given society" (p. 167). It is essential to understand the significance of language practices in constructing social structures. With regard to schooling, any understanding of the mental functioning of individuals must be predicated on an understanding of how they are situated culturally, historically, and institutionally.

Despite the idea that language can serve as a neutral means for transmitting disembodied information, "there is no such thing, in reality, as decontextualized communication—meaning is always a matter of contextualizing signs within shared mental models and social contexts.... All communication conveys emotion and a sense of social identity" (Gee, 1996, p. 157). Language, including one's perception of oneself as a user of language, is inseparable from identity and class and is, therefore, inseparable from relations of power. Students and teachers who do not perceive themselves as effective, empowered writers will not enact written literacies that reflect authorial agency. If teachers define the process of writing and students define their identities as writers on the basis of the examinations, then students are likely to react with resistance to pedagogies that are alienating and hegemonic in nature. Resistance to schooling on the part of students diminishes their possibility to achieve success in an economy marked by the new capitalism. Given these conditions, the technology of the examinations may limit the possibilities that students and teachers imagine with respect to writing as a means of empowerment.

DISCOURSE AND DIALOGICALITY

Vygotsky (1986) linked sociocultural influences with individual mental functioning by considering mental functioning as mediated and shaped by sociocultural contexts. Wertsch (1991) extends this point of view by invoking Bakhtin (1973, 1981, 1986), who conceived of meaning in language as grounded in voice and dialogicality. Bakhtin describes the social influences on discourse as resulting in "multivoicedness"—a sense that language is never an individual, uni-dimensional expression. Bakhtin conceives of meaning as "an active process, not a static entity. He insisted ... that meaning can come into existence only when two or more voices come into contact" (Wertsch, 1991, p. 52). Bakhtin's understanding of multivoicedness and the social language in our mouths and minds involves not only the voices of production but also the voices being addressed.

For Bakhtin, multivoicedness is preceded by the notion of dialogicality. According to Bakhtin, discourse is primordially dialogic in nature; in fact, "any true understanding is dialogic in nature" (Wertsch, 1991, p. 54). This is because any interaction carries with it the "simultaneous presence of both the transmitting and transmitted voices" (p. 55), in an immediate as well as a sociocultural, historical sense. The concept of multivoicedness is multifaceted in terms of writing instruction. Students and teachers enter language arts classrooms with their own versions of and senses of "voice." Multicultural, holistic approaches to writing instruction focus on developing student writers without marginalizing the sociocultural context of students' voices. Traditional schooling tends to emphasize the acquisition of academic language with minimal consideration of the significance of students' sociocultural languages. One aspect of multivoicedness, then, involves its recognition in the classroom. In addition, teachers' voices require critical consideration, since pedagogical interactions might be dialogical or parallel. Teachers must understand and appreciate the place of multivoicedness in apprenticing young writers if dialogic pedagogies are to occur.

Bakhtin's dialogic orientation facilitated his construction of a linguistic framework that differentiated between national languages and social languages. While the character and functions of national languages are important, it is the notion of social languages that is most useful in the context of this study. Wertsch describes how Bakhtin links discourse and social languages: "For Bakhtin, a social language is a discourse peculiar to a specific stratum of society within a given social system at a given time" (Wertsch, 1991, p. 57). Bakhtin argues that language users invoke social languages even as social languages shape their utterances. Moreover, because people use language to construct meaning, "an individual is constituted by language and culture which can only be maintained and renewed in communities he is a part of" (p. 69). These communities can be understood as social constructions of class because discourses are produced and consumed by and through interrelations of social class in families, in social institutions like schools, and through popular culture.

Freire (2003, 2004) asserts the significance of the connections among knowledge, power, and dialogue in the pursuit of social justice. Like Foucault (1993), who argues that resistance is a constituent of power, Freire maintains that the knowledge possessed and enacted by marginalized and oppressed people is real; however, it is silenced and rendered invisible by those in power. The route to social change, according to Freire, lies in action that is rooted in dialogue. A dialogic approach to learning in which the culture of learners is explicated and validated provides the possibility for transformational educational experiences and eventual liberation.

Since social class backgrounds of students affect their experiences of schooling, it is not surprising that social class has been historically connected to educational achievement and economic success. From the standpoint of social justice, the problems with these conditions are evident. But economic issues are also relevant in terms of lost potential. For example, Anyon (1981) demonstrated that the schooling experiences of students in schools serving families of different social classes were essentially stratified according to social class, that is, without significant family and/or community intervention students would leave their schools with widely disparate "portfolios." Livingstone and Sawchuck (2000) argue that incomplete images of working-class culture are perpetuated through academic portrayals, which ignore the creative cultural practices of the working class. This results in both "wasted knowledge and denied recognition" (p. 10).

Discourse, in both its broad social sense and in a more narrow linguistic sense, is deeply connected to social class and schooling. Members of social classes live in and construct identities that are, in part, linguistically oriented – marked and shaped by shared social languages. Gee (2004) argues that schools, which emphasize academic language, are inadequate in ameliorating discursive inequities. A dialogic approach to literacy practices does not perceive diverse, poor, or working-class literacies as deficient. Instead, literacies are understood to represent "deep levels of identity and epistemology, and thereby the stance that learners take with respect to the "new" literacy practices of the educational setting" (Street, 2005, p. 140). In this study, data analysis indicates that dialogic pedagogical interactions are a rare phenomenon. In general, students (and student writers) repeat the words and ideas of authorities (teachers and texts). Teachers and texts replicate the content and skills mandated by the state. Narrowed curriculum and minimal competencies tend to result from these monologic encounters; therefore, class stratification is reinforced.

Since schools mirror the hegemonic nature of society in the United States, working-class students resist activities that seem exploitative and meaningless—activities students perceive as imposed by authorities who are complicit in the denigration of working-class identity. Student resistance, as a reactive performance, results in denial of additional skills and credentials. As a result, resistance can reinforce and even exacerbate class stratification, since resistance to literacy instruction leads to weakened skills and diminished opportunities for educational advancement.

REFERENCES

Apple, M. W. (1982). *Education and power*. Boston, MA: Routledge and Kegan Paul.

Apple, M. W. (1996). *Cultural politics and education*. New York, NY: Teachers College Press.

Apple, M. W. (2001). *Educating the "right" way: Markets, standards, god and inequality*. New York, NY: Routledge-Falmer.

Apple, M. W. (2003). *The state and politics of knowledge*. New York, NY: Routledge-Falmer.

Anyon, J. (1981). Elementary schooling and the distinction of social class. *Interchange, 12*, 118-132.

Bakhtin, M. M. (1973). *Marxism and the philosophy of language* (L. Matejka & I. R. Titunik, Trans.). New York, NY: Seminar.

Bakhtin, M. M. (1981). *The Dialogic Imagination* (C. Emerson & M. Holquist, Trans.). Austin, TX: The University of Texas Press.

Bakhtin, M. M. (1986). *Speech genres and other late essays* (V. W. McGee, Trans.). Austin, TX: University of Texas Press.

Beach, R., Parks, D., Thein, A., & Lensmire, T. (2007). High School Students' Exploration of Class Differences in a Multicultural Literature Class. In J. Van Galen & G. W. Noblit (Eds.), *Late to Class: Social Class and Schooling in the New Economy* (pp. 141-166). Albany, NY: State University of New York Press.

Bernstein, B. (1973). *Class, codes and control* (Vol. 2). London: Routledge & Kegan Paul.

Diamond, I., & Quinby, L. (1988). *Feminism and Foucault: Reflections on Resistance*. Boston, MA: Northeastern University Press.

Dorn, S. (2003). High-stakes testing and the history of graduation. *Education Policy Analysis Archives, 11*(1). Retrieved from http://epaa.asu.edu/epaa/v11n1/

Dorn, S. (2007). *Accountability Frankenstein: Understanding and Taming the Monster*. Charlotte, NC: Information Age.

Escobar, A. (1995). *Encountering development: The making and unmaking of the Third World*. Princeton, NJ: Princeton University Press.

Finn, P. J. (1999). *Literacy with an attitude: Educating working-class children in their own self-interest*. Albany, NY: State University of New York Press.

Foucault, M. (1993). Power as knowledge. In C. Lemert (Ed.), *Social theory: The multicultural and classic readings*. Toronto, Canada: HarperCollins.

Freire, P. (2004). *Pedagogy of indignation*. Boulder, CO: Paradigm.

Friere, P. (2003). *Pedagogy of the oppressed* (M. B. Romos, Trans. 30th anniversary ed.). New York, NY: Continuum International.

Gee, J. P. (1996). *Social linguistics and literacies: Ideology in discourses*. Bristol, PA: Taylor and Francis.

Gee, J. P. (1997). The new literacies and the "Social Turn" [Electronic Version]. Retrieved http://www.schools.ash.org.au/litweb/page300.html

Gee, J. P. (2004). *Situated language and learning: A critique of traditional schooling*. New York, NY: Routledge.

Giroux, H. (1992). *Border crossings: Cultural workers and the politics of education*. New York, NY: Routledge.

Giroux, H. A. (2003). *The abandoned generation: Democracy beyond the culture of fear.* New York, NY: Palgrave MacMillan.

Gunzenhauser, M. G. (2006). Normalizing the educated subject: A Foucaultian analysis of high-stakes accountability. *Educational Studies, 39*(3), 241-259.

Hayek, F. A. (1996). *Individualism and economic order* (reissue edition ed.). Chicago, IL: University of Chicago Press.

Hillocks, G. J. (2002). *The testing trap: How state writing assessments control learning.* New York, NY: Teachers College Press.

Ketter, J., & Pool, J. (2001). Exploring the Impact of direct writing assessment in two high school classrooms. *Research in the Teaching of English, 5,* 344-393.

Lemke, J. (1995). *Textual politics: Discourse and social dynamics.* London: Taylor and Francis.

Livingstone, D. W., & Sawchuck, P. (2000). Beyond cultural capital theory: Hidden dimensions of working class learning. *Review of Education, Pedagogy and Cultural Studies, 22*(2), 121-146.

MacLeod, J. (1995). *Ain't no makin' it: Aspirations and attainment in a low-income neighborhood.* Boulder, CO: Westview Press.

National Writing Project, & Nagin, C. (2006). *Because Writing Matters: Improving Student Writing in Our Schools.* San Francisco, CA: Jossey-Bass.

Neill, M., & Gayler, K. (2001). Do High-Stakes Graduation Tests Improve Learning Outcomes? Using State-level NAEP Data to Evaluate the Effects of Mandatory Graduation Tests. In G. Orfield & M. L. Kornhaber (Eds.), *Raising Standards or Raising Barriers* (pp. 107-126). New York, NY: The Century Foundation Press.

Nelson, G. L. (2001). Writing beyond Testing: "The Word as an Instrument of Creation." *English Journal, 91*(1), 57-61.

New York State Education Department. (1999). DESCRIPTION OF SURR SCHOOL GROUPS. Retrieved from http://www.emsc.nysed.gov/nyc/PDFs/SURRDescr.pdf

Nichols, S. L., & Berliner, D. C. (2007). *Collateral damage: How high-stakes testing undermines education.* Cambridge, MA: Harvard Education Press.

Orfield, G., & Kornhaber, M. L. (Eds.). (2001). *Raising standards or raising barriers.* New York, NY: The Century Foundation Press.

Popham, W. J. (2001). *The truth about testing: An educators call to action.* Alexandria, VA: Association for Supervision and Curriculum Development.

Shor, I. (1997). What is critical literacy? *Journal for Pedagogy, Pluralism & Practice, 1*(4), 1-26.

Smith, F. (1986). *Insult to intelligence: The bureaucratic invasions of our classrooms.* Portsmouth, England: Heinemann.

Sowell, T. (1996). *The vision of the annointed: Self-congratulation as a basis for social policy.* New York, NY: Basic Books.

Street, B. V. (2005). Recent applications of new literacy studies in educational contexts. *Research in Teaching of English, 39*(4), 417-423.

Touraine, A. (2001, Aug). *Beyond neoliberalism.* London: Polity.

United States Department of Education. (2003). *No Child Left Behind.* Retrieved from http://www.ed.gov/nclb

von Mises, L. (1997). *Human action: A treatise on economics* (4th rev. ed.). San Francisco, CA: Fox & Wilkes.

Vygotsky, L. (1986). *Thought and language* (A. Kozulin, Trans.). Cambridge, MA: The MIT Press.

Wertsch, J. V. (1991). *Voices of the mind: A sociocultural approach to mediated action.* Cambridge, MA: Harvard University Press.

Wiggins, G. (1998). *Educative assessment.* San Francisco, CA: Jossey-Bass.

Willis, P. (1977). *Learning to labor: How working class kids get working class jobs.* New York, NY: Columbia University Press.

Weedon, C. (1987). *Feminist practice and poststructuralist theory.* Oxford, England: Blackwell.

CHAPTER 2

THE STUDY

INTRODUCTION

In 2003, Giroux published a scathing revelation regarding the effects of the current political climate on public education and the young people intended to be served by its system. Giroux made connections between the deteriorating state of public education in the United States and an economic climate where inequities in income and wealth are increasing at an unprecedented rate, leaving those near the bottom struggling to survive. As politicians authorize economic policies that favor the wealthy and powerful, government has reduced investment in public services (including education) that benefit the poor and working class (Giroux, 2003). These conditions leave public schools in poor and working-class communities scrambling to provide adequate educational opportunities for already disadvantaged students.

Along with academic content, public schools are charged to provide their students—particularly those from lower-income families—with a variety of social services, including meals, health care, and counseling. Layered onto this difficult task are federal and state accountability reform initiatives. As resources for public schools have diminished, government control has increased, specifically in the form of common standards and high-stakes assessments. This has been tolerated by the public, at least in part, because current educational reform initiatives have been presented using rhetoric that is infused with a message that *promotes* the very opposite

Power, Resistance, and Literacy: Writing for Social Justice, pp. 19–39
Copyright © 2011 by Information Age Publishing
All rights of reproduction in any form reserved.

of the actual consequences of the reform. No Child Left Behind (NCLB), for example, the federal legislation emblematic of the accountability-based reform movement, purports (as its name implies) to alleviate social and economic inequities by providing all children with educational opportunities that will foster their eventual success. Supporters of NCLB, as well as the current administration's *Race to the Top* initiative, claim that accountability measures based on high-stakes assessments will improve public schools, particularly for poor and minority students. However, decades of research reveal evidence that contradicts this claim: students in schools serving poor and working-class communities are most likely to be harmed by high-stakes assessment-based reform (Brantlinger, 2007; Dorn, 2007; Nichols & Berliner, 2007).

Giroux (2003) describes how current political conditions, marked by a withdrawal of public commitment to social justice, affect public schools and those who function within them.

> The first casualty is a language of social and political responsibility capable of defending those vital institutions that expand the rights, public goods, and services central to a meaningful democracy. This is especially true with respect to public schooling and the debate over the purposes of education, the role of teachers as critical intellectuals, the politics of the curriculum, and the centrality of pedagogy as a moral and political practice. (p. 74)

Giroux's words suggest a frame for the arguments that will be presented in this book. The NCLB legislation and its state level counterparts have had powerful effects on perceived educational purposes, pedagogical practices, and curricula. As the language of accountability and reform saturates public schools, students and teachers construct their identities, define what it means to teach and learn, and generate conceptions of literacy.

To complicate matters, working-class students are experiencing a reconstruction of their class identities vis-à-vis the economic system. As the economy completes its shift from industry-based to service-based, the remnants of structures which shaped traditional working-class identities are vanishing. Economic changes in the United States have been particularly detrimental for working-class families, whose standards of living have declined steadily since the 1970s (Beach, Parks, Thein, & Lensmire, 2007; Ehrenreich, 2001; "Twenty-Five-Year Slide" 2003). During the post-World War II era in the United States, a period which Gee (2004) refers to as the "old capitalism," members of the White working class benefited from the growth of manufacturing and industry. Employment in this sector of the economy provided decent wages (enabling working-class families to exist on one income), good benefits (such as health insurance, paid sick leave and vacation time, and a pension upon retirement), and job stability—all accessible without credentials related to higher education.

The White, working-class identity has been historically marked by alienation from daily labor, which was perceived as instrumental for achieving personal goals rather than a means of self-actualization. In addition, the working-class identity was constructed *in opposition to* management. Willis (1977) and Weis (1990) demonstrated that both of these characteristics that is, alienation from labor (including academic work) and antagonism toward authority, were paralleled within working-class schools.

Changes in the economy have produced changes in the construction of working-class identities. Identities are constructed within and against particular cultural contexts, and economic shifts have prompted reconfigurations of class relations in terms of gender and race as well. The "new capitalism" does not offer the types of employment that fostered the development of the hegemonic White masculine working-class identities. Globalization has enabled manufacturers to operate in developing countries where business and labor costs are considerably reduced, causing a steep decline in the living standards of both middle-class and working-class families. According to Gee (2004), to succeed in the new capitalism workers must be more flexible, more knowledgeable, and more collaborative. The job market is extremely competitive, and workers will need an orientation toward lifelong learning and cooperation with colleagues at all levels of the organizational hierarchy.

It is evident that certain aspects of working-class identities cultivated within the old capitalism will be detrimental to students who must survive in the economy of the new capitalism. Students must be engaged with learning, not alienated from it and resistant to it. They will require critical thinking skills, intrinsic motivation and facility with new literacies. As college admission becomes more competitive and economic inequities are amplified, students will need to construct identities based on a portfolio of experiences that will enable them to become productive participants in the new capitalism (Gee, 2004; Sacks, 2007). The questions were explored by the study on which this book is based include the following: are public schools in working-class suburban communities preparing students for the current and future economies? Does schooling in a working-class high school contribute to the reproduction of class stratification or provide opportunities that ameliorate individual, structural, and social inequalities? Does the discourse of schooling in this setting promote pedagogies that foster social reproduction or those that might transform social inequalities?

The study explored how teachers and students in a predominantly White working-class first-ring suburban high school experience and articulate academic practices related to writing. Practices of literacy incorporate and (re)produce relations of power. The ethnographic study focused on structural and curricular factors that influence academic practices of writing, as well as the ways in which expressed and lived identities of faculty and youth influence, and are influenced by, these practices. State and federal reform initiatives currently reflect a strong emphasis on student writing, and standardized assessments in every discipline incorporate some form of writing. Writing practices and policies are impacted by these changes, and this study investigated how practices of writing in this school relate to social class(es) and discourses of empowerment and/or disempowerment among students and faculty. The following questions guided my research:

- How do teachers and students in a predominantly White working-class first-ring suburban high school experience and articulate academic practices related to writing?
- What factors (structural, curricular, expressed and lived identities of faculty and youth) influence these practices? How do these practices relate to social class(es) and discourses of empowerment and/or disempowerment among students and faculty?

Significant issues that emerged from the exploration of these questions include the effects of the state and federal high-stakes assessment reform efforts on teachers and working-class students, the political rhetoric of reform and how this rhetoric conflicts with reality, and the powerful consequences of this reform on the discourse of writing in this school. In short, data from this study indicate that reform based on standardized assessments results in increased student resistance which leads to alienation from potentially empowering experiences of literacy.

Writing, as a representation of language and thought, is an essential and visible aspect of identity. Therefore, it is critical to consider how writing is conceived and conveyed within the school and explore how writing has been affected by high-stakes assessments. Giroux (2003) contends that the "hidden curriculum," traditionally perceived as the cultural messages related to class, culture and *habitus* that are instilled by schools along with the content and skills that comprise the overt curriculum, has been appropriated by the discursive power of state examinations which now serve to define what it means to teach, to learn, to think, and to be eligible for upward mobility in the current society. In this milieu, it is important to understand how students and the teachers in a working-class high school construct their identities and negotiate their relationships, particularly with respect to teaching and learning writing.

SOCIAL CLASS, SCHOOLING, AND
PROCESSES OF EXCLUSION

Exclusion and Stratification

Mechanisms of exclusion, which serve to reinforce class stratification, exist throughout society. Capitalism perpetuates and often exacerbates inequalities associated with stratification. Brantlinger (2007) notes that currently in the United States "capitalism does reign and schools mirror, or reproduce, its social order" (p. 237). Because schools mirror society, mechanisms of exclusion are prevalent in schools. Brantlinger explains how the dynamics of schooling operate vis-à-vis power and opportunity in a capitalistic society:

> Bourdieu defines capital as the "capacity to exercise control over one's own future and that of others as a form of power" (Calhoun, LiPuma, & Postone, 1993, p. 4). Additionally, school quality varies according to the economic capital, or financial status, of clientele (Burton, 1999; Kozol, 1991). Hence, rather than being a leveler, education gives rise to, and perpetuates, inequalities....The fact that students do not have equal chances because playing fields are unequal is ignored as is the emotional impact of having subordinate status. (pp. 237-238)

Moreover, "Bourdieu argues that because social positions are relational and interdependent, the dominant class not only controls Others, but their power depends on Others' subordination" (Brantlinger, 2007, p. 239). Therefore, differential opportunities, which position some for success and restrict others, are inherent to schooling in a capitalistic society.

Processes of exclusion in schools include differential aspirations and expectations, tracking, various forms of high-stakes testing, differential access to academic knowledge, and differential access to college counseling (Van Galen & Noblit, 2007). Processes of exclusion in schools result in differential opportunities for students, that is, students are provided and denied opportunities based, in part, on the nature of the schooling they experience.

(Re)Constructing the White Working Class

Citing Apple, Brantlinger (2007) states that "social class is an analytic construct, but also a set of relations that exist outside our minds" (p. 263). That is, class is constructed by groups of individuals and, simultaneously, identities are subjectified by the practices and delineations of the classes to which they belong. In a similar vein, Weis explains her understanding of class construction.

> Like Walkerdine, Lucey, and Melody (2001), I understand social class to be the "social and psychic practices through which ordinary people live, survive and cope" (p. 27). This involves understanding "the practices of living, the process of subjectification and the formation of subjectivities." ... I, like E. P. Thompson (1966) and other more culturally driven theorists, stretch understandings of class so as to include the practices of everyday living—practices that are both engaged in by, and simultaneously encircle, men, women, and children on a daily basis. Under this formulation, class is "lived as an identity designation and not simply as an economic relation to the means of production." (Walkerdine et al., 2001, as cited in Weis, 2004, p. 4)

This sociocultural understanding of class emphasizes the importance of its development as a context-specific endeavor. Members of a particular social class affect and are affected by relations of class. Everyday activities, interests, aspirations, understandings, and beliefs are intertwined with class status; dynamics as central to identity as language and thought are connected to discourses which are features of social class. How people use language as a means of thought and communication, then, is deeply tied to class experiences and relations.

With economic shifts, representations of social class and the associated identities can undergo significant changes. Because identity is "situated within historically contingent, culturally constructed worlds" (Brantlinger, 2007, p. 241), its construction is intimately related to social class. Weis (1990) describes the interrelating dynamics among identity, class and society. She states that individuals' identities construct and are constructed by the cultural space they inhabit because "society is the material accomplishment of conflicting groups struggling for control of the field of historical cultural action" (p. 4).

The United States enters the first decade of the twenty-first century experiencing the synergistic effects of capitalism and globalization. Weis (2004) explains the extent of these effects on the White working class.

> What was once referred to as deindustrialization by American economists in the 1980s is now understood to be a fundamental shift in the local economy, one which represents a radical break with past practice.... As a consequence, the former working class is in competition with routine production workers all over the world, most of whom will work for a fraction of what the American, British, or Australian worker (even nonunionized worker) demands. Given this situation, the old collective bargaining agreements (what we can call the "capital-labor accord") are useless—leaving routine production workers without a stable foothold in the economy (pp. 9-10). Capitalism has been

demonstrated to exacerbate class stratification in ways that are detrimental to poor and working-class people. Capitalism coupled with globalization has had a profound impact on the White working class.

The White working class is experiencing a major transformation. Brantlinger (2007) notes that "as labor unions are quashed and working-class economic and political clout declines, the collective and personal agency of the working class dissipates" (p. 241). As manufacturing jobs disappear and knowledge-based employment dominates new capitalism, education has become essential to economic and class-based sustenance (not to mention upward mobility). However, as the market has become more competitive, public financial support for poor and working-class students to extend their education has declined. Beach, Parks, Thein, and Lensmire (2007) describe the effects of this dynamic.

> These shifts have placed working-class people in a double-bind. On the one hand, the transformation from manufacturing to "knowledge-economy" jobs requires increased higher education beyond high school. On the other hand, cuts in state and federal spending have resulted in large increases in tuition at state colleges and universities, pricing many working–class students out of higher education. (p. 142)

The financial obstacle to higher education is one challenge faced by working-class students as they imagine future possibilities in the new capitalism. Another involves their experiences of secondary schooling. Historically, working-class schools have contributed to the construction of identities that position students for employment in the old capitalist system. It is common for working-class students to experience alienation from the process of learning and develop attitudes of opposition toward authority. Such dispositions will not serve them well in the new economy where engagement with knowledge is valued and collaboration with colleagues at all organizational levels is essential.

The White working class has historically been defined and perceived through the perspective of a hegemonic male worker—the breadwinner on whom the family depended for sustenance and protection from the (usually) racially marginalized "Other." However, recent work by Weis (2004), Walkerdine, Lucey, and Melody (2001) explores the reconception of the working-class identity inclusive of race and gender. Walkerdine et al., in particular, underscore the challenge of defining a secure working-class identity at a time when the characteristics that serve as boundaries of its class formation have all but disappeared. Drawing on Marx, Walkerdine et al. explain that actually Marx argues that the working class was made through the struggle of the proletariat to recognize itself as a class, which necessitated a recognition and consciousness of its historic and revolutionary mission. Therefore, the working class did not automatically exist in any straightforward sense: it was not simply produced by its relation to the means and ownership of production. In this sense we can begin to understand the working class is not an unproblematic designation of a real group of people whom we might struggle to describe adequately. Rather the working class is a group of people who exist historically and culturally, and their designation is heavily contested. This is not the same as saying that the materiality of their oppression and exploitation is non-existent, but that their materiality is made to signify in and through the discursive practices in which it is produced. (p. 14)

The material evanescence of the working-class identity is evident, particularly as globalization and capitalism combine to marginalize the male labor power though which, historically, this identity has been defined. But the disappearance of the masculine power associated with the White working class cannot be equated with the disappearance of the White working-class identity. In fact, issues of race and gender come into sharp relief as the traditional White working-class male identity recedes into the past.

The White working-class identity has defined itself *against* three primary Others; these relate to authority, race, and gender. The first, located in the economic realm, is management. The White working-class identity is constructed in an attitude of resistance to the authority which, in the workplace, is represented by management. (In other settings, such as schools, working class resistance is transferred to authority figures like teachers and principals.) Historically, White male working-class identities have also been constructed against feminine and racialized "Others" (traditionally Black and Brown minorities). Weis (2004), Walkerdine, Lucey and Melody (2001) have demonstrated that the construction of the White working-class identity has shifted, particularly with respect to the gender.

Walkerdine, Lucey, and Melody (2001), in discussing the identity construction among working-class adolescent girls in Great Britain, describe how economic changes have resulted in the feminization of the work force. Although this phenomenon may appear to represent empowerment for women, in fact it represents a change in the contours of working-class identity. Walkerdine et al. explain how this is possible.

Women are being allowed to enter the professional and managerial labour market at precisely the time when the status of professions in particular is changing.... Professionals now have far less status and are paid far less than the new elite in the financial and multinational sectors. Women are thus being allowed to enter the professions at precisely the time when these professions are being devalued and high-flying men are going elsewhere. (pp. 7-8)

The new economy, assert Walkerdine et al., requires individuals to construct an identity that can be described as "an autonomous, self-invented subject" (p. 8). The kind of self-transformation required to be successful in the new economy is traditionally associated with femininity. This identity is inconsistent with a traditional working-class identity with respect to class cohesion i.e., the working-class identity is traditionally forged within the significance of community. Success in the new economy, then, requires relinquishing both the security of hegemonic masculinity and the solidarity of community.

Weis (2004) explores the consequences of the economic forces facing the White working class. In her longitudinal ethnographic study, she determined that working-class identities are being reformed and reconstructed, particularly with respect to gender. The feminization of the workforce has allowed properly credentialed working-class women to have access to jobs that provide benefits and security, although the jobs do not offer much chance for upward social mobility. Most of these women, however, have achieved a level of economic independence that many of their mothers did not have. Working-class men who have both working partners and an educational credential are able to maintain what Weis calls "settled" lives. On the other hand, men and women who have not been able to redefine themselves as "autonomous, self-invented subjects" struggle to hold jobs and to obtain necessities such as food, clothing and shelter on a regular basis. Members of the working class who do not construct identities consistent with the new economy and who continue to reject femininity and resist authority fall into the category Weis terms "hard livers."

In addition, Weis (2004) found the dynamics of the racial boundaries had changed only with respect to their target (Arabs, rather than Blacks, were identified as the "Other" in the community being studied). Rather than seeking solidarity with those whose economic and political interests might parallel their own, members of the White working class, then, persist in constructing identities in opposition to racialized "Others."

The first-ring suburban school where this study was conducted serves a community that is predominantly White and working-class. Issues of gender and race intersect with the economy and mirror those explored by Weis (2004) and Walkerdine et al. (2001).

Social Class and Schooling

Weis (2004) asserts that categories of social identity such as class are socially constructed, fluid, and flexible; however, they "*become* 'real' inside institutional life, leading to dire political and economic consequences" (p. 13). Because schools are powerful social institutions, social class and schooling are mutually influential. Brantlinger (2007) notes that "social class has a major cultural significance in the construction of identity and, in turn, influences school relations in school and in community life" (p. 240). Factors that affect student access to various opportunities are both material and nonmaterial. Students who attend schools that serve middle-class or upper-middle-class populations tend to have access to superior facilities as well as higher expectations and expanded forms of academic knowledge. They are exposed to school personnel and classmates whose narrated aspirations include elite colleges and postgraduate plans. These students' experiences of schooling enable them to imagine for themselves a future which incorporates elements that will prepare them for their middle-class or upper-middle-class existences.

The converse is true as well. If students' everyday experiences of schooling (e.g., exposure to poor facilities and lower levels of academic knowledge) reinforce lesser aspirations for educational and occupational goals, then students will be unlikely to imagine themselves in a future beyond that with which they have familiarity. While the material aspects of differentiation that result in exclusion are evident, nonmaterial factors are significant and—because of their apparently insubstantial nature—difficult to identify and to interrupt. Aspirations and beliefs are constructed by individuals as they interact in various realms of society, and mechanisms of stratification feel natural and normal. They are part of one's "habitus." All social institutions contribute to the perpetuation of social stratification; however, institutions of schooling do so despite being charged to ameliorate inequalities. It is troubling when instructional activities purported to lead to empowerment instead exacerbate inequalities, contributing to unequal outcomes for students. Working-class students' experiences of literacy, particularly writing, provide an example of this phenomenon.

Writing as a Process of Exclusion

Writing contributes to processes of exclusion in schools because schooling contributes to the construction of writers whose identities facilitate the reproduction of social stratification. Writing is essential to thinking; it shapes conceptual thoughts and allows writers to frame, reframe, extend and critique ideas. Given the significance of writing, it is important to consider what happens to thinking when writing is experienced as an alienating activity, disconnected from the self and disconnected from the possibility of empowerment. What happens when processes of schooling facilitate and enforce conceptions of literacy that reify social stratification by making class-based empowerment impossible? What happens when opportunities are excised by preventing the types of critical thinking necessary to challenge the status quo effectively?

STUDY SETTING

On paper, Pontiac High School (To ensure confidentiality, pseudonyms are used for the research site as well as all participants) exemplifies several principles of progressive education. Its size, among "small school" enthusiasts, is considered ideal; enrollment in Grades 9 through 12 hovers at about 800 students. Serving a community that is primarily White and suburban, with a small (about 5%) but growing minority population, Pontiac High School is often described as the most sought after public district in Borderburg, a large first-ring suburb of a deindustrializing rust-belt city in the northeast United States—a city I will call "Lakefront City." But there are indications that conditions in this suburban public school are less than idyllic. In the post-Columbine tradition, the school has adopted strict security-related tactics and procedures. There are security cameras inside and outside of the building which are monitored and reviewed regularly. A door monitor buzzes in visitors, who sign in and wear a bright yellow rectangular "Visitor's Pass." Borderburg police officers are a frequent and administratively endorsed presence in the halls of Pontiac High School, and the district Code of Conduct is repeatedly referenced by teachers and administrators as they seek to regulate students. These initiatives might be perceived as successful in that fights between students are rare and incidences of cigarette smoking on school grounds (by students and adults) are virtually nonexistent. Zero tolerance policies, in addition to semi-annual sweeps of the school by Borderburg police officers accompanied by drug dogs, are credited with the few reports of drug use or sale on campus. The emphasis on control and regulation is evident in even the most mundane of communications. For example, the letter the principal sends to parents and students welcoming them to a new school year devotes fully half of its space to student discipline. An excerpt from the August, 2007 letter follows:

> Maintaining a safe and orderly environment for our students remains a primary concern. Cell phone usage and text messaging have created disruptions during the instructional day. Please be aware that any student

use of cell phones during the instructional day is prohibited by board policy.... Dress code will also be strictly enforced. Dress code expectations are reviewed with students, and any questions regarding acceptable dress can be answered by calling the office, or by speaking with a staff member. Although infrequent, physical altercation/fighting will not be tolerated. These incidents will result in a report being filed with the Borderburg Police Department, an out-of school-suspension, and a social suspension.... Our Code of Conduct will continue to direct our actions. (Principal, 2007)

Although the letter goes on to indicate that "the vast majority of students at Pontiac High are well-behaved and respectful," the emphasis on discipline is unmistakable. It is noteworthy that a letter meant to welcome students and their families to a new school year invokes board policy regarding cell phone use, dress code, the police department, and the school's code of conduct. These initiatives of control might be perceived as indicative of the fact that this public high school serves a working-class community in an inner-ring suburb.

Because Pontiac High is located in a first-ring suburb, it embodies characteristics of both urban and suburban school cultures. The racial and ethnic composition of the student body resembles the primarily White populations of the region's suburban communities; however, disciplinary policies and procedure as outlined above indicate a sense of the need for "cracking down" on students to maintain control (Lipman, 2003). Lipman links economic globalization to an "increased policing of youth through zero tolerance school discipline policies" (p. 81). Significantly, she demonstrates that regulation of youths is enacted in ways consistent with social class stratification i.e., schools serving minority and low-income youths impose more restrictions on both students and teachers than schools serving middle-class youths. Regulation of teachers tends to involve accountability mechanisms based on high-stakes tests. Regulation of students involves both curricular discipline and strict rules on conduct, dress, and language. An attitude of zero-tolerance drives the school's code of conduct, police officers work closely with school administrators and, as data analyzed in this study will reveal, examinations dominate curriculum and instruction at Pontiac High.

It is noteworthy that this school has enacted zero tolerance at the same time as its student population is undergoing a small but significant shift in racial composition, with the Black student population rising from 1.8% in 2000 to 5.2% in 2005 (*New York State District School Report Card Comprehensive Information Report*, 2007). In a community historically considered racist (Kraus, 2000), school discipline policies may also represent an intensified, school-oriented replication of "border-patrolling" that characterizes the White working class (Orfield, 2002; Weis, 1990) and persists in the wider community of Borderburg (Kraus, 2000). Kraus describes Lakefront City as "one of the most segregated cities in the United States" (p. 1). The structural racism that results in this condition affects surrounding suburbs as well (Orfield, 2002). Like many first-ring suburbs, Borderburg has experienced a shift in the racial composition of its residents (Orfield, 2002). In 2000, the town's population was 94.9% White, 2.9% Black, and 0.9% Asian. In 2005, however, census results show a population that is 92.2% White, 5.0% Black, and 0.6% Asian ("Factfinder," 2007). Moreover, because increased regulation of students is linked to racial minorities, heightened efforts to control students may well be related to the increasing representation of racial minorities within the student body. Whether the increased regulation of youths at Pontiac High is related to accountability reforms, White working-class border-patrolling, an increasing minority population, or a combination these factors, the emphasis on control provides an indication that the school culture at Pontiac High inclines toward working-class, urban rather than middle-class, suburban norms.

As an inner-ring suburb, this community is undergoing socioeconomic shifts reflected in national metropolitan polarization as families seek to escape substandard urban schools and are able to access affordable housing in school districts such as the one being studied (Orfield, 2002). As Orfield notes, schools are particularly interesting sites for understanding demographic trends. "Schools are the first victim and the most powerful perpetuator of metropolitan polarization. Local schools become socioeconomically distressed before neighborhoods become poor; rising poverty among a community's school children predicts the future of its adults" (p. 3). This site is of particular interest because it offers the possibility of understanding how students and teachers in this working-class community perceive schooling and social class, and how their experiences and practices of writing reinforce and/or interrupt structures that maintain social class composition.

FIELDWORK, DATA COLLECTION, AND DATA ANALYSIS

Fieldwork

This study considers the meanings that students and teachers in a particular setting ascribe to their experiences of writing instruction and academic writing in school. The setting itself is relevant because the White working class, which is prevalent in the backgrounds of the faculty and the district's community, is undergoing significant transformations in the new economy. An additional aspect of this study involves the multilayered nature of schooling and its role in class construction. Schools, as social institutions, influence the opportunities available to students and teachers.

This study delves into the everyday activities and discussions of academic writing and the pedagogies that support or constrain it in this particular setting. Writing both constitutes and is a constituent of thought. Writing affects and is affected by one's use of language. Language, an element of discourse, is a signifier and a component of social class. This study explores the interconnectedness of written language, schooling, and social class in order to understand how students and teachers in this predominantly White inner-ring suburban high school use written language as they construct identities in the new economy

Since this study aims to unpack the multilayered meanings that underlie the daily experiences of students and teachers in this specific setting, critical ethnography is the ideal methodological approach.

Data Collection

In order to understand how students and teachers in this school experience and practice writing and how these experiences and practices relate to identity construction and the structures of schooling and social class, I used ethnography, employing non participant and participant observation, interviews, and document analysis. Because I am deeply connected to the research site, I was there every school day, from 7:00 A.M. to 3:00 P.M. from early September through late June.

Observation is an essential component of critical ethnography. Because my intent was to develop deep understanding of the everyday experiences of students and teachers at this particular site with respect to writing instruction, it was essential for me to be immersed in the culture of the site. As a teacher in this building and a member of the community, I am utterly familiar with the research site; however, the comfort of such familiarity is not equivalent to deep understanding. In addition to the access and knowledge provided by my experiences as a faculty member in the building, I was seeking to pick up on themes that swirled around the school on a daily basis—themes that might be so familiar as to be rendered invisible, *and* themes that I might never have noticed until I investigated more carefully using the eyes and ears of a researcher.

Prior to in-depth interviews, I observed classes in each of the four core subject areas—English language arts, social studies, science, and mathematics—focusing on the classes of the teachers whom I intended to interview. To set up interviews, I sent an e-mail message to all teachers of these subjects who taught students in Grade 11, the level I had targeted for student participants. My intention was to provide optimal opportunities for data to intersect, that is, by interviewing students and teachers whose day-to-day activities might overlap, I could maximize the likelihood that some of their experiences might reflect emerging themes for analysis.

I did not specifically seek out composition-oriented instruction or activities because I hoped to observe how writing is treated as an everyday academic activity. It was important to observe English language arts classes as well as classes in other disciplines for two reasons. First, "writing across the curriculum" is a movement that is well-established and gaining ground. Second, required Regents exams in every subject area now include a writing component. Classroom observations were intended to provide insight into whether these writing components influence instruction. In addition, observing across subject areas allowed me to reflect on whether writing activities and experiences exhibit consistency or variety in terms of purposes, priorities, and perceptions of composition. Within the school setting, I tried to act as a participant observer, acting most often as unobtrusive observer in classrooms. This method allowed me to observe and record how writing processes and products are treated in classes and to describe the everyday practices of teachers and students regarding academic writing.

In addition to observing classes, I also attended meetings of the faculty, English department meetings, and other relevant committees within the school. I spent time with teachers and administrators as they discussed student achievement, curriculum development, and assessment activities. I participated in the administration and scoring of the commencement level New York State English Language Arts Regents Examination (administered in Grade 11) and reviewed written components of Social Studies and Science Regents Examinations. Although these are activities that I participate in as a part of the faculty, during the span of the study I also served as an observer. I took notes at each meeting, again writing as copiously as possible to transcribe words and events as they occurred. I found that this type of notetaking enabled me to observe more effectively for two reasons: first, I was less likely to participate if I was engaged in recording field notes; and second, documenting verbal exchanges as fully as possible enabled me to maintain a level of distance from the proceedings rather easily. I listened in a more detached manner than I would have if I had not been attempting to chronicle events and discussions. Once again, I reread notes directly after each meeting to ensure future legibility and to capture key ideas as the study progressed.

Since I was employed by the school, I naturally participated as necessary, serving as a scorer on the state examination, offering to record minutes at some meetings, and adding to discussions as necessary. However, an overarching goal was to seek deep comprehension of the nature of daily interactions in the school. Participant observations at meetings provided valuable insights into the attitudes of teachers toward their colleagues, their students, the community, and their profession. Serving as a participant-observer during these activities allowed me to consider the effect of structural and curricular factors on students' and teachers' experiences of academic writing. Furthermore, my observations provided essential groundwork for the development of interview questions as well as clues about emerging themes relevant to data analysis.

The second method of data collection focused on semi-structured in-depth interviews. Like participant and nonparticipant observation, interviews provide an essential perspective for critical ethnography. Through semi-structured, in-depth interviews, I explored the experiences of students and teachers vis-à-vis academic writing in this setting. For this study, I interviewed 20 students (10 female and 10 male) in Grade 11 and 21 teachers (including the school librarian) across the four "core" subject areas (English language arts, social studies, science, and mathematics). Students in Grade 11 offer an interesting perspective in several ways. They have attended school long enough to be able to reflect on and articulate their experiences in a meaningful way. They are beginning to consider their lives post-high school, but are not as focused on it (especially in the fall semester) as seniors would be. Furthermore, in this school, students take the New York State Regents Examination in English Language Arts in January of their junior (11th grade) year, so these students will be exposed to the most immediate effects of this high stakes exam which they must pass (with a score of at least 65%) in order to graduate.

By using first quarter English language arts grades, I selected students who reflected a variety of ability levels and in the school. Because the class is composed almost equally of males and females, I attempted to select an equal number of males and females in each category. Aside from gender and achievement criteria which I intended to replicate, I selected students at random.

I also conducted in-depth interviews with teachers in the areas of English, social studies, science (primarily chemistry and applied science, since most 11th grade students are enrolled in one of those two classes) and math. I conducted in-depth interviews with five teachers from each of the four subject areas as well as the school librarian. In-depth interviews focused on experiences and practices of academic writing, the purposes and processes of writing, teachers' and students' perceptions of themselves as writers, and the influences of curriculum and assessment on school-based writing. All interviews were audiotaped with permission of the participants; for students, written permission from parents was also secured.

The interview questions (see Appendices A and B) were predetermined and were developed based on classroom observations as well as a previous, small study conducted with English teachers and 11th grade students at the same school.

The final method of data collection involved document analysis. I analyzed numerous documents related to school-based interactions that involve writing. Such documents included letters to parents and students, course syllabi, class assignments/projects, written products by students and teachers, published school writing guidelines, assessment rubrics, and New York State Regents Examinations. In addition, I asked students to bring with them to their interviews two writing samples: (1) a piece of "typical" school writing, and (2) a piece of writing that was meaningful to them. (Of the 20 student participants I interviewed, 15 brought with them samples of writing as requested. The others generally referred to documents they recalled during the relevant parts of the interview protocol.) These documents provided a useful starting point in discussing writing instruction, meaningful (and less meaningful) writing with students. In addition, they offered a concrete glimpse of how writing is assigned, conducted, and assessed in this setting.

After collecting the documents described, I read, reread, and sorted them into categories prior to coding. Documents that were directly connected to interviews and observations were copied and placed with the relevant transcripts and field notes so that data could be considered in both contexts (i.e., as "documents" to be analyzed and as supplementary and pertinent to the analysis of interviews and field notes). I examined, read and coded all documents to explore the ways in which academic discourse is used and evaluated, and what uses of language are privileged, silenced, and subjugated within the school.

Data Analysis

All observations and document analyses were recorded as field notes and expanded as narratives. Interviews were audiotaped and transcribed. To ensure confidentiality, pseudonyms are used for all participants, for the school district for Borderburg, and for Lakefront City. To facilitate analysis, notes and transcriptions were imported into Nudist data analysis software. When data collection was complete and transcriptions and field notes were imported, I read and analyzed data to identify topics for coding (Bogdan & Biklen, 2003; Stake, 1995; Weis, 2004).

To develop and facilitate analysis of codes, I used constant comparative methods, which enabled me to "establish analytic distinctions—and thus make comparisons at each level of analytic work" (Charmaz, 2009, p. 54).

To establish codes, I first read, word-by-word and line-by-line, through about one-third of each type of data, making notes on themes that emerged in order to create tentative coding categories. This close reading was intended to "make fundamental processes explicit, render hidden assumptions visible, and [provide] new insights] (Charmaz, 2009, p. 55). Prior to reading the one-third of each type of data, I sorted interview transcripts, field notes, and documents so that a representative sample of participants and settings might be reflected in the codes. Using the constant comparative method, recurring themes and motifs related to my research questions were then identified as codes.

A categorized system of 81 codes emerged from the data, and all data were coded; double—and triple-coding occurred in some places. Coded chunks were organized through the software program, and I printed data from each code then created file folders housing these data. Individual codes had between 4 pages and 150 pages of data. I read data in every folder and took notes on emerging themes. I read and re-read the pieces while thinking about the themes before putting them back into their narrative form.

Data were considered in the contexts of social class and identity, as well as the social implications of discourses and composition. In the following chapters, examination of these concepts is interconnected with pedagogical theory in order to reflect on how experiences and practices of academic discourse affect learning, schooling, and identity construction.

Situating this Study

In this study I sought to bring together some of the essential elements that affect the educational experiences of young people in a working-class high school serving a first-ring suburban community. These Millennial youths in the first decade of the twenty-first century face particular challenges: the sweeping changes of new capitalism that affect their families and await them in the workforce, increasing disparities in income coupled with waning political commitment to social services, and escalated accountability pressures with respect to standardized testing in public schools. It is true that the experiences of students in working-class schools has been examined for decades; however, the distinct experiences of young people in this political and cultural milieu are important to explore. In addition, this study is unique in that it explores the experiences of students and teachers in this setting through their practices of writing and writing instruction, thus providing a particular focus on discursive performances that relate to the construction of identity.

This study also considers the experiences of teachers in this setting. Teachers are significant because the identities they construct have profound effects on their interactions with students. The role of teachers is undergoing a profound shift as the pressures of high-stakes tests come to be perceived as "normal." Teachers are experiencing a sense of deprofessionalization as they are re-socialized toward the working-class aspects of their occupation. Since many teachers were raised and educated in working-class communities, their schooling has provided little experience with empowering literacies. Although their backgrounds are predominantly working-class, teachers perceive themselves as having moved beyond the working class, particularly with respect to education and income.

As teachers' self-perceptions shift toward the middle class, they may define themselves against working-class Others—a group which includes their students and the families in this working-class community. Weis (2008), quoting conservative columnist David Brooks (2005), asserts that escalating economic disparities are affecting social class, particularly regarding education:

> Economic stratification is translating into social stratification. Only 28 percent of American adults have a college degree, but most of us in this group find ourselves in workplaces in social milieus where almost everybody has been to college. A social chasm is opening up between those in educated society and those in noneducated society, and you are beginning to see vast behavioral differences between the two groups. (as cited in Weis, 2008)

It is critical that educators and educational researchers grasp the complex forces that are shaping our field, as well as our future. The identities that are being constructed in school—identities that are affected by how young people perceive themselves as literate, liberated citizens – will influence the character of our nation in the twenty-first century. This book, through its discussion of the study, attempts to offer a glimpse into that character.

REFERENCES

Beach, R., Parks, D., Thein, A., & Lensmire, T. (2007). High school students' exploration of class differences in a multicultural literature class. In J. Van Galen & G. W. Noblit (Eds.), *Late to class: Social class and schooling in the new economy* (pp. 141-166). Albany, NY: State University of New York Press.

Bogdan, R. C., & Biklen, S. K. (2003). *Qualitative research for education: An introduction to theory and methods* (4th ed.). Boston, MA: Allyn and Bacon.

Burton, R. L. (1999). A study of disparities among school facilities in North Carolina: Effects of race and economic status. *Educational Policy, 13,* 280-295.

Brantlinger, E. (2007). (Re)Turning to Marx to understand. In J. Van Galen & G. W. Noblit (Eds.), *Late to class: Social class and schooling in the new economy* (pp. 235-268). Albany, NY: State University of New York Press.

Brooks, D. (2005, September 25). The education gap. *The New York Times, Section 4,* 11.

Calhoun, C., LiPuma, E., & Postone M. (Eds.). (1993). *Bourdieu: Critical perspectives.* Chicago, IL: University of Chicago Press.

Charmaz, K. (2009). Shifting the grounds: Constructivist grounded theory methods. In J., A. Morse (Ed.), *Developing grounded theory* (2nd ed.) Walnut Creek, CA: Left Coast Press.

Dorn, S. (2007). *Accountability Frankenstein: Understanding and taming the monster.* Charlotte, NC: Information Age.

Ehrenreich, B. (2001). *Nickel and dimed: On (not) getting by in America.* New York, NY: Metropolitan Books.

Factfinder. (2007). Retrieved from http://factfinder.census.gov/servlet/ACSSAFF-Facts?_event=&geo_id=16000US3615000&_geoContext=01000US%7C04000US36%7C16000US3615000&_street=&_county=borderburg&_cityTown=borderburg&_state=04000US36&_zip=&_lang=en&_sse=on&ActiveGeoDiv=&_useEV=&pctxt=fph&pgsl=160&_submenuId=factsheet_1&ds_name=DEC_2000_SAFF&_ci_nbr=null&qr_name=null&reg=null%3Anull&_keyword=&_industry=

Gee, J. P. (2004). *Situated language and learning: A critique of traditional schooling.* New York, NY: Routledge.

Giroux, H. A. (2003). *The abandoned generation: Democracy beyond the culture of fear.* New York, NY: Palgrave MacMillan.

Kozol, J. (1991). *Savage inequalities: Children in America's schools.* New York: HarperCollins.

Kraus, N. (2000). *Race, neighborhoods, and community power: Buffalo politics, 1934-1997,* Albany, NY: SUNY Press.

Lipman, P. (2003). Cracking down: Chicago school policy and the regulation of Black and Latino Youth. In K. J. Saltman & D. A. Gabbard (Eds.), *Education as enforcement: The militarization and corporatization of schools* (pp. 80-101). New York, NY: RoutledgeFalmer.

New York State District School Report Card Comprehensive Information Report. (2007). Albany, NY: New York State Education Department.

Nichols, S. L., & Berliner, D. C. (2007). *Collateral damage: How high-stakes testing undermines education.* Cambridge, MA: Harvard Education Press.

Orfield, M. (2002). *American metropolitics.* Washington, DC: Brookings Institution Press.

Principal. (2007). Welcome letter. Unpublished letter. Pontiac High.

Sacks, P. (2007). *Tearing down the gates: Confronting the class divide in American education.* Berkeley, CA: University of California Press.

Stake, R. E. (1995). *The art of case study research.* Thousand Oaks, CA: SAGE.

Thompson, E. P. (1966). *The making of the English working class.* New York, NY: Monthly Review Press.

Twenty-five-year slide in the workers' standard of living. (2003, May-June). *Spark.* Retrieved from http://www.the-spark.net/csart233.html

Van Galen, J. A., & Noblit, G. W. (Eds.). (2007). *Late to class: Social class and schooling in the new economy.* Albany, NY: State University of New York Press.

Walkerdine, V., Lucey, H., & Melody, J. (2001). *Growing up girl: Psychosocial explorations of gender and class*. New York, NY: New York University Press.

Weis, L. (1990). *Working class without work: High school students in a de-industrializing economy*. New York, NY: Routledge.

Weis, L. (2004). *Class reunion*. New York, NY: Routledge.

Weis, L. (Ed.). (2008). *The way class works: Readings on school, family, and the economy*. New York, NY: Routledge.

Willis, P. (1977). *Learning to labor: How working class kids get working class jobs*. New York, NY: Columbia University Press.

CHAPTER 3

SOCIAL CLASS, WRITING INSTRUCTION, AND IDENTITY CONSTRUCTION

While it is clear that the way people think affects their language use, it is a more subtle notion that the ways people use language affect their thinking. Since writing shapes thinking, classroom experiences and practices of writing can have a profound influence on students' academic achievement, identity formation, and social class identification. Emphasizing this connection between writing and thinking and the importance of this idea for educators, Moffett (1988) equates writing with inner speech:

> Educators would do best ... to conceive of writing, first of all, as full-fledged authoring, by which I mean authentic expression of an individual's own ideas, original in the sense that he or she has synthesized them for him or herself.... Presupposing true authorship ... acknowledges that *any* writing (emphasis in original) about whatever personal or impersonal subject, for whatever audience and purpose, can never comprise anything but some focused and edited version of inner speech. The chief reason for defining writing as a revision of inner speech is to ensure that writing be acknowledged as nothing less than thinking, manifested a certain way, and to make sure that it is taught accordingly (pp. 88-89)

Writing instruction can expand or restrict possibilities for ways of thinking and imagining one's self and one's place in the world. Students' experiences of writing affect their understanding of language use. People who do not understand written discourse as a means of discovery and a means of enacting agency lose the opportunity to develop access to those aspects of empowering discourse. Effective instruction, effective pedagogies, can enable students to develop a conception of language that is empowering. Effective teaching can provide students with the understanding that language is a tool for critical thinking, and that understanding is the first step toward empowerment.

Strategies exist for teaching composition as an act of empowerment. A wealth of research offers educators theoretical and practical approaches for doing so (Atwell, 1987; Fanselow, 1992; Finn, 1999; Hillocks, 1986; Marinara, 1997; Moffett, 1988). Empowering pedagogical approaches to composition involve dialogue, authenticity, and sociocultural sensitivity.

Composition, as a concrete manifestation of stratified social discourses, can be an instrument of liberation or domestication (Finn, 1999). School experiences have a powerful influence on the development of young people as writers; consequently, it is conceivable that writing instruction impacts identity development. Katznelson and Weir (1985) state the importance of language as a factor in identity construction: "Language neither precedes other human activities nor just reflects material realities. It is the hinge between social reality and social consciousness" (p. 210). Hawkes (1999) explains the ideological and political foundations of writing instruction.

> The American state enjoys, then, a degree of ideological unanimity of which Stalin could only dream. Composition, which constantly boasts of teaching students how to think as well as how to write, is an ideological apparatus for the inculcation of the doctrine that every individual is unique but also equal. The contradiction between individualism and egalitarianism is erased by the imposition of an ideology so uniform that it is no longer recognized as such. Through its emphasis on self-expression, composition inadvertently lays bare the objectification of the postmodern subject. (para. 14)

If the dominant view of education defines its processes as centered on the transmission of skills, discourse becomes reduced to "communication skills," basic language uses consistent with literacy for domestication (Finn, 1999). This perception of writing instruction undermines the possibility of student empowerment because of three fallacious assumptions: that communication skills are freely transferable, that discourse involves a simplistic model of acquisition, and that discourse is primarily a matter of mastering technique.

Notions of writing that do not reflect full authorship relate to both "institutional convenience and the materialistic framework of schooling"

(Moffett, 1988, p. 88). Moffett notes that, in fact, it is the materialism that places the institution over the individual, form over content.

> Generally, the materialistic bias of our cultural practically forces us to prefer the visible domain of language forms ... to the invisible domain of thought, which is still a scary can of worms. But teachers have no business preferring either and have no choice but to work *in the gap* (emphasis in original) between thought and speech. Writing is a manifestation of thought, but, however tempting we cannot deal with it only as it finally manifests itself visually in writing. (p. 89)

The key issue, then, is to be able to look at the writing process before it becomes visible and material. Moffett continues:

> If we concentrate our forces on fostering the highest development of inner speech, we will automatically not only teach excellence in writing, but lift other subjects along with it into a new learning integration, for the quality an qualities of inner speech determine and are determined by all mental activi- ties.... We have to consider writing in relation to the rest of the curriculum. Because inner speech is the matrix of spontaneous discourse that can be composed in any direction and that reflects any externalities, it allows us to integrate all discursive learning. (p. 93)

Identities are socially constructed and fluid. Empowering uses of language can facilitate the development of student agency by validating critical construction of meaning. If, however, language is perceived primarily as a means of replicating authoritative views, if it is taught as a formulaic discipline to which only the privileged and educated have access, if it is assessed for form over content and facility with "old" printcentric concep- tions of literacy, then students will learn that language is a weapon—a force to constrain them rather than an instrument of power to which they might gain access.

TEACHER EXPECTATIONS AND SOCIAL CLASS

School experiences are comprised, to a great extent, of interactions between students and teachers; many of these interactions take place through and around processes and products of written discourse. In addition, teachers' perceptions of social class, particularly as it relates to discourse, affect the experiences and practices of both writing and writing instruction. Because teachers' social class is connected to their beliefs about and experiences with discourse, the social class of teachers impacts the writing instruction they provide to students. That is, the social class of teachers impacts their ability to assist students in becoming powerful writers, thinkers and people (Anyon, 1981; Borkowski, 2004; Delpit, 1992; Finn, 1999; Lareau, 2003; Marinara, 1997). Panofsky (2004) explains: "The practices and representations organized by social class construct distance or proximity between the students and work through teacher-student interaction to differentiate student experiences" (p. 5). Understanding the role of proximity in pedagogic interactions is central to instructional effectiveness (Vygotsky, 1986).

Many contradictions occur in classroom interactions. Teachers, in the process of schooling, reinforce working-class norms at the same time as they reject them rhetorically. That is, even as they reject working-class values in written discourse, teachers frequently perform in ways that are in accordance with working-class values. For example, they tend to accede to authority figures and they belong to professional collective bargaining units (teacher unions). In terms of education and cultural capital, however, teachers are not categorized as working class. Grimm (1998) quotes Loewen (1995) in asserting that two social processes occur in schools to perpetuate dominant ideologies of individualism and equal opportunity: allegiance and socialization.

> Educated adults usually have higher incomes than those without education but in America, we are taught in school to believe that one earns successful positions through virtuous behavior and individual characteristics rather than through one's parents' social position. As a result, educated adults "have a vested interest in believing that the society that helped them be educated and successful is fair" and thus they "are more likely to show allegiance to society" than to be critical of it. (p. 7)

It is possible that teachers, in considering issues of social class, may feel conflicting allegiances among which they must choose. "Choosing," of course, implies conscious critical consideration, which may or may not be part of teachers' personal experiences or professional practices.

In school, teachers and students are immersed in a particular culture of academic discourse. Lankshear (1998) describes this as institutional deficiency, stating, "Schools are seriously out of touch with the discursive universe beyond their gates" (p. 4). Teachers are also implicated as having inadequate understandings of how narrow definitions of knowledge and literacy can "subvert learning for life" (p. 4). She further argues that as it reproduces dominant ideologies "School-based literacy ... undermines independent thought (because) when only dominant academic literate standards are valued, they create logical hierarchies" (p. 5). Such hierarchies become naturalized and seem normal through ideological discourses.

In schools, the regulatory formal structure of schools privileges individual meritocracy over the collective and students' intellectual selves are of greater concern than their social or emotional needs. Understanding writing as a means of discourse can begin to mend working-class students' fragmented experiences of schooling. In classrooms, there is often a tension between students' social motivations and academic learning. Ideally, by recognizing discourses as social constructions, these tensions can be minimized if writing is taught as a social process that includes interaction among students and includes them as expert users of new literacies. As Moffett (1988) claims, "Since discourse is ultimately social in origin and in function, it seems a shame to fight those forces that could be put to such excellent use in teaching the subject" (p. 119). Despite its potential for application toward collective purposes, writing is perceived as autonomous and individual.

Teacher expectations for students have been shown to be closely related to cultural characteristics that can be attributed to social class, but are instead perceived as student-based deficiencies. Relevant characteristics on which working-class students are judged negatively by teachers include language, subcultural values, and material factors; each and all of these contribute to lowered expectations.

The education of students in the United States is profoundly influenced by social class (Anyon, 1981; Finn, 1999; hooks, 1994; Weis, 2004). Paradoxically, Americans' belief in the equality of educational opportunity and the attendant social mobility has not diminished. Educators, in particular, typically attribute educational failure to deficiencies in students rather than the structural inequalities of the American educational system. The social class backgrounds of students and teachers influence their classroom interactions. Teachers convey different expectations based on characteristics that can be attributed to cultural capital, which is based to a great extent on social class experiences (Anyon, 1981; Bourdieu, 1993; Delpit, 1992; Lareau, 2003). Teachers tend to be profound believers in education as a neutral, meritocratic force toward social mobility (Apple, 2001; Mitchell, 1994) and teachers with working-class backgrounds may narrate particularly strong beliefs in this area. These beliefs may serve to reinforce teachers' perception of the need to promote the virtues of academic writing without developing an understanding of its ideological underpinnings. Furthermore, student resistance to the restraints of academic writing may produce "basic writing" pedagogical approaches which have been shown to exacerbate student engagement with school as well as their access to empowering discourses based on their own experiences (Borkowski, 2004; Brooks, 1987; Finn, 1999; Friere, 2003; Heath, 1983). While teachers tend to localize success or failure within individual students, structural and cultural factors are influential.

Panofsky (2004) explains that while students are perceived as initiating relationships with teachers who are characterized as neutral representatives of educational institutions, the relationship, in fact, develops in reverse: "Differential treatment is *not* in response to students; it is initiated by school personnel" (p. 10).

The identity construction of students in this setting is complicated when students resist the authority of teachers who perceive themselves as offering opportunities that will improve students' life chances. Teachers' identity construction is further complicated by the fact that their professional identities (which exist, in part, in opposition to working-class Others) hinge on the very performance of their (sometimes resistant) students. It would seem clear that teachers have multilayered reasons to encourage students to shed aspects of working-class identity that act in opposition to academic achievement. They are liable to embrace students who comply and reject those who resist. Although these dynamics are certainly not new, they are undoubtedly exacerbated by the current political and economic pressures. Teachers of all four core subjects— veterans and novices—and students across the spectrum of achievement —top scholars and dropouts—narrate similar perspectives of the effects of testing on curriculum in general and writing in particular. Their ideas shed light on the practices of writing in this school and how these practices illustrate and reinscribe the way students and teachers imagine their futures.

DEMORALIZATION AND ANXIETY

Reforms connected to high-stakes assessments rely on the external pressure of examinations to motivate teachers and students. Nichols and Berliner (2007) condemn this approach, noting that it results in demoralization and anxiety. They assert that "tests that attempt to control behavior ultimately undermine self-motivation in the area being tested. These tests reduce investment and commitment to the goals of the activities." (p. 148). Demoralization is coupled with stress. Given the range and significance of consequences associated with these assessments, it is not surprising that anxiety is associated with them.

Teachers experience anxiety as they navigate the dilemmas associated with standardized assessments and experience pressure to raise student achievement. Teachers are demoralized by their inability to reconcile dilemmas effectively on the basis of their professional expertise. Students narrate anxiety about performance on examinations and are demoralized by exam-related instruction that results in self-doubt regarding their ability as writers. Nichols and Berliner (2007) are clear in their assertion that reforms based on high-stakes testing are unfair in their application of consequences.

It is one thing that teachers are being evaluated on the basis of student test scores but yet another to humiliate and devalue them by judging performance for which they are at most co-creators. They are clearly not solely responsible for that performance, but teachers and schools are judged as if they were. Do physicians get punished when their patients supersize their food portions and develop diabetes? Do dentists get punished if their patients will not brush after every meal? This peculiarity of the teaching profession adds to the anxiety teachers feel. (p. 151)

Teachers at Pontiac High narrate anxiety regarding individual accountability for student performance on state assessments. Social studies teacher Gary Ventura describes the stress of being held individually accountable for students' assessment scores.

Gary Ventura: Nichols I think there's just so much stress—with No Child Left Behind, and you have to show adequate yearly progress, and all these things that have been set forth by the government—that there's so much pressure on this test, that's what the teachers are striving for. If this kid doesn't get 65, then they're thinking, "Does this measure teacher accountability? If the kids don't perform, then the teacher's done," or something like that—it's a mess!

English teacher Roger Johnson describes the conflicts he feels regarding the state's ELA exam given during grade 11 (junior year). He narrates a vague sense of the district level consequences imposed by the state for poor performance, and then shifts from discussing what "they" need to what "we" need. Mr. Johnson acknowledges that the test's significance, for him, is situated in the authority of district administrators who have the capacity to penalize him for unacceptable student performance.

Roger Johnson: In the junior year you are teaching Regents and … I have mixed feelings about that. Because on one hand it's an important test in terms of my bosses.

JG: Your bosses being?

RJ: The principal probably. The superintendent. I don't know the ins and outs of that but I know we need to have certain scores. And so the dilemma for me is (that) I know (administrators) need that. If I'm in their shoes, I can understand that. If we don't get certain scores we lose money, or whatever it is. It doesn't look good. In terms of marketing, we need (good examination results) to bring in people in the district, so there's that piece. Another piece is that we give (the examination) in January (instead of June). As a junior teacher that gives me half the time to prepare students.... (There is also) the understanding that these scores count and that we need bottom line scores. I shouldn't say bottom line scores; we want our scores to keep rising and rising and rising. And the whole question is, if that's what they are telling us to do, how to best do that. Or how to do that if there are going to be consequences. One year we did have lower scores and there were consequences, I remember. And we were kind of told—I felt the perception that our scores have to be higher and we need to do something about it.

Gunzenhauser (2006) notes that "It is the task of the examination to remake the individual" (p. 250). Despite reservations about the effectiveness and utility of the examination, Mr. Johnson has allowed his professional goals and expectations for students to be appropriated by it. Mr. Johnson's professional identity is influenced by his inability to reconcile the demands of the assessments with his desire to provide effective writing instruction. It is also important to note that Mr. Johnson does not describe himself as teaching "to the" Regents examination, but as "teaching Regents," a discursive move that reinforces the extent to which the state controls the classroom.

JG: So, are we collaborators...?

RJ: That's the dilemma I guess. Are we adding to the problem? Well, I guess part of me is practical. And I like my job. It's hard, but if my boss is giving me an ultimatum, I guess I am going to abide by it. I am realistic and I am not going to fight battles I know I can't win. At the same time, is there a way to do two things at once? In other words, is there a way of being able to teach writing that will allow them be successful? And that's tested? I am not going to change it, so then I just have to deal with it. I am not going to change it; it's not going to go away. But if I don't say anything about (the examination in my classes), I don't think my kids will be successful (on it) and that will translate in real terms to—I think, no one says it—but I think it would translate to me. I would be held accountable. If my kids were getting

> fifties I definitely think (I'd be asked), " Where are
> all these fifties coming from?" Somewhere down the
> line, someone will say, "Mr. Johnson, all your kids
> are getting fifties. What's going on? Ms. Lawrence's
> classes, they are doing well, so...."

Mr. Johnson, sensitive to the detrimental effects of the ELA examination, narrates a sense of futility and powerlessness with respect to the state reform ("I'm not going to change it"). Mr. Johnson's perception of his dilemma is upheld by Dorn (2007), who asserts that it is a "natural response" of teachers to do what is necessary for their students (and themselves) to avoid negative consequences (p. 153). Nichols and Berliner (2007) also note that such hypocritical actions have negative effects on educator morale.

In discussing his concerns about having his students' scores compared with those of Ms. Lawrence's students, Mr. Johnson suggests the sense of competition central to the high-stakes reform movement (Dorn, 2003, 2007; Jackson, 2003; Nichols & Berliner, 2007; Popham, 2001). Competition is detrimental to the educational process in that it improves neither teaching nor learning, undermines confidence of teachers and students, and heightens anxiety. Moreover, a competitive approach to learning privileges individual accountability rather than emphasizing the notion that individuals operate within a system of structures and institutions that influence their performance. Nichols & Berliner (2007) explain that

> individual workers are usually doing their best and ... what prevents them
> from doing better is the system in which they work. The solution, therefore,
> is not to set individuals in competition with one another but to organize
> their work so they can collaboratively improve the system. For the most part,
> however, teachers and administrators have been excluded from discussion of
> how to improve the American educational system. Instead, school improve-
> ment has been mandated by politicians who believe in high-stakes testing as
> a powerful instrument of school change. They ignore the fact that ... high-
> stakes testing invariable leads to a system of perverse incentives. High-stakes
> testing adds a layer of worry, anxiety, and stress to what teachers see as an
> undervalued, underpaid, and undersupported profession. (p. 147)

Apple (2001) predicts just such an effect as a consequence of the growing neoconservative movement in the United States. He states that

> Under the growing conditions of regulated autonomy, teachers' actions are
> now subject to much greater scrutiny in terms of process and outcomes....

> Such a regime of control is based not on trust, but on a deep suspicion of the motives and competence of teachers. (p. 51)

According to Apple (2001), neoconservatives expect that the problem of incompetent teachers will be solved by "a strong and interventionist state that will see to it that only 'legitimate' content and methods are taught. And this will be policed by statewide and national tests of both students and teachers" (p. 51). The narrations of students and teachers at Pontiac High clearly indicate that Apple's prediction has come to fruition. State mandates drive the actions of school administrators and directly affect the daily interactions of students and teachers.

English teacher Hillary Lawrence narrates dissatisfaction with the district administration's directives regarding the ELA examination. Like Mr. Johnson, she expresses a sense of powerlessness.

Hillary Lawrence: Obviously, if we are given writing instructions from administrators that we need to fulfill a certain writing requirement or it has to be done using a certain time frame, then we do that. Because that's what we do. In my own mind I am struggling with the concept of the January Regents exam. I believe that if we let our students have that extra set of instruction till June we will be better off.... But that is not my call. So I think that has impacted my selection of things I am going to do in class.... We could be better served, but if we are doing it this way, we're doing the best we can.

Mr. Ryan, chairperson of the department, echoes Ms. Lawrence's words with respect to managing professional dilemmas associated with Regents examinations.

JG: Where does writing fit into your curriculum?
SR: (Laughs) K to 11? Well, K to 11, I think we're structuring it very much in terms of New York State Standards and in terms of the measure that the state and our school board is concerned with. So is writing far more substantially altered? Yes! I'm sorry, it's that parallel tasking, okay? I'm not teaching creativity when I'm teaching parallel tasking. I'm not teaching intellectual thought. I'm teaching a pedestrian way of approaching things

> that will meet the needs of this standard. Oh well!
> So that's what I do. Thank you very much!

JG: You're obviously not happy about it. How do you reconcile what you want to be doing with what you're doing?

SR: (Laughs) I don't like getting e-mails (from administrators)—how 'bout you?

Both Ms. Lawrence and Mr. Ryan refer to examination-based writing instruction as detrimental to teaching and learning. However, it is clear that they have adopted this approach ("That's what we/I do.") Despite feeling conflicted about the exigencies of the exam and its administration, pressures from the state and local authorities cause all of these teachers to resolve the dilemmas in favor of the examination. It is clear that the examination has become, in Gunzenhauser's (2006) words, "an instrument of discipline" (p. 252). As a result, Gunzenhauser states that

> Teachers and administrators are acquiescing to the power of high-stakes testing, despite what educators believe and have learned in their professional lives, but teachers and administrators do not appear to have much choice. (p. 245)

UNDERMINING CONFIDENCE

The examination has explicit effects on the teachers who administer and score it as well as the students who complete it. Sarah Milton, a math teacher in her first year at Pontiac High, describes how the ELA Regents exam she took as a junior in high school changed her opinion of herself as a writer.

Sarah Milton: I'd always gotten good feedback (on my writing). Actually, … up until 10th grade, I always got good grades and I thought I was a good writer. And I took the Regents exam? And I got—like, a 70-something.

As a student, Ms. Milton was involved in the first administration of the state's high-stakes Regents examination. At that time, neither teachers nor students had a clear picture of what the exam would be like or how it would be scored. Despite twelve years of schooling during which her grades on writing assignments were good, Ms. Milton's performance on this one examination undermined her confidence. Instead of considering the examination an anomalous event, it became an instrument that redefined "good" writing and redefined Ms. Milton's perception of herself as a writer. Gunzenhauser (2006) describes this effect: "The examination thus effects a reversal of power relations—he measurement supplants the self, and measuring becomes the project of the school" (p. 251).

Chloe, whose average in English has dropped over ten points during her junior year, explains how in-class preparation for the English Regents examination undermined her perceptions of her own writing skills.

> **JG:** What do you think your teachers' expectations are for writing?
>
> **Chloe:** I think, I know, they want you to do your best so they are going to teach you their little tricks and their little ways and what they think the Regents is looking for.
>
> **JG:** Can you tell me about the tricks?
>
> **Chloe:** You get starter sentences for our body paragraphs. You have to, obviously, say what the book is and the author, but you have to say the literary element in the first sentence and you have to say whatever the element is, you have to use it for a character or maybe, if it's conflict, you have to describe the conflict and then you have to say how it relates to the quote. So the trick is to write the certain sentence. There's like two sentences in your body paragraph that are supposed to be written. So we had notes on them.
>
> **JG:** Do you know them?
>
> **Chloe:** Yeah.
>
> **JG:** What are they?
>
> **Chloe:** Usually it's, "In the play or book," and then you say the book. Then you say, "By so and so, the literary element— characterization or something—can be used to prove the quote true." Then the second sentence would be like, "For example, in Macbeth, Lady Macbeth was persua- sive," and you would say how it proves the quote true.
>
> **JG:** I'm amazed. You just rattled that off the top of your head.
>
> **Chloe:** It's been drilled in my head since September, so….
>
> **JG:** I hope you're not worried about the exam.
>
> **Chloe:** I am, but I'm trying not to be.
>
> **JG:** Do you think you could take the Regents exam without all the preparation, without, say, having that (starter) sentence memorized in your head?
>
> **Chloe:** Well, before I learned about that sentence, the starter sentence, I was like, "Yeah, I could do this." I thought I was a pretty good writer, I thought I had the main idea of

what I was supposed to do. But after all the preparation, I was like, "Oh, I guess not." I had to go back and rethink and just kind of look at what I was writing and I was, like, "Guess that wasn't what I was supposed to be writing." At a time I thought I was good, but not anymore.

JG: You really don't think so anymore?

Chloe: No. Not if I were to just dive right in and take (the ELA examination), probably not if I didn't have what we were learning now. Because what (the English teachers) tell us is, "Oh, the grading is going to be based on this, and if you don't have this then you'll automatically get a 3 out of 6." It's scary, so you want to do exactly what they tell you to do.

Chloe's perception of herself as a writer was altered by the prescriptive nature of the examination and the preparation associated with it. She states that instruction geared for the writing examination diminished her confidence in her writing abilities. Despite her effortless recitation of the "starter sentence," she remains anxious about exam. Moreover, as a writer, she has become utterly dependent on her teachers (who function as pawns of the state and its examinations). This conception of writing, wherein authority for language and thinking is situated in authority figures rather than learners, reinforces a working-class approach to schooling and literacy (Anyon, 1981; Finn, 1999; Weis, 1990).

Dylan discusses how the writing he did to prepare for the Regents examination diminished his motivation to the point that he simply stopped trying.

Dylan: Essays just got really boring. We'd come in every day and, say, write an essay on Macbeth, write an essay on The Crucible. I wouldn't even create them, I just kind of take my time and think about what I'm doing after school, that kind of thing.

JG: You can write an essay without your brain....

Dylan: These ones I can because they keep telling us to write it again after writing pretty much the same essay ten times. It's easier to come up with it; I just throw out big words and stuff. Your hand gets tired when you're writing the same essay every day. It's get annoying having to do over and over again. I stop trying in class when it's really not affecting anything at all.

Nichols and Berliner (2007) describe this result as an amotivational effect, stating that high stakes tests "lead to a withdrawal of effort, to not caring what happens" (p. 149). Dylan is an avid reader who loves to write at home, but finds examination-based writing demoralizing and meaningless. Again, students at Pontiac High are alienated from the process and products of learning. Weis (1990) argues that working-class schools reinforce the *form* of schooling rather than the process of learning or the substance of what is learned. Writing at Pontiac High displays a similar orientation in that the *form* of writing is privileged over the content or substance of the written product. The narrations of these students reflect the likelihood that working-class norms of learning and literacy are being reproduced (or even exacerbated) in this setting.

STUDENT ANXIETY

According to Nichols and Berliner (2007), "students … feel increased anxiety and stress as a result of the pressures to perform on tests. The pressure is all around them, as symbolized by the posters on walls everywhere" (p. 156). Stress and anxiety affect learning and affect students' perceptions of the purposes of and for writing. Paige's perspective of writing invokes deficit thinking; she associates writing not with its possibilities, but with the hazards of being unskilled.

> **JG:** So do you think that Regents exams have affected the writing that you do in school?
>
> **Paige:** Yeah. Definitely. On most Regents exams, … you have to write on everything now. If you can't write, you're in trouble. If you don't know how to write, you're going to have a problem.

Chloe, Andrew, and Riley narrate anxiety and pressure related to their performance on high-stakes assessments. For Chloe, the examination is more "real" than her classroom writing.

> **JG:** What affect, if any, do you think New York State exams have had on you as a writer?
>
> **Chloe:** I think that when we do our essays in class, it's kind of like we don't take things seriously but when the exam hits us we're like, "well this is for real, we have to do really good on this."

Andrew narrates pressure from both teachers and parents.

> **JG:** Do you think New York State exams have had an ef-
> fect on you as a writer?
>
> **Andrew:** I think so, yeah, because how much pressure they put
> on us for actually taking the exam and everything....
> **JG:** Where do you get that pressure from?
> **Andrew:** I think probably the teachers the most and then i
> comes down to the parents who actually want you to
> do good in school.

And Riley describes the negative effects of examination related stress on learning and on her personal well-being.

> **JG:** Do you think Regents exams have affected the writing
> you do at school?
> **Riley:** Actually, yeah, because you have to practice for the
> English and as the Regents comes closer and closer,
> you're stressing yourself on doing good on the exam,
> doing good on the writing, and it's not good to stress
> yourself. I learned that because my freshman year on
> the global (examination) I actually did okay on the
> essay but I could have done better if I wasn't stressing
> so much over it. So it does affect the writing you do
> in school because if you're practicing for it you're like,
> "Oh my God, the Regents is coming. The Regents is
> going to be asking questions a lot harder than this, es-
> says a lot harder than this." And it does (cause stress)
> ... I know it does to me. I've been stressed out about
> this English one and last night it was difficult for me
> to sleep. I felt like throwing up....

Students experience anxiety because their performance on high-stakes tests has material effects on their schooling as well as on their possibilities for future education. Dorn (2007) reveals the fallacious assumptions that underlie this aspect of high-stakes assessment based reform.

> Research evidence does not currently support the claims of its advocates
> that high-stakes accountability improves student achievement. The theory of
> action behind the argument for consequences assumes ideas about motiva-
> tion that are not supported by research or experience.... The psychological
> model of high-stakes accountability rooted in fear and material interest has
> little foundation. (p. 144)

CONCLUSION

Despite the lack of evidence supporting a positive correlation between high-stakes assessment based reform and student achievement, students and teachers are subjected to the disciplinary regulations of Regents examinations. These examinations have significant social and emotional effects on teachers, including deprofessionalization and disempowerment. In addition, expectations for student achievement in writing are reduced to standardized, assessment driven goals, further diminishing teachers' authority. Furthermore, the imposition of standardized expectations precludes dialogue necessary for effective writing instruction. Writing instruction is reduced to test preparation, which results in demoralization and anxiety.

The social and emotional consequences of high-stakes assessments at Pontiac High are not limited to individuals. Identities are constructed through daily interactions that are influenced by hegemonic relationships and reinforced by discourses of social class. Likewise, norms of social class are constructed and reconstructed through institutional norms and practices. The regulatory aspects of assessment-based state reform contribute to the social class shifts that are occurring in the new economy. Teachers are being resocialized toward working-class identities. Although these circumstances allow for the possibility of collective interactions among working-class students and teachers (e.g., both groups narrate frustration with the pressures of state examinations), the ideology of individualism privileged by standardized assessments results in increased regulation and educational experiences that are alienating for students. Institutions, like schools, change and are changed by the forming and re-forming identities of those who participate in (and are regulated by) its daily activities. Teachers and students narrate institutional effects which contribute to redefinition of identities. Social and emotional effects will be further explored in the next chapter.

REFERENCES

Anyon, J. (1981). Elementary schooling and the distinction of social class. *Interchange, 12,* 118-132.

Apple, M. W. (2001). *Educating the "right" way: Markets, standards, god and inequality.* New York, NY: Routledge-Falmer.

Atwell, N. (1987). *In the middle: Writing, reading, and learning with adolescents.* Upper Montclair, NJ: Boynton/Cook.

Borkowski, D. (2004). Not too late to take the sanitation test: Notes of a non-gifted academic from the working class. *College Composition and Communication, 56*(1), 94-122.

Bourdieu, P. (1993). Structures, *habitus*, practices. In C. Lemert (Ed.), *Social theory: The multicultural and classic readings* (pp. 479-484). Boulder, CO: Westview Press.

Brooks, D. (2005, September 25). The education gap. *The New York Times, Section 4,* 11.

Delpit, L. (1992). Acquisition of literate discourse: Bowing before the master? *Theory Into Practice, 31,* 296-302).

Dorn, S. (2003). High-stakes testing and the history of graduation. *Education Policy Analysis Archives, 11*(1). Retrieved from http://epaa.asu.edu/epaa/v11ni/

Dorn, S. (2007). *Accountability Frankenstein: Understanding and taming the monster.* Charlotte, NC: Information Age.

Fanselow, J. F. (1992). *Contrasting conversations.* White Plains, NY: Longman.

Finn, P. J. (1999). *Literacy with an attitude: Educating working-class children in their own self-interest.* Albany, NY: State University of New York Press.

Friere, P. (2003). *Pedagogy of the oppressed* (30th anniversary ed.) (M. B. Romos, Trans.). New York, NY: Continuum International.

Heath, S. B. (1983). *Ways with words: Language, life, and work in communities and classrooms.* New York, NY: Cambridge University Press.

Grimm, N. M. (1998, April). *Redesigning academic identity kits.* Paper presented at the Conference on College Composition and Communication, Chicago, IL.

Gunzenhauser, M. G. (2006). Normalizing the educated subject: A Foucaultian analysis of high-stakes accountability. *Educational Studies, 39*(3), 241-259.

Hawkes, D. (1999). Composition, capitalism and the new technology [Electronic Version]. *Bad Subjects, 44.* Retrieved from http://bad.eserver.org/issues/1999/44/hawkes.html

Hillocks, G. J. (1986). *Research on written composition: New directions for teaching.* Chicago, IL: ERIC Clearinghouse on Reading and Communication Skills: National Institute of Education.

hooks, b. (1994). *Teaching to transgress: Education as the practice of freedom.* New York, NY: Routledge.

Jackson, S. (2003). Commentary on the rhetoric of reform: A twenty-year retrospective. In K. J. Saltman & D. A. Gabbard (Eds.), *Education as enforcement: The militarization and corporatization of schools.* New York, NY: Routledge-Falmer.

Katznelson, I., & Weir, M. (1985). *Schooling for all: Class, race, and the decline of the Democratic ideal.* Berkeley, CA: University of California Press.

Lankshear, C. (1998, May). *Frameworks and workframes: Literacy policies and new orders.* Keynote address, Australian College of Education, Canberra.

Lareau, A. (2003). *Unequal childhoods: Class, race, and family life.* Berkeley, CA: University of California Press.

Loewen, J. W. (1995). *John Brown, big brother, memory hole, Why is history taught like this? What is the result?* excerpted from the book *Lies my teacher told me: Everything your American history textbook got wrong.* New York, NY: Touchstone Books.

Marinara, M. (1997). When working class students "do" the academy: How we negotiate with alternative literacies. *Journal of Basic Writing, 16,* 3-16.

Mitchell, J. P. (1994). Money, class, and curriculum: A freshman composition read-
    ing unit. Unpublished Journal Article accepted to *Writing on the Edge*, Uni-
    versity of Mississippi.
Moffett, J. (1988). *Coming on center* (2nd ed.). Portsmouth, England: Boynton/Cook.
Nichols, S. L., & Berliner, D. C. (2007). *Collateral damage: How high-stakes testing
    undermines education*. Cambridge, MA: Harvard Education Press.
Panofsky, C. P. (2004). The relations of learning and student social class: Toward
    re-socializing sociocultural learning theory. Retrieved from http://issuu.
    comgfbertini/docs/the_relations_of_learning_and_student_social_class=a-
    p&wmode=0
Popham, W. J. (2001). *The truth about testing: An educators call to action*. Alexandria,
    VA: Association for Supervision and Curriculum Development.
Vygotsky, L. (1986). *Thought and language* (A. Kozulin, Trans.). Cambridge, MA:
    The MIT Press.
Weis, L. (1990). *Working class without work: High school students in a de-industrializing
    economy*. New York, NY: Routledge.
Weis, L. (2004). *Class reunion*. New York, NY: Routledge.

CHAPTER 4

HIGH-STAKES TESTING

Social and Emotional Effects

> High-stakes testing often harms students' daily experience of learning, displaces more thoughtful and creative curriculum, diminishes the emotional well-being of educators and children, and unfairly damages the life-chances of members of vulnerable groups. (NCTE, 2007)

> That's all (my teachers) have been saying since freshman year, "The ELA, the ELA. You have to practice for the ELA." I'm like, "all right!" (Paige, an 11th grade student commenting on the English language arts (ELA) Regents examination during an in-depth interview)

Compulsory curricula and high-stakes assessments are part of the coercive discursive structure of schooling. State mandated, standards-based curricula and the associated high-stakes examinations are powerful structural factors that contribute to the identity construction of students and teachers. Gunzenhauser (2006) asserts that the "high-stakes accountability movement has appropriated the technology of the examination to redefine the educated subject as a normalized case" (p. 241). Such a redefinition displaces alternative modes of accountability, "such as community responsibility of equitable educational opportunities" (p. 241). Moreover, a standardized or "normalized" representation of what it means to be an educated person inevitably precludes possibilities not

---

Power, Resistance, and Literacy: Writing for Social Justice, pp. 59–78
Copyright © 2011 by Information Age Publishing
All rights of reproduction in any form reserved.

associated with hegemonic, normative expectations. This is detrimental to poor and working-class students, whose native discourses and identities may not align with the middle-class norms of schooling privileged by examinations (Dorn, 2007; Hillocks, 2002; Nichols & Berliner, 2007; Sacks, 2007).

High-stakes tests and the curricula that support them affect the ways students and teachers define themselves, relate to one another, and experience schooling. In addition, standards-based reform initiatives that rely on high-stakes assessments affect how students and teachers perceive and practice thinking and writing in school (Hillocks, 2002).

The discourse of schooling has been infiltrated by the rhetoric of high-stakes assessments and, as Gee, Hull, and Lankshear (1996) note, practices of discourses relate directly to identity formation. Experiences of writing connect to discourse and identity because "the 'world on paper' is important: how we think and write about the world has a great deal to do with how we act in it and, thus, what becomes reality" (p. 25).

The redefinition of identities in association with high-stakes examinations is particularly pertinent for students and teachers in working-class schools because poor and working-class schools experience more negative consequences from such assessments (Dorn, 2007; Gunzenhauser, 2006; Nichols & Berliner, 2007; Orfield & Kornhaber, 2001). At Pontiac High, the narrations of students and teachers indicate that the social class signifiers connected with the working class are reinforced by the discourse of high-stakes assessments. However, the demise of traditional working-class employment and the consequential reconstruction of the White working-class identity shift the context in which these signifiers perform. In the past, white working-class resistance to academic norms did not preclude the possibility of earning a living wage in an industrial setting. In the new economy, these opportunities are scarce and resistance is particularly perilous. Unfortunately, students and teachers narrate the sense that assessment-based reform reinforces pedagogical approaches that seem to foster resistance to rather than engagement in educational activities.

Teachers and students at Pontiac High are consistent in their descriptions of particular effects of high-stakes tests, and their descriptions are consistent with the scholarship on this topic. In addition to the redefinition of identities in terms of education, the effects of high-stakes standardized testing include deprofessionalization of teachers and narrowing of curricula. In general, at Pontiac High School, high-stakes testing reinforces a non-dialogic, instrumental approach to teaching and learning and a domesticating approach to writing. Therefore, rather than promoting empowering literacies, these assessments contribute to the reproduction of social class in this setting.

TESTING AT PONTIAC HIGH

Test results embed inequalities of race, ethnicity, and poverty. (Orfield & Kornhaber, 2001, p. 18)

Despite the well-documented limitations and potential harm of assessment-based reform, in 1999 (prior to No Child Left Behind [NCLB] legislation) New York State implemented graduation mandates that require students to pass examinations in the following content areas in order to earn a high school diploma: English language arts, global history and geography, United States history, science, and mathematics. In a review of state assessments, Hillocks (2002) described New York State's requirements as "the most demanding examination regimen we have seen in this study" (p. 137). The exams, called "Regents" exams because they are administered by the New York State Board of Regents, include specific regulations for educators regarding administration, scoring and reporting.

Teachers and administrators at Pontiac High have felt the disciplinary effects of standardized reform initiatives. These disciplinary effects influence the daily interactions of schooling, reinforcing economic stratification based on social class (Nichols & Berliner, 2007). Nichols and Berliner argue that

> The power elite in this society, along with the vast middle and upper-middle class whose children now attend good public schools, see high stakes testing as working to their own children's advantage.... High stakes testing blends with their self-interest because it forces a kind of education on the children of the poor that ensures that they cannot compete with the children of the wealthy. (pp. 22-23)

Pontiac High serves a working-class community in an inner-ring suburb of a rust belt city experiencing severe economic decline. These conditions make it much more likely that high-stakes tests will influence the discourse of schooling at Pontiac High through daily practices of teachers and their interactions with students (Nichols & Berliner, 2007; Sacks, 2007).

Gunzenhauser (2006) invokes Foucaultian notions of power and discipline in describing the effects of high-stakes assessments on public schools and the people who operate within them.

> As Foucault articulates, the examination is one of the most powerful tools of normalization. For Foucault, normalization is one of the effects of an expanded disciplinary apparatus found manifest in public schools. It is an example of what happens when "disciplinary power [becomes] an

'integrated' system, linked from the inside to the economy and to the aims of the mechanisms of power that it brought with it." (p. 249)

Brantlinger (2007) explicates the connections between and among school experiences, high-stakes accountability based reform (in this case, federal No Child Left Behind legislation), social class, and the economy. She first points out that this reform movement rests on students, who are expected to achieve social mobility through education despite the impediment of powerful structural factors which tend toward replication of the status quo (Foucault, 1983, 1993).

> No Child Left Behind is based on the premise that closing the educational achievement and attainment gap between classes will reduce economic and social disparities. The message is that it is up to poor children to replicate the achievement patterns of their higher-income counterparts if they are to become as one with the middle class. (Brantlinger, 2007, p. 238)

Next, Brantlinger (2007) reveals the fallacious nature of a high-stakes assessment-based reform strategy from an economic perspective, describing its inevitable effects on students and teachers.

> Prescribed remedies, however, inevitably solidify rather than reduce disparities. Solutions that call for increasing the ranks of the educated class as a way to end poverty do not take into account (1) that people with high school diplomas and even college degrees are unemployed or underemployed, (2) that there are not enough professional and other college attainment-based careers for all citizens, and (3) that working-class labor is needed. Tightening school standards and demanding higher test scores has negative repercussions, including social and emotional stress for both teachers and students and narrowing the schools' focus to measurable skills and knowledge. (p. 239)

Students and teachers Pontiac High, whose faculty's origins are primarily working-class, narrate both of these effects, describing social and emotional stress as well as narrowing of the school's focus to preparation for high-stakes assessments. As the pressures of the new economy increase social stratification, shifting class relations among teachers and students are evident. All of these factors affect the identities that students and teachers construct as they negotiate experiences of schooling. It is noteworthy that students at all levels of achievement narrate anxiety about state examinations and dissatisfaction with the writing and writing instruction that accompany the assessments. Likewise, teachers narrate anxiety and frustration about the effects of examinations on curricula and autonomy. This chapter explores the social and emotional effects of high-stakes testing on students and teachers at Pontiac High. Chapter 5 will reveal the reductive effects of standardized assessment-based reforms on curriculum and instruction and how these effects influence identity construction.

Areas of social and emotional stress related to high-stakes assessment include deprofessionalization of teachers as well as demoralization and anxiety affecting both teachers and students.

DEPROFESSIONALIZATION OF TEACHERS

The teaching profession has always displayed characteristics that cross over boundaries of labor classes (Katznelson & Weir, 1985; Robertson, 2000). For example, the employment conditions of K-12 teachers couple professional-class educational requirements with working-class schedule restrictions. Despite such inherent conflicts, the autonomous nature of the daily activities of teachers have enabled them to resist top-down reform efforts by, quite literally, closing their classroom doors. Robertson claims that

> in a very real sense, teachers remain committed to a notion of occupational autonomy. Closing the classroom door on the intrusions of the outside world is, for teachers, symbolic. It is the exercise of organizational power—the ability to control one's labour and the stuff of professionalism—a claim that runs the long and jagged vein of teachers' occupational history, particularly since the mid-19th century. (p. 2)

Recent accountability measures, however, have undermined the sense of autonomy which is a key aspect of teachers' professional identities. Mandatory assessments provide a window through which snapshots of student achievement are captured for publication. This intrusion has had a profound effect on teachers' perceptions of their professional autonomy, particularly with regard to setting purposes and expectations for themselves and their students.

Nichols and Berliner (2007), in considering the effects of the high-stakes standardized assessment-based reform movement, describe the teaching profession as having

> been changed in some ways from being associated with the proud title of "educator" to that of "trainer," a title that evokes working with dogs and other animals. Teachers of some subjects are now script readers, curriculum and testing technicians, not professionals in the sense in which the term

is usually used. Disciplinary regulations associated with this shift in professional identities can be linked directly to high-stakes assessments. (p. 146)

Although all of New York State's examinations include written components, the English Language Arts examination focuses on writing. New York State's commencement examination in the area of English Language Arts is composed of four tasks to be completed in two three-hour sessions on consecutive days. Every element of examination administration is prescribed: directions are scripted for teachers to read; exams must be given only during the time allotted; and, at completion, both students and teachers must sign oaths attesting to the integrity of exam administration. Exams may not be opened from sealed wrappers prior to designated starting times, and scoring materials may not be reviewed by teachers until students have finished writing exams. Finally, in order to facilitate publication and analysis of regional and state data, teachers must fill in standardized "bubble sheets" with scoring data about each student's performance on every task. Before examinations are even begun, much less scored, the authority and control of the state education department are conspicuous and palpable.

The scoring procedure is also highly regulated. The state-published *Information Booklet for Administering and Scoring the Regents Comprehensive Examination in English* is 16 pages long and includes two scoring grids which must be photocopied and completed by all participating scorers (teachers). The scoring keys are voluminous; none has fewer than 100 pages. Each of four student essays must be graded by two different scorers. Scoring directions require that districts make every effort to avoid having teachers rate their own students' work. Obtaining a final score for the four-part examination involves the following:

> Add all four essay scores together. (If the total essay score ends in .5, that score should be rounded up to the nearest whole number at this time.) Write that score in the box labeled "Total Essay Score." (The maximum total essay score is 24.) Add the number of correct answers for the multiple-choice questions on the three parts. Write that score in the box labeled "Total Multiple Choice." (The maximum total multiple-choice is 26.) To determine the student's final examination score, use the chart located at the end of the Scoring Key and Rating Guide for Session Two, or on the Department's website: http://www.emsc.nysed.gov/osa/. Locate the student's total essay score across the top of the chart and the student's total multiple-choice score down the left side of the chart. The point where those two scores intersect is the student's final examination score. The chart below illustrates the format of the chart. The chart included with the actual Scoring Key and Rating Guide will include scores ranging from 0 to 100 within the cells of the chart. Because the scaled scores corresponding to raw scores in the conversion chart may change from one examination administration to another, it is *crucial*

(all emphases in original) that, for each administration, you use *only* the conversion chart provided in the scoring materials for that administration to determine the student's final score. (New York State Education Department, 2004)

For each exam administration, scorers must be retrained with new anchor papers and scores are determined through an exam-specific "scoring scale." This discourse of control, with its consequential reduction of writing assessments to numerical values, gives the impression of operational efficiency and accuracy. This precision is a pretense, since the tests are riddled with limitations and flaws (Dorn, 2003, 2007; Jackson, 2003; Nichols & Berliner, 2007). Their effects, however, are powerful. High-stakes tests increase accountability while simultaneously reducing teachers' authority (Dorn, 2003, 2007; Nichols & Berliner, 2007).

In *Working Class Without Work*, Weis (1990) revealed the nature of power relations among students, teachers, and administrators in a working class school. Weis showed how the focus on regulation and control creates an environment in which form dominates over substance. At the brink of the twenty-first century, power relations in the working-class school Weis studied replicated relations of labor that were consistent with working-class work. Teachers exerted control over the labor of students and administrators exerted control over the labor of teachers. The result of these conditions is, inevitably, a sense of alienation from labor—in this case, the labor of *learning*. Weis asserts that when

> teachers perceive that there is too much administrative (read management) control over what has come to be defined as the instructional/educational area. This ultimately serves to alienate teachers from their labor, to some extent, and undermines the notion that education acts to move individuals I to true professional positions.... The political climate undermines the notion of a meritocracy; the perceived heavy-handedness of management erodes the idea that they have moved into a profession. (p. 148)

Twenty-five years later, the most significant change with respect to power relations in this working class school involves the *extent* of the control and alienation, which has magnified with the increased participation of the state as "assessor." One way that teachers have historically exerted control over students is through grades, which are generally tied to tests. A key aspect of teachers' professionalism involves their ability to decide *what* sorts of knowledge should be tested as well as *how* to test students to determine their achievement. The extent to which school and district administrators participated in these decisions could vary widely. Now, with the implementation of standards-based high-stakes testing, the state —through policies, reporting requirements, and administrators—wields unprecedented power in the day-to-day operations of schools, particularly those that serve poor and working-class communities.

The interactions among students, teachers, administrators, and state education officials are analogous with respect to power and regulation. Teachers and administrators maintain the same types of controls that Weis identified over 20 years ago. Because teachers and administrators regulate the mechanisms necessary for students to earn the credentials for a diploma, students wishing to do so are always subjugated to their authority. Now, however, there are additional regulatory mechanisms related to state assessments. Both students and teachers are judged by student performance on state assessments, which are tightly controlled in administration and scoring. Assessments affect students directly because graduation is dependent on obtaining a passing level performance. Assessments are used by administrators to tighten control of teachers because teachers are judged on the basis of their students' performance. State assessments, therefore, influence the actions of the administrators who then increase their regulation of teachers. The regulation is direct in terms of the scoring, administration, and reporting procedures that teachers must adhere to. The regulation infiltrates the classroom when it involves submission of curricular materials and assessments that must show alignment with state assessments. The interactions described highlight the realities of shifting class relations within working-class schools. As public school teachers become increasingly subject to state control (through regulatory assessments), their role becomes more aligned with working-class norms. Although these conditions might seem to foster possibilities for *connecting* with their working-class students, teachers increase control and regulation, resulting in increased alienation and exploitation of students.

Nichols and Berliner (2007) maintain that high-stakes assessment-based accountability movements like NCLB result in deprofessionalization of teachers. They assert that

> high stakes testing is attacking the professionalism of our teachers, those to whom we have entrusted both the socialization and the education of our next generation. We hold the simple view that teachers are special people in a democracy, and as such, most of them have earned the right to our respect. But listening to teachers across the country makes us aware that their treatment under NCLB is simply as "pawns." (p. 145)

Teachers in all subject areas in which assessments are administered experience a loss of autonomy as they function in the shadow of these examinations.

State regulations are fortified and personalized when they are enforced by district administrators. An e-mail exchange between Pontiac's district assistant superintendent for curriculum and the chairperson of the English department demonstrates how regulations related to high-stakes assessment affect the daily activities of teachers and reinforce the hierarchical relationships between administrators (who must ensure compliance with regulations) and teachers. In his e-mail message (which was copied to the building principal), the district administrator describes his concerns about the English department's level of compliance with assessment-based regulations. The e-mail message was subsequently forwarded to high school English teachers by Stan Ryan, the department chairperson.

Please respond to the following:

1. Do you have scoring teams or is the department one scoring team? In other words, are you scoring tasks one and two simultaneously and tasks three and four simultaneously or do you score each task as a department?
2. If you have scoring teams, please tell me who are on the teams for each task, 1-4.
3. Who is doing the training? (For the department and/or for each team?)
4. Where are you scoring?
5. How were you going to do the training @ 12:00 if the universal admissions deadline is 2:00 and the training papers aren't available until after 2:00?
6. Are you using independent rating sheets that are NOT (all emphases in original) viewed by the other rater?
7. Please describe the rating process in terms of paper exchange and score reporting for each task.

It is recommended by SED (the State Education Department), in order to assure consistency among the raters, that training occur before each task. Training could take up to two hours for each task. The scorers must have a universal vision of what a 2 is, a 3, a 4 and so on. Teachers must have a vision of what the STATE says is a 2, 3, 4, to be fair to our students. It is possible that you could use four days to correct the examination.

Stan Ryan responded with an e-mail message that clarified scoring plans in compliance with state (and district interpretations of) regulations. The exchange concluded with this message sent from the assistant superintendent to Mr. Ryan, who forwarded it to the department:

Thank you for your response. You raised my level of concern yesterday when you said that you were starting training at 12:00 and may be correcting papers at the end of session one. Your response clarifies your intent as well as confirms the correct scoring procedure. Again, just to reiterate, training occurs before each task, the training should not be split (begin one day, finish the next), and it continues until there is a clear vision by all raters of the state's expectations.

This highly regulated set of practices related to assessment administration is an example of what Nichols and Berliner (2007) refer to as an "effect of high stakes testing on the profession at large" (p. 167). They assert that

> As the high stakes programs continue, the role of "teacher" as a professional with decision making responsibility seems likely to be sufficiently downgraded to such an extent that they will end up resembling technicians and trainers. (p. 168)

Indeed, state distributed scoring materials consistently refer to teachers as "raters" who require hours of "training" prior to scoring an examination which assesses content in their area of specialization. Authority regarding assessments and accountability is plainly situated in the state and enacted through its publications and local administrators. Moreover, the extent to which compliance is expected by state officials and monitored by local administrators indicates some skepticism as to the ability or willingness of teachers to behave as professionals, that is, to be autonomous as they enact their professional identities. This deprofessionalization connected to high-stakes tests is consistent with the assertions made by Dorn (2007), who states that "testing has influenced modern accountability ... by denigrating the authority of classroom teachers" (p. 40).

The relationship between teachers and administrators (and administrators and the state) clearly demonstrates adherence to a working-class sense of labor and knowledge. Weis (1990) asserted that the theme of "control" was central to both knowledge and labor, that is, teachers exert control over what counts as knowledge (and, thus, the "labor" of students) and administrators exert control over the labor of teachers. In this era of high-stakes testing, the state, through its assessments, has secured control of knowledge. In addition, state guidelines now permeate the ways in which administrators exercise control over the labor of teachers.

Jackson (2003) probes the potential long-range effects of high-stakes testing on the professionalism of teachers.

When one considers that becoming an educator, a teacher in particular, is not based on training and the transmission of strategies, tactics, and internalization of best practices, but rather academic and professional preparation to understand and negotiate the complexities of teaching and learning as well as work within complex and dynamic organizations that have particular cultures, then one has to question what will be the future for those who see education as holistic, intended to engender intellectual, affective, ethical, aesthetic, as well as physical development of others, and not merely to pass tests? (p. 235)

Teachers' professionalism is centered, to a great extent, on their ability to make decisions with respect to teaching and learning based on their education and experience. A sense of deprofessionalization results when goals and expectations are determined and measured exclusively by an outside entity.

EXPECTATIONS FOR STUDENTS AS WRITERS

Expectations are a politically dynamic factor in education. One way that high-stakes assessments deprofessionalize teachers is by restricting their ability to set and measure expectations. Dorn (2007), like Brantlinger (2007), notes that recent reforms have shifted expectations from schools to students, further diminishing teachers' control. While schools have long been charged to encourage economic and social progress, the high-stakes testing movement, by using students' scores on standardized assessments as the basis for demonstrating achievement *and* earning credentials, sets the expectations for achievement explicitly on students. Using student test scores to assess accountability has significant consequences for teachers as well, a condition which Nichols and Berliner (2007) describe as unfair and unreasonable.

> Teachers are put in the precarious position of putting their livelihoods squarely on the shoulders of students. That is, unlike so many others whose work is evaluated based on their performance, teachers succeed or fail based on the performance of others! (p. 150)

Teachers are disempowered by high-stakes assessments in two ways: First, expectations are standardized rather than dependent on their professional expertise; and second, teachers are held accountable for test scores which they, at best, coconstruct with students (Nichols & Berliner, 2007). Although their perceptions of the rigor of state expectations vary, both teachers and students at Pontiac High describe how expectations for learning and for writing were shaped and limited by high-stakes tests. This is problematic because effective education requires ongoing professional dialogue about purposes and expectations; high-stakes tests preclude such dialogue. Gunzenhauser (2006) emphasizes the significance of this development stating that "high-stakes accountability has so dominated discourse and practices in public education that dialogue about the purpose and value of education has been circumscribed to dangerously narrow proportions" (p. 242). The preclusion of professional dialogue is an effect of high-stakes testing which influences both the identities of teachers and the daily activities within classrooms.

Veteran English teacher and department chairperson Stan Ryan articulates a belief in the espoused intention of the reform, which is to improve education for disadvantaged students. However, he also states that the standardized assessment-based reform has been detrimental to students, especially those with the most academic potential. He believes that mandatory testing may have raised expectations for lower-achieving students, but has lowered expectations for students in general.

> **Stan Ryan:** The state (reform) ... certainly ... has worked on the lower half and has said some very meaningful things about the fact that you can't let that lower half or lower third or lower ten percent disappear. There's no factory for them to go and sweep. I get that—okay? It's not a hard deal.... But what about the other students who you used to look at and say, "We are going to advocate their success and we are going to stimulate their success and we are going to do things to encourage them to be more successful?"... The only criterion we have for success at the high school is the (ELA) Regents (examination) which is what? It's a minimal competency exam.

Although he sees it as harmful to high-achieving students, Mr. Ryan narrates a belief that this reform is beneficial for the "lower half." He points to the espoused economic aims of high-stakes reform, which are typically well-publicized by politicians and the media, as a favorable aspect of the initiative (Gunzenhauser, 2006). It is widely believed that reform movements like NCLB legislation have positive effects for impoverished children; however, high-stakes assessments typically sort children on the basis of their socioeconomic status and exacerbate rather than ameliorate social stratification (Nichols & Berliner, 2007). Students in the "lower half" are generally most harmed by high-stakes assessments (Dorn, 2007; Nichols & Berliner, 2007).

Mr. Ryan's perceptions about the potentially deleterious effect of reduced expectations on high-achieving students may have merit (Dorn, 2007); however, his belief in the beneficial effects on the "lower half" is unfounded. In fact, the reverse has been shown to prevail in that high-stakes assessments have far more negative consequences for students from poor and working-class families than for students from middle – and upper-class families (Dorn, 2007; Hillocks, 2002; Nichols & Berliner, 2007; Sacks, 2007). Moreover, it is noteworthy that Mr. Ryan blames school personnel, including himself, as responsible for accepting what he acknowledges as deficient expectations based on what he calls a "minimal competency exam."

Hillocks (2002), having analyzed the effect of standardized writing assessments in five states including New York, concurs with Mr. Ryan's evaluation of the examination. He identifies significant discrepancies between examination rhetoric with respect to the rigor of critical thought required and the anchor papers intended to demonstrate proficiency on examination tasks. In short, New York's commencement level English Language Arts examination *appears* much more difficult than it actually is. Hillocks explores this inconsistency.

> We have to ask why this great chasm exists between the expectations we see in the language of the prompts and criteria and the reality of their application as seen in the benchmark papers. It cannot be that this clear disparity has gone unnoticed by players in the New York state assessment system. I suspect the gap is intentional.
>
> Why? As in other states, there is a need to convince citizens that the state assessments are as demanding and rigorous as the Regents' goals suggest they will be. Politicians need to claim that their educational efforts will lead to excellence. At the same time, if the assessments do not seem to demonstrate improvement, they become a liability to political careers. If the testing program is really rigorous, it is likely to reveal weak performance, a disaster for any politician claiming education as his chief priority. For the politicians and bureaucrats, it will be far safer to claim high standards and rigorous assessment, and cut a great deal of slack in the implementation. The pompous language of the prompts and criteria, while undoubtedly confusing for students, give the impression of living up to the goals set by the Board of Regents. (p. 151)

Despite documented flaws in their development and implementation, high-stakes tests permeate the discourse of schooling at Pontiac High. Gunzenhauser (2006) describes a particularly insidious effect of high-stakes tests on schools mandated to implement them.

> schools seem to be falling back on a "default" philosophy of education, a nonreflective, nondialogical approach to schooling in which external constraints determine the purpose and value of education (p. 245)

Expectations for writing in courses that do culminate in state Regents examinations are shaped by the examinations. In social studies and English language arts classes, writing assignments parallel examination tasks in terms of format and are rated numerically based on state-published rubrics.

Mr. Ryan, chairman of the English department, asserts that the ELA examination sets low standards for writing and thinking and that school personnel have been complicit in the denigration of writing instruction by acceding to the low standards set by the state rather than expecting more from students.

> **JG:**   Have New York State exams affected writing instruction?
>
> **Stan Ryan:** We think we've done enough when a child has a 4. We think he's met our criteria. He's met the school's criteria. And we will get from every single person here in an administrative fashion that they're satisfied if they've got a 4. I have yet to have any principal come in to question me about it if the high 4 is there. They don't have to have a 5 or a 6. Nobody is asking for a 5 or a 6, as long as they get the 4, because that's the, that's the number cruncher. You don't get extra points for the 5 or the 6, you just need to get the high 4—that's it.... It's mediocrity.
>
> **JG:**   And the exams have contributed to that ... mediocrity?
>
> **SR:**   It's the two hands washing each other. And we'll turn out exactly what we set out to do.

Mr. Ryan complies with the expectations of the examinations even though he articulates their negative effects. Gunzenhauser (2006), discussing the effects of high-stakes testing, anticipates this development. He states that, "It is my contention that high-stakes accountability overlays a discourse that pervades discussions (by educators, researchers, policymakers, and the general public), even by those who are well aware of the limitations of testing" (p. 243).

Mr. Ryan describes conditions in which the "external constraint" of the examinations has been allowed to set expectations for student writing. Describing it as contributing to the systemic production of "mediocrity," Mr. Ryan believes it is evident that state expectations dictate the assessment of student writing. Their rhetoric resounds with the notion that written products can be reduced to numbers, scores that are based on state-provided rubrics. Calling for training in writing *instruction* for teachers rather than training that focuses on *scoring*, Hillocks (2002) describes how this misplaced emphasis influences writing instruction. "States merely offer training for scoring the writing resulting from state prompts. The workshops on scoring indoctrinate the teachers into the state's way of thinking about writing...They do not deal with teaching" (p. 205). The widespread acceptance of examination-based expectations for writing is significant because these conditions stifle professional discussion about writing instruction and assessment. Gunzenhauser (2006) writes that "In the context of high-stakes accountability, the examination has a particularly effective role to play to foreclose dialogue about student learning. Schools are encouraged to talk about scores rather than students, scores rather than learning" (p. 249). When writing is assessed strictly in relation to a task-oriented rubric, writing as thinking is discouraged and the development of critical thought is inhibited (Hillocks, 2002).

In addition, the reduction of writing—a process that is essential to deep and critical thinking—to a set of discretely assessed skills reinforces working-class perspectives about teaching and learning. Reinforcing the findings of Weis (1990), teachers and students in this working-class school reveal a focus on form over substance and "getting by" (in this case, achieving a "4" on a prescribed task as scored by a prescribed rubric) is perceived to be sufficient.

STUDENT PERCEPTIONS OF TEACHER EXPECTATIONS

Students across levels of achievement describe expectations for writing as being tied directly to state assessments. Echoing the descriptions of teachers, students' descriptions of school-based writing are infused with references to state standards and rubric-based scores.

Writing is closely linked to thinking and, as an aspect of language, to identity. The prevalence of a definition of writing established strictly in association with assessments is significant in that it limits the possible definitions of "self" that can be developed in relation to language, writing and schooling. Gunzenhauser (2006) states that this is a predictable result of high-stakes assessment.

> Using the technology of the examination, educators are encouraged to remake the individual as a set of attributes, each assessed by its deviation from the normal. The individual becomes a case, a normalized educated subject.... High-stakes testing solidifies the normalization of the subject and forecloses educational possibilities. (pp. 242-243)

Teachers' expectations for students as writers have been shaped by state examinations and students have internalized these expectations as they construct their identities as writers.

While the general sense that state standards drive writing instruction is prevalent, students have also adopted the language of numerical, rubric-based scores in assessing their writing and assessing themselves as writers.

Samuel, who is barely passing 11th grade English, writes regularly outside of school for personal purposes. He experiments with poetry, enjoys blogging, and creates elaborate written scenarios for an online fantasy game. However, when asked to describe himself as a writer, Samuel makes an immediate link to the Regents rubric as his performance indicator.

> **JG:**   How would you describe yourself as a writer?
> **Samuel:**   Excellent. I can throw upper 4½, 5 papers out there.

The manner in which Samuel, and students like him, depict their ambitions with respect to academic writing suggests that the high-stakes ELA examinations have, in fact, limited the imagined possibilities of these young writers.

Students who understand the process of writing, and themselves as writers, primarily in terms of their performance on standardized assessments are not developing to their potential as fully literate human beings. Such development requires—writing and reading in the six intertwined worlds that we now inhabit: the personal, the cultural, the educational and professional, the economic, the civic, and the cyber. Each of these requires its own set of processes and skills, and attaining them represents a highly demanding educational goal. (Alsup et al., 2006, p. 283)

At best, examination-based writing relates to a small part of the "educational" world of literacy, just one dimension of a multidimensional approach to literacy. Proficiency in this aspect of writing is not sufficient for success beyond the examination itself. Moreover, since this approach to writing is predominant, it precludes the possibility of transformational pedagogical approaches that might enable students to find the voices they need in order to engage in the dialogue necessary for dialogic classroom interactions.

Furthermore, on a broader scale, this approach to writing alienates students from thinking and learning. Weis (1990), in her ethnography set in a working-class high school, found school personnel complicit in the encouragement of working-class identities of students: "the school simply demands passivity ... in order to pass" (p. 92). Despite the fact that examination content does not reflect the skills necessary for success, the belief that passing is enough is prevalent among the working-class students at Pontiac High. A major shift in perspective, however, involves the fact that state examinations have replaced teachers as the regulators of knowledge.

STUDENT PERCEPTIONS OF TEACHERS

Public school teachers, as agents of the state, are obliged to fulfill state mandates. However, mandates are problematic when they conflict with professional and ethical beliefs. This is not a new dilemma. Alsup et al. (2006) state that it is a "paradoxical challenge" for teachers to "function effectively in an educational system that we believe they must also try to change and improve" (p. 284). Teachers at Pontiac High are typical in that they have chosen to help students achieve in the current system, which (particularly at schools serving poor and working-class students) means focusing on examination requirements. Unfortunately, this focus does not support the type of transformational literacy in which teachers and students develop consciousness of their own potential as agents of change.

Teacher expectations for students have significant effects on teaching and learning. Expectations affect how each perceives and interacts with the other. Students echo the examination-based nature of expectations for writing at Pontiac High; these expectations influence the relationships students and teachers form and perform within. If teachers do not enact the critical stance necessary to seek change, it seems unlikely that students will. Therefore, it is not surprising that the fact that high-stakes assessments set the goals and expectations for learning affects students' perceptions of their teachers.

Samuel affirms the prominence of the state's influence on teachers' use of writing in school. Although sympathetic to their situation, he perceives teachers as pawns of the state.

> **JG:** What do you think are your teachers' expectations about writing?
>
> **Samuel:** When it comes to English they're very strict—very ridiculously strict—but you gotta do it. And when it comes to teachers, they're just doing their job. If it comes to writing, they just, you know, they give you an assignment because New York State says you have to. I mean, it all goes back to New York State.

Samuel narrates a sense of his teachers' relative powerlessness in the context of state jurisdiction. Nichols and Berliner (2007) explain the how this attitude emanates from an environment permeated by high-stakes tests.

> It is hard to build responsibility in our youth, or require it of our teachers, if we choose to control the behavior of both through high-stakes testing. And when students end up believing ... that their teachers are helpless to change things, ... we have undermined a profession that could serve our nation better. (p. 170)

Samuel perceives teachers' subjugation to the technology of state assessments, a condition Apple (2001) anticipates to be a result of standards-based reform. Apple states that "such policies lead to the 'deskilling' of teachers, the 'intensification' of their work, and the loss of autonomy and respect" (p. 51). The perception that teachers serve as pawns of the state who obediently pass along examination-based "knowledge" to students who are meant to unthinkingly reproduce it reinforces a working-class approach to knowledge revealed by Anyon (1981) and bolstered by Weis (1990). Weis and Anyon assert that working-class schooling encourages a perception that knowledge is accessed through authorities and exists outside of the "self." Learners reproduce knowledge; they do not construct it.

Teachers and students at Pontiac High extend this interpretation, establishing the fact that that high-stakes assessments promote conditions in which the relationship between the state and teachers parallels the relationship that exists between teachers and students. While each of these sets of relationships are dialectical (i.e., it is conceivable that teachers might challenge the state's conception of knowledge; instead, their passivity strengthens the hegemonic power relations that obtain), they overwhelmingly reflect a working-class orientation toward knowledge, learning, and schooling. While the reality that working-class schooling does not encourage students to construct knowledge is well documented, the prevalence of high-stakes tests has exacerbated conditions to a point where *teachers* do not construct knowledge either. Like their working class students, they simply interact with the knowledge that is sanctioned by the state. Given these conditions, it is unlikely that Samuel's teachers will be able to instill elements of empowering literacies through classroom interactions. Instead, working-class norms of schooling—which do not promote success in the new economy—are reproduced and inequalities are exacerbated by high-stakes examinations.

Chloe relates a deep association between writing instruction and Regents examinations. According to her, teachers describe the purpose of writing instruction as preparation for state (Regents) assessments.

> **JG:** So what's the role of your teachers in making writing instruction better?
>
> **Chloe:** The teachers? Just basically how to write the Regents, because that's what I've been told by our teachers, "Well, I'm here to teach you how to write for the Regents because you have to pass this in order to graduate." So it's like, if you don't pass it, you can't just write…. You have to write what they tell you for the Regents. If you write something that you want to write about, you can't because it's not what they want…. We have to write for the Regents because it's something we

have to do. If you don't do it, you can't graduate. You
can't get into college.

Chloe's narration emphasizes the disciplinary power that is exerted by
high-stakes assessments over classroom interactions. She describes teachers as restricting students' writing in the service of the Regents examinations i.e., because of the examinations, students cannot write about things
which interest them. Moreover, although Chloe is in no danger of failing,
she is influenced by the threat that failing the exam will prevent her from
graduating and attending college. Chloe's perceptions of her teachers' attitudes toward state assessments reinforces Gunzenhauser's (2006) assertion that "the most effective discipline occurs through the actions of the
disciplined self" (p. 249).

CONCLUSION

In the working-class high school where this study took place, instructional
practices privileged an autonomous, monologic approach to literacy exemplified by pedagogies that are likely to reproduce class stratification
rather than interrupt it. Teachers and students have accepted and adopted expectations for writing based on high-stakes tests. This condition
precludes dialogue about teaching and learning and contributes to the
redefinition of self by both students and teachers. Institutional effects of
high-stakes testing, which include narrowing of curricula and teaching to
the test, will be explored in the following chapter.

REFERENCES

Alsup, J., Emig, J., Pradl, G., Tremmel, R., Yagelski, R. P., Alvine, L., et al. (2006).
The state of English education and a vision for its future: A call to arms.
English Education, 4(38), 278-294.

Apple, M. W. (2001). *Educating the "right" way: Markets, standards, god and inequality.*
New York, NY: Routledge-Falmer.

Brantlinger, E. (2007). (Re)turning to Marx to understand. In J. Van Galen &
G. W. Noblit (Eds.), *Late to class: Social class and schooling in the new economy*
(pp. 235-268). Albany, NY: State University of New York Press.

Dorn, S. (2003). High-stakes testing and the history of graduation. *Education Policy
Analysis Archives, 11*(1). Retrieved from http://epaa.asu.edu/epaa/v11n1/

Dorn, S. (2007). *Accountability Frankenstein: Understanding and taming the monster.*
Charlotte, NC: Information Age Publishing.

Foucault, M. (1983). The Subject and Power. In H. L. Dreyfus & P. Rabinow (Eds.), *Michel Foucault: Beyond structuralism and hermeneutics*. Chicago, IL: University of Chicago

Foucault, M. (1993). Power as knowledge. In C. Lemert (Ed.), *Social theory: The multicultural and classic readings*. Toronto, Canada: Canada HarperCollins.

Gee, J. P., Hull, G., & Lankshear, C. (1996). *The new work order: Behind the language of new capitalism*. Sydney, Australia: Westview Press.

Gunzenhauser, M. G. (2006). Normalizing the educated subject: A Foucaultian analysis of high-stakes accountability. *Educational Studies, 39*(3), 241-259.

Hillocks, G. J. (2002). *The testing trap: How state writing assessments control learning*. New York, NY: Teachers College Press.

Jackson, S. (2003). Commentary on the rhetoric of reform: A twenty-year retrospective. In K. J. Saltman & D. A. Gabbard (Eds.), *Education as enforcement: The militarization and corporatization of schools*. New York, NY: Routledge-Falmer.

Katznelson, I., & Weir, M. (1985). *Schooling for all: Class, race, and the decline of the democratic ideal*. Berkeley, CA: University of California Press.

National Council of Teachers of English. (2007). On urging reconsideration of high stakes testing. Retrieved from http://www.ncte.org/about/gov/cgrams/126092.htm

New York State Education Department. (2004). *Information booklet for administering and scoring the regents comprehensive examination in English*. Retrieved from http://emsc33.nysed.gov/osa/inform/DET%20541E%200604.pdf

Nichols, S. L., & Berliner, D. C. (2007). *Collateral damage: How high-stakes testing undermines education*. Cambridge, MA: Harvard Education Press.

Orfield, G., & Kornhaber, M. L. (Eds.). (2001). *Raising standards or raising barriers*. New York, NY: The Century Foundation Press.

Robertson, S. L. (2000). *A class act: Changing teachers' work, the state, and globalisation* (Vol. 8). New York, NY: Falmer Press.

Sacks, P. (2007). *Tearing down the gates: Confronting the class divide in American education*. Berkeley, CA: University of California Press.

Weis, L. (1990). *Working class without work: High school students in a de-industrializing economy*. New York, NY: Routledge.

CHAPTER 5

RESTRICTED LITERACIES

In its present state, American education cannot be a vehicle for the kind of social transformation we envision, because the current trajectory of school reform in this country has been in the direction of narrowing the curriculum rather than broadening and deepening it. (Alsup et al., 2006, p. 285)

In the society we live in, especially in New York State where Regents exams drive all, (high stakes state assessments) drive curriculum. They drive instruction. (Excerpt from in-depth interview with social studies teacher Gary Ventura)

NARROWED CURRICULUM

When teachers feel that they lack the time necessary to cover the content that will be assessed on state examinations, they tend to restrict the curriculum in order to focus on the content and skills that are prescribed by test makers (Dorn, 2007; Hillocks, 2002; Nichols & Berliner, 2007). In a structuralist sense, definitions of what counts as knowledge are regulated by what is counted for credit on state assessments. This contrasts with a sociocultural framework "in which mental activity is distributed and shared between the teacher and student participants" (p. 209) and knowledge is developed through joint activity. Definitions of what counts as knowledge and how learning is assessed are central to decisions regarding

Power, Resistance, and Literacy: Writing for Social Justice, pp. 79–106
Copyright © 2011 by Information Age Publishing

curriculum. Robertson (2000) describes the relationship between high-stakes assessment-based reform initiatives and school curricula.

> curriculum changes (such as national curriculum, testing, and so on) have increased the technical elements of teachers' work and reduced the professional elements. In other words, the spaces available for professional autonomy are reduced as a result of the impositions of standardisation and normalisation processes—measurement, hierarchy and regulation—on classroom practice. (p. 142)

An important aspect of teachers' professional identities involves curriculum-related decision making. Robertson (2000) argues that part of the professional autonomy of teachers is based on "trust that the professional will make expert decisions within a framework which has been sanctioned by the state" (p. 155). However, recent reform initiatives centered on high-stakes standardized assessments minimize decision-making potential by maximizing the control of the state-sanctioned "framework," that is, state standards and the correlated assessments. Teachers at Pontiac High narrate little room for meaningful decision making, and blame state assessments for this condition. Their daily interactions with students, however, are permeated by these power relations and, as Gunzenhauser (2006) explains, the identities of teachers and students are affected: "Foucaultian power gets exercised in the small, day-to-day decisions that support larger power apparatuses; … teachers' actions are prime examples of the ways in which selves are constrained and normalized" (p. 255).

Teachers in each of the four core subject areas agree about the powerful influence of state assessments on curricula. Whatever their impressions of the state reform initiative, teachers (like Gary Ventura, whose excerpt introduces this section) state that Regents exams drive curricula and instruction—the "what" and "how" that is the essence of classroom interactions.

Science teacher Michael Simon describes the effects of New York State examinations on curriculum and instruction, narrating effects on both *what* is taught and *how* it is taught.

Michael Simon: If I didn't have a core curriculum (in Regents courses), … we could teach any curriculum we want; we can go about teaching that topic how we want. We would make the assessment for that. We wouldn't have to gear it towards a regent's exam at the end of the year…. Whereas with regents exams, all of our assessments throughout the year have to be geared toward that regent's exam... at the end of the year.

Nichols and Berliner (2007) anticipate this effect of standardized assessment-based reform.

Teachers, in particular, are disenfranchised from their profession when they are told what to teach, how to teach, and judged solely on the academic outcomes of their students. NCLB and the high-stakes testing that accompanies it impoverishes their lives. For many teachers, it has taken away the joy of teaching. (pp. 169-170)

Blake Oliver, also a science teacher, admits that limitations based on standardized assessments can minimize the complexity of curricular decision making.

Blake Oliver: I think when you teach Regents people will gripe about it, "Oh, we have to do this, and we're handcuffed by having to do this." There's also comfort in that for a Regents teacher. I know exactly what I have to do... The state tells you exactly what you have to do.

The restrictions on curriculum produced by high-stakes tests, while making their work less complicated, also result in the loss of teachers' academic, pedagogical and interpersonal expertise (Dorn, 2007). In an environment dominated by high-stakes tests, curriculum and instruction are not responsive to the needs of communities or students.

During the past eight years, math teachers have had to make significant changes to their curriculum in response to New York State examinations. A new curriculum, accompanied by a different series of assessments, is currently under development. In considering the effects of these changes on her teaching, math teacher Judy Hanley describes lowering expectations.

JG: Has your teaching changed?
Judy Hanley: My teaching has changed, yes. I tend to shy away from the more complicated details and the derivations of formulas and just provide them with how to use the formulas and their application. So that has changed. I try to keep it simple.

Social studies teacher and department chairperson Linda Roberts narrates a clear belief with respect to the connection between state examinations and the curriculum she teaches. She appreciates the public accountability that is associated with state examinations, but also describes a nuanced understanding of the many factors that affect student performance—an understanding that she does not seem to think is common even among teachers in her own department.

Linda Roberts:	We are teaching to the test.
JG:	What does that mean?
LR:	That means that at the end of the year, let's face it, these kids have to take a test. When they look at the results of this test, the community, the school board, looks to see how they did on those tests and they're listed and we are graded according to how our students do. I think it was in the newspaper. Our U.S. (History examination) grades were fabulous; our global grades are terrible. But what it doesn't say is that these kids have had U.S. History most of their lives in school. They had two years of it in middle school, it's personal, it's what they know, and we have good grades. The other thing I will mention, when you're talking about 11th graders, is that a lot of the (low-achieving) students – how should I put it? —have left, dropped out of school, moved on. And when you get to 11th grade, (the ones remaining) are here for the long haul. In 9th and 10th grade there are kids that aren't going to go all the way through school. They're going to drop out and they're gonna go for a GED (high school equivalency credential) because they're hitting their heads against the wall and they can't pass that global exam. So by 11th grade students are a little bit more focused and I think that's another reason why (scores are) so good. Trust me, it's not because of us (social studies teachers), but don't quote me on that. Because we think we are the best.

Ms. Roberts is candid in discussing noninstructional factors that affect student scores. Student scores on the U.S. History exam tend to be very good; in the past three years, about 92% of students who take the examination have scored 65% or higher (65% is a passing score.). Global history results are not as good; during the same time frame, about 84% achieved passing scores. Ms. Roberts reveals some mitigating factors: students are much more familiar with United States history, both from their school experiences as well as their everyday exposure to such information. In addition, the populations of students for these examinations differ because the students in grade 10 (when the Global examination is administered) include students who are likely to drop out of school and are just waiting to do so. On the other hand, students in Grade 11 (when the U.S. history examination is administered) generally expect to graduate.

Dorn (2007), Jackson (2003), and Nichols and Berliner (2007) – among many others—maintain that high-stakes assessments provide simplistic measures of a complex combination of individual, institutional, and systemic attributes. Ms. Roberts articulates sophisticated understandings of the myriad dynamics that affect student performance and ought to affect her decisions about curriculum and instruction. Regrettably, instead of being able to apply her knowledge and experience to the "what" and "how" of her classroom, she describes herself as "teaching to the test." English teacher June Summers also describes her curriculum as driven by the state examination. Although she maintains that the exam is deficient, she asserts that her professional performance, as well as the performance of her students, is assessed on the basis of the examination and, therefore, the examination affects the type of writing that is emphasized in the English department.

> **JG:** Have the New York State exams affected our curriculum?
>
> **June Summers:** I think so. I think it drives our curriculum. Obviously, our test results are very important. And we're measured by those results, unfortunately, and our students' success is measured by those results.... So, as a result, you end up teaching to the exam. All the writing we do is very, very structured because of the Regents exam. As much as we say we don't teach to the exam, we do teach the exam. And essentially the Regents exam is a "fill in the blank" test, I tell the kids.

Reinforcing Ms. Summers' perceptions, Jackson (2003) notes that high stakes assessment-based reform creates conditions in which "teachers are to be scrutinized and regulated with their performance assessed in relationship to the test scores of their students" (p. 228). Because test scores are so critical, teachers focus instruction on the content and format of the tests, even as they the deficiencies of the test itself.

In addition, Ms. Summers' assertion regarding the formulaic ("fill-in-the-blank) nature of the examination is reinforced by Hillocks (2002), who critiques New York's state English Language Arts examination as essentially lacking rigor. Hillocks notes that higher-order thinking skills (e.g., analysis) are alluded to in the examination instructions but are absent from the anchor papers used for scoring student work. Hillocks describes how one anchor paper fails to realize the expectations set forth by examination instructions.

> The *sine qua non* of analysis is that it reveal something that was not previously known.... The top rated paper (for the June 1999 ELA examination) in response to the speech about the Suzuki method is not an analysis. It only summarizes the speech.... For the Regents examiners, summary qualifies as in-depth understanding. (p. 146)

Ms. Summers' contention that the curriculum is driven by the examination implies, then, that a structured, formulaic approach to writing, one which does not foster higher cognitive thinking, is prevalent in her department.

TEST PREPARATION AND WRITING INSTRUCTION

A significant negative effect of high-stakes testing involves an intensive instructional focus on test-preparation. Dorn (2007) distinguishes between meaningful instruction and test-preparation, describing the latter as follows:

> I am speaking here of activities that are not justified as legitimate instruction, regardless of the label. If certain activities simply stop after annual testing or would not exist if the test were suddenly switched to a different format or emphasis (let alone if testing were removed entirely), then we can label that activity test preparation rather than instruction. (p. 21)

A concentration on test-preparation is a reductive approach to education. It reinforces an instrumental attitude to schooling and a domesticating approach to writing, wherein facts and format are privileged over discovery and inquiry. While several teachers at Pontiac High identify limitations of test-preparatory writing instruction, they acknowledge applying it, thereby enacting a test-based approach to writing. Hillocks (2002) describes this development as typical.

> Few teachers (have) special training in composition and rhetoric that might enable them to conduct a detailed critique of the assessments. Indeed, it is much more common for the state assessment to become the theory of writing upon which teachers base their teaching. (p. 198)

Although writing is typically viewed as the province of English teachers, the current push toward accountability has raised awareness of the need for all teachers to foster literacy. This movement opens the possibility that writing, if approached from a sociocultural perspective, can be used to facilitate learning across curricular areas. In this vein, Newell (2005) asserts that

> when writing is construed as specialized genres that offer new ways of know-ing and doing, the role of "literate thinking" is expanded and deepened to include both the learning of content and the process of critical analysis. However, given that transmission views of teaching and learning are current-ly the common sense of schooling and the larger culture of which schools are a part, to implement writing-to-learn reforms requires a new perspec-tive—which John Mayher (1990) has called "uncommon sense"—to guide teaching and learning toward constructivist orientations. (p. 237)

A social constructivist approach to writing instruction is inherently grounded in the experiences of students and involves authentic meaning making. This is significantly different from a the structuralist approach exemplified by the transmission model of writing instruction, in which knowledge exists outside of the learner and is repeated to demonstrate understanding. However, as Hillocks predicted, the examinations provide the basis for teachers' approach to writing and thus reinforce a structural-ist perspective which operates in opposition to the perspective called for by Mayher. The standards-based examinations support what some believe is a "common sense" approach, one consistent with the status quo. Across curricular areas, literacies are defined as and therefore restricted by ex-amination-based writing tasks.

RESTRICTED LITERACIES

The types of writing privileged by examination-based instruction are not conducive to dialogic, transformational literacies. Instead, students repeat memorized formats and restate information provided in authoritative texts—both characteristics of domesticating writing instruction typical of working class schools (Finn, 1999) and consistent with a structuralist epistemology. Teachers in mathematics, science, and social studies state that writing instruction is influenced by how writing is used on Regents examinations. In science and math, they are expected to be able to explain their processes of determining answers. In social studies, students work on thematic essays and DBQs. In each case, definitions of literacy are manifested and regulated by high-stakes examinations.

The narrations of students and teachers at Pontiac High provide evidence that printcentric, linear literacies predominate. Personnel and practices at Pontiac High cling to a structuralist epistemology in which examinations drive curricula and instruction, leaving little space for the literacy culture that exists beyond school walls. Miller and Borowicz (2005) explore the burgeoning crisis created by these conditions.

> The literacy of school usually differs from the New Literacies needed in the 21st century workplace *and* (emphasis in original) from the blogs, zines, and video games around which Millennial youth affiliate. Key to the current educational context is understanding that beyond the school walls many adolescents use the New Literacies to negotiated meaning in digital communities, not just to read print text but also to "read" the images and sounds of the fast-changing real and virtual worlds. Unfortunately, the school focus on mostly print-based literacy can cut students off from the multimodal resources they increasingly use—or would like to use—for making sense of the world outside of school. (p. 2)

Although writing is not heavily weighted on the state mathematics examination, math teachers have been affected by the inclusion of writing on their state examinations. The written components of the mathematics examinations refer specifically to the need for students to "explain" their process of problem solving. In short, students are expected to script their procedures. Like teachers in other subject areas, math teachers have adopted an approach to writing that mirrors the examination expectation. Amy Wells provides one example of this phenomenon.

> **JG:** Where does writing fit into your curriculum?
>
> **Amy Wells:** Now, on the actual questions on the exams, it isn't just "find your answer," it's "find your answer and explain." So we do a lot of explaining....
>
> **JG:** Do you think New York State exams have impacted the writing you use in your classes?
>
> **AW:** Absolutely. Because, like I said before, now there are actual, not just "find the answer" but "find the answer, explain your steps." I mean, they have to actually be able to read and write on all the Regents exams now. And that's changed since I started.

New York State science Regents examinations now require students to provide short written responses to particular test items. The intent of state officials is to develop cross-curricular writing proficiency. Science teacher Miranda Schmidt is clear about the effects of this initiative on the writing that occurs in her curriculum.

> **JG:** Where do you think writing fits into your curriculum?

Miranda Schmidt: I think that we're getting them used to the exam.

Mr. Simon, also a science teacher, states that because of the curricular restrictions of the Regents examination, he incorporates more writing in non-Regents (Applied Science) course than in his Regents chemistry course.

JG:	Where does writing fit in your curriculum?
Michael Simon:	The Applied Science course it is very writing intensive. Every week, we do research and writing and summarizing on articles on line. Chemistry is more of, just the short answer questions with the writing or explanation answers or explaining your thoughts, the process of getting to that answer.
JG:	To what extent is that based on the Regents exam?
MS:	A lot because most of the exam, I think fifty out of the eighty-five points is multiple choice questions. Then the rest of it is math problems with the other thirty-five points come from math problems with answers, they have to have a specific answer or set up a problem correctly. Some of them are one-word answers or two-word answers or one-sentence answers and that's about it.
JG:	That's the extent of the writing they do?
MS:	That's the extent of the writing on the exam.

Mr. Oliver, who teaches Earth Science, discusses the effect of this examination on writing instruction in his classroom.

JG:	Where does writing fit into your curriculum?
Blake Oliver:	(In) Regents (classes), writing is part of the final exam, but it's much more guided. We're driven towards the exam.
JG:	What does it look like on the final exam?
BO:	Most of the exam is about fifty questions; about fifty percent are multiple choice. That is driven by reading, obviously and the other fifty percent, well, includes fifteen percent for a lab exam. The written response is never essay writing, it's always application and it includes diagramming, graph drawing—no more than a sentence or two. And I've told you my own troubles with this,

being driven towards the exam. I don't consider
myself a slave to the exam, but I guess I do teach
to it. So when we get down to preparation in
class throughout the year. I wind up saying to
the kids for a text response or a lab response:
"I'm interested in the key words. I want you to
follow the directions first, so if you are asked to
use complete sentences, use complete sentences.
If you are asked to make reference to page 7
from the reference tables, you have to do that."
You know, it's technical or scientific writing....
Sometimes they miss the key word. And the
grading on the exam is very deliberate in saying,
there are a variety of responses, but they must
include, this phrase, or they must include this
word.

What is described as "writing" on the science examinations is described
as resembling little more than a short answer (perhaps a complete sentence or two) constructed response to a question. Since this is interpreted
by teachers as the state's expectation, it is adopted by teachers as their
expectation for writing in Regents classes.

Social studies teacher Sean Thomas describes the influence of the state
examination on writing instruction in his classes.

> **JG:**   Have New York State exams influenced your use
> of writing?
>
> **Sean Thomas:**   I think I definitely spend more time on DBQs
> and thematic essays, just because they're such
> a major part of the final exam. I hate to teach
> to the exam, but sometimes you just don't have
> choice. When there's that much writing on it with
> the thematic and the DBQs, you really don't have
> a choice.

Social studies teacher and chairperson Linda Roberts describes how
test-preparation dominates her approach to writing in her classes.

> **J:**   Do you think your approach to writing would change
> if you didn't have the tests?
>
> **Linda Roberts:**   Definitely. I would not have just total (test-oriented)
> assessments.... I'm telling you, we talk about this a
> lot (in the department): "Wouldn't this be a great

idea"? And we look at each other. " But it's not on
the exam so why would we do it?"

Social studies teachers describe writing as an important part of
their curriculum. Its significance is closely associated with the state
examinations. This may appear to be a positive development; however,
the writing privileged by the social studies examinations is not conducive
to critical thinking or dialogic inquiry. Hillocks (2002) states that exam-
based writing of this nature causes teachers to "focus on the study of
models and teaching the structure of various kinds of writing so that their
students learn what goes where in a ... paper, but not on the production
strategies necessary to thinking through problems" (pp. 200-201). In
addition, writing prompts that expect students to restate expository
information negate the likelihood of deep thinking or epistemological
inquiry (Hillocks, 2002).

The students, too, see the limited forms of writing they do in school.
Cameron, whose first quarter grades in social studies and English classes
are below 50, describes examination based writing in social studies classes
as repetitive and restrictive.

> **Cameron:** I just don't like doing thematic essays. It's one sub-
> ject and it's like everybody's doing the same thing.
> It's not a variety. It's like you're doing the same thing
> everybody else is.
>
> **JG:** Right. And you don't like that because...?
>
> **Cameron:** Because it's like, say if you were to write it, a teacher's
> going to read it and then they're going to read the
> same thing (from every other student). It's, like, re-
> petitive. I just feel like when I'm doing it I'm repeat-
> ing what other people are saying and I just like to
> add my own thing.

Cameron's sense that school-based writing requires repeating the words
of others emphasizes the lack of inquiry and engagement. This type of
writing reinforces the perspective that knowledge exists outside the self
and is apprehended or accessed, not constructed through interpretation
and dialogue (Hillocks, 2002).

It is evident that teachers have resolved the dilemma about whether
to teach students or teach to the test in favor of boosting students' test
scores. Using parallel tasks similar to those on the exams as the basis for
writing instruction reinforces a narrow, instrumental view of writing; however, such an approach is perceived as effective in improving performance
on the examination. According to Popham (2001), if the test-preparation

activities do, in fact, result in higher test scores then it is likely that the test does not assess or address critical thinking. Noting that "repetitious instructional activities tend to deaden learning" (p. 21), he states that

> one fairly certain way of telling whether a high-stakes test is a winner or a loser is to see if unexciting drill activities can actually *raise* (emphasis in original) test scores. If so, the test is almost certainly inappropriate—measuring only low-level outcomes. (p. 21)

Thus, by focusing on test preparation to improve test scores, teachers simultaneously reinforce restricted conceptions of literacy and lower level thinking skills. Once again, Popham (2001) emphasizes this point. "What's assessed in a high-stakes testing program not only restricts the curricular content areas, it restricts the nature of the cognitive operations students face" (p. 20) To a student like Cameron, that is very evident.

Although teachers of math, science, and social studies describe test-based writing activities, English classes involve the most explicit explanations of this phenomenon. This is particularly troubling because English language arts is the class in which writing is perceived to be a critical component of the curriculum.

English teacher Hillary Lawrence states that the preponderance of the writing she assigns students is intended to prepare them for the Regents examination.

> **JG:** And what kinds of writing assignments do you give?
>
> **Hillary Lawrence:** Almost all them have to do with literature-based questions to prepare for the Regents exam.

English teacher Cindy Reynolds corroborates Ms. Lawrence's perception of the influence of the ELA Regents examination on writing instruction. Although the commencement level examination is administered in grade eleven, students begin practicing examination-based writing prompts in ninth grade English classes.

> **JG:** Have the New York State exams influenced your writing instruction?
>
> **Cindy Reynolds:** Yeah. That's all we do.
>
> **JG:** Can you say more about that?
>
> **CR:** All of our assessments have to look like the exam, so even if you wanted to have kids write a poem for an end of the unit assessment, we're technically not supposed to because it has to

> parallel what's on the exam. (This happens) even
> in ninth grade so they get used to the literature
> or to the language and the expectations.

Ms. Reynolds notes that administrators expect assessments in English classes to correspond to one of the four essay writing prompts on state examinations. Nichols and Berliner (2007) cite American Educational Research Association (AERA) guidelines in critiquing the state for administering assessments that enable this practice.

> The AERA says that "because high-stakes testing inevitably creates incentives for inappropriate methods of test preparation, multiple test forms should be introduced on a regular basis, to avoid narrowing of the curriculum toward just the content sampled on a particular form." (p. 180)

Because the state examinations do not undergo substantive changes and multiple formats are not distributed, it is expedient for district administrators to require teachers to develop and administer unit assessments that mirror examination questions. These assessments are called "parallel tasks," and they serve as the primary form of writing and measure of progress in Grades 9, 10, and 11 language arts classes at Pontiac High.

Stan Ryan, chairperson of the English department, affirms the prevalence of writing assignments whose format and content parallel those of Regents exam tasks. When asked how students respond to writing assignments in his class, Mr. Ryan replied:

> **Stan Ryan:** Think about it. From grade three through ten, everything
> has been defined (by the exam) and we keep going with
> this parallel tasking right to the point that now the child
> says, "Which one of the tasks am I doing today?"

Since they explicitly emulate examination questions in design, parallel tasks function as teacher-developed test preparation materials. Popham (2001) derisively describes such materials as "an endless array of practice exercises—and the closer the practice items are to the items on the 'real' high-stakes test, the better" (p. 21). Parallel tasks reinforce the phenomenon described by Luna and Turner (2001)

> Trying to prepare students for a standardized exam that presents knowledge of literacy as a set of answers to separate test questions, ... English teachers seem to have moved away from a more holistic, constructivist approach to teaching and toward a transmission model involving more direct instruction.

Thus, ... teachers' experiences highlight a pedagogical (and ethical) dilemma created by the high-stakes testing movement. (p. 80)

The focus on parallel tasks means that students learn to think about writing in school as a narrow, subject-oriented activity. Writing is taught as the mastery of four specific formulaic assignments. Nichols and Berliner (2007) describe a key distinction with respect to test preparation, noting that "there is a fine line between teaching to the test and teaching the test itself" (p. 122). It seems undeniable that when writing instruction is reduced to the point that it consists of four text-based tasks, that line has been crossed.

English teacher June Summers describes the reductive effects of the state examinations on writing instruction and independent thinking.

> **JG:**   Has your writing instruction changed since you've been here?
>
> **June Summers:**   Well, my writing instruction's been pretty much straight the same since I started 'cause it's for the Regents exam. It's always for the Regents exam. Each marking period each one of the exemplar papers we do is modeled after the Regents exam. All the parallel assessments modeled after the Regents exam. So the students know the Regents exam. They can spit it back out at you, which is wonderful, but I don't know if it's the "end all be all"... I don't mind the exam, but I think there are some flaws with the exam, and I think we've all realized that, regardless of which exam's being offered. Social studies is, "Can you find the line and write it?" That's not, that's not independent thought. That's not encouraging independent thinkers, which is what we want to encourage. And our exam does allow for more freedom of thought. But, at the same time, I think it's still very fill-in-the-blank-ish.

Ms. Summers expresses a sense that the type of writing assessed on the state examination reinforces a domesticating form of writing, one that does not promote critical thinking. Hillocks (2002) explains that such a development is not uncommon in circumstances where high-stakes tests dominate the discourse of writing instruction.

When states establish writing assessments and determine certain categories of writing to test, they privilege the selected categories in the eyes of the schools and teachers. When school scores are reported to a central authority and compared to the scores of other schools, the procedure of testing and reporting demands attention to what it taught. Teachers teach what is on the test and ignore what is not. When Illinois, New York, Texas, and many other states exclude imaginative literature from the assessment, they send a message that teachers do not have to include such writing in their curricula. They sabotage their own goals for creative thinking. (p. 204)

Enacting the dilemma expressed by Luna and Turner (2001), English teacher Roger Johnson distinguishes between assigning writing and teaching writing. He narrates a lack of confidence in the test-based approach that dominates writing instruction at Pontiac High, noting that the Regents examination ignores many aspects of literacy.

Roger Johnson: I don't think our English department teaches writing too much. Honestly, we give out a lot of essays. We assign essays but there is little of teaching writing. The test is okay.... But I think there are so many different types of writing that the kids could do.

Mr. Johnson continues, discussing the limitations of the types of writing assessed on the state examination. In this excerpt, he refers to the essays in part two of the ELA Regents examination, which he describes as a peculiar type of writing that is unlikely to be applicable to most students' lives.

RJ: The part twos … it's kind of a weird type of writing. Taking these literary elements and using them … It's kind of forced to me. I don't think they will be doing that like outside of here. I don't think anywhere except at graduate level English program will (they) ask you to talk about literary elements in this sense.

The prevalence of such parallel tasks in English classes at Pontiac High is verified by students as well. Their experiences corroborate what Nichols and Berliner forewarn: that teachers are not just teaching *to* the test, they are *teaching the test*. When asked to discuss a typical piece of writing they might do in school, several students discuss a particular part two examination task entitled the "critical lens." The writing prompt asks students to interpret a quotation (the "critical lens"), develop analytic criteria based on the lens, and then analyze two pieces of literature (that they have previously read) using the established criteria. In addition, students must identify and discuss literary elements from each work they discuss. This task is presented as rigorous and multifaceted. Hillocks (2002) provides an explanation of its espoused expectations.

> The final of the four prompts (on the ELA commencement examination) requires students to interpret a "critical lens" in such a way that the interpretation establishes criteria for the subsequent analysis.... The language calls for clearly establishing the "criteria for analysis," using the criteria to "make insightful analysis," and "making use of a wide range of relevant and specific evidence." (p. 149)

The anchor papers provided for scoring this task, however, reveal the fallacious nature of these expectations. Having studied the anchor papers, Hillocks (2002) discovered that "the 'criteria for analysis' turn out to be not criteria at all.... In fact, 'interpretation of the critical lens' appears only to call for rephrasing in one's own words" (p. 150). Restating the words of an established authority—in this case, the texts provided by state examinations—is a fundamental characteristic of a structuralist approach to literacy and writing instruction, and it is this type of instruction that is reinforced by the state's examination.

STUDENT PERCEPTIONS OF WRITING IN SCHOOL

> In my most cynical moments, I wonder if the master plan is to train people not to think (Hillocks, 2002, p. 204)

> **JG:**   What effect, if any, have New York State exams had on you as a writer?
> **Alexis:**   Time limits. 'Cause that's really where they all come from.... I think it's extremely important that I become a good, fast, writer for college. I don't really know what sort of real life application I have, for the ability to write an excellent essay in forty-five minutes. But, that's what I have to do, so that's what I have to get good at. (Excerpt from student interview)

Emphasizing the powerful impact of state assessments on conceptions of literacy, students describe the characteristics of the critical lens writing task effortlessly. By expressing their familiarity with its format and the ease with which they can replicate it, students indicate the prevalence of writing instruction that is formulaic, representing a linear reproduction of established facts—an approach indicative of structuralist epistemology. Characteristics of assessment-based writing assignments are narrated by students at various levels of academic achievement. Alexis, whose comments open this section, is on track to take Advanced Placement (AP) English (a college level class) next year. Her average is in the mid-90s, so while her description of writing is not consistent with empowering literacies, her approach is effective with respect to school-based achievement (as measured by grades).

Taylor's average in English class is in the high 90s. When asked about the types of writing she does in English class, she refers exclusively to test-preparatory assignments.

> **JG:** What kinds of essays are you doing in English?
>
> **Taylor:** We have ones from previous Regents exams. They'll give you a piece of writing and you've got to make all the information click together and put it into a certain (format).
>
> **JG:** Can you tell me about the typical piece of writing that you brought with you?
>
> **Taylor:** Yeah. I brought an English essay that I had to write. It's a critical lens. You had to compare two books to a quote that we got: "It is preoccupation with possession, more than anything else, that prevents men from living freely and nobly." I used Macbeth and The Green Mile, and we had to use literary elements and support to either agree or disagree (with the critical lens quote) using quotes from both books.
>
> **JG:** Why did you select that as a typical piece of school writing?
>
> **Taylor:** Most of my essays that I've written are critical lenses where you have to use novels, because basically that's what we were doing for English before the ELA (Regents examination). I've been doing that since last year, too, because that was what every single paper was on.
>
> **JG:** Can you describe how you wrote it?
>
> **Taylor:** We had to write the introduction and you had to make sure you had all the information that you needed in each paragraph.... One body paragraph was on.... Macbeth and I had to use literary elements, and then supporting details for each one. Then in the next paragraph I had to do the other book the same way.

Before she even sees the assigned question for a task four essay, Melissa predicts the structure of her essay and, in general, the content of each paragraph. The notion that the process of writing primarily involves filling in blanks and reorganizing information contradicts sociocultural, constructivist notions of literacy and learning. While the types of assignments provided on state examinations might be useful in assessing basic language and organizational skills, they do not offer engagement in literacies that support deep understanding or development of empowering literacies (Finn, 1999). Newell (2005) explains that

> The underlying assumption that frames this discussion is that the extent to which information is manipulated enhances topic understanding.... In general, engagement is associated with the constraints of the writing task.... Accordingly, the greater the range of composing processes a writing task engenders, the more likely the writer will focus on the relationships among the ideas that give them coherence an structure, and thus develop more coherent topic understanding. A second assumption is that different tasks focus the writer's attention in specific ways, and the effects of writing on learning from text are limited to the ideas that are expressed during composing. (p. 238)

It is evident, then, that merely repeating and reorganizing information does not involve true meaning making. In fact, according to Newell (2005), superficial writing tasks undermine students' ability to learn from and/or about the ideas they repeat and minimally manipulate.

Students' experiences of writing at Pontiac High are saturated with examination-based tasks. School-based literacies are restricted by the nature of the examinations and, as a consequence, students' developing proficiency as writers and thinkers is diminished.

A general question about writing in school prompts Jesse, whose first quarter average in English class was 70, to refer to preparation for the Regents exam, particularly the critical lens. He states that the writing assignments he gets are driven by the requirements of the examination.

> **JG:**   What kinds of writing assignments do you get in school?
> **Jesse:**   Basically, this year it's all been critical lens because we're preparing for the Regents. So they are trying to get us to remember all the things we did in high school, all the literature work, and combine it together to make a critical lens essay. Because that's what we need for the Regents.

Chloe, whose English average hovers near 90, also describes the critical lens task as typical of school-based writing. Although she does not name the task, she describes it as ubiquitous and confirms its formulaic format.

> **JG:**   So this (referring to the essay Chloe brought to the interview) is a typical piece of school writing. Can you tell me what class it's for?
>
> **Chloe:**   This is for English. It was that task where you have to prove a quote. He gives you a quote and then you have to reword the

> quote and then you have to prove the meaning of it, prove it
> with the book.

JG: Why did you select it as typical?

Chloe: Because it's just what we do every day. Every single day in
class, every week, essays, essays, essays.

JG: Can you describe how you wrote it?

Chloe: I think the big thing is figuring out what the quote means, so
you write that down. Then you have to get literary elements
from the book to prove the quote and that's what you write in
your body paragraphs. So, your quote's in the first paragraph
and in the body paragraphs you're proving that.

Chloe indicates that her role in this process of writing is to uncover
the meaning that is latent in the critical lens quote. She does not perceive herself as an active agent in constructing knowledge, but instead
describes her task as "figuring out" what the quote she is given "means."
Later in the interview, Chloe describes her aversion to writing critical lens
essays, citing their restrictions on personal expression as well as their boring, repetitive nature.

JG: Is there any type of writing you don't like to do?

Chloe: The Regents writing.

JG: Tell me about that writing.

Chloe: It's easy to write if you get the idea, but it can get repetitive.
It's really boring, and I kind of want to write my own thing
but you have to stick to writing about the book, and there's
things you can and can't do. I don't like getting limits on
what you have to write.

JG: Tell me some of those things you can and can't do.

Chloe: You're not supposed to write plot summary and things like
that. You have to prove the main point of the quote they give
you for task four. It's easy, but I like to write to get the message that the book that you're writing about was sending. But
because you have to use elements that are mostly characterizations of a character, it's not really the theme of the book.

Chloe hints at the possibility of using writing to seek understanding
("I like to write to get the message that the book that you're writing about
was sending"). However, she sets this possibility in opposition to the type
of writing she is allowed by the critical lens prompt, the structure of which
(e.g., "you have to use elements that are mostly characterizations of a
character") prevents her from engaging with what she sees as the real
theme of the book – perhaps the meaning she has constructed as a reader

and a writer. Furthermore, the prevalence of examination rhetoric with respect to writing is emphasized by Chloe's fluid familiarity with the other ELA examination tasks.

> **JG:**   How about the other tasks?
> **Chloe:** Task one is a listening task. They read a passage or an essay that someone wrote and then you write notes on it. Then they give you another task that says "write in letter format" about an issue. You have to base your essay on a chart that they give you and a passage. On task three they give you your topic for you to write about and two (reading) passages and then you have to prove that topic.
> **JG:**   Do you have any challenges or difficulties with writing?
> **Chloe:** Not really.... Because it's so repetitive you just have to get in your mind of what you have to write and once you memorize the format for it, you can write it.

The practice of writing as repeating the words of authorities is consistent with a structuralist epistemology and represents a stark contrast with the dialogic notion of "curriculum as conversation" articulated by Newell (2005).

The notion of writing as a means for learning content and procedures appropriate to a domain is based on the metaphor of "curriculum as conversation." "When we take this metaphor seriously, the development of curriculum becomes the development of significant domains of conversation and [writing] becomes a matter of helping students learn to participate in conversations within those domains (Applebee, 1996, as cited in Newell, 2005, p. 244). Students describe writing as an exercise in repetition rather than a means of expressing or developing ideas. At best, concepts are repeated and information is reorganized. This approach to writing is reminiscent of reading from a script rather than engaging in a conversation or a dialogue.

Despite diverse levels of achievement, students are consistent in their critiques of assessment-based writing. Olivia, who is barely passing English this year, describes the critical lens essay as too structured and restrictive of the personal expression that would typify writing as a means of curricular "conversation."

> **JG:**   What kinds of writing do you do in school?
> **Olivia:** The mandatory stuff, the essays that we have to do for English, for history, the critical lens.... I don't really like them. I think there's too much structure to them. You can't really say what you want to say. It pretty much tells you what has to be

said and how it is. I don't think there's enough freedom to say what your opinion really is.

JG: And what kinds of writing do you most dislike?

Olivia: Essays, especially the critical lens (essays) because they're the most structured ones where you can't really say much....

JG: What do you mean by "the most structured?"

Olivia: There's not much that you can really say. It's pretty much a set format. You read the quote, you interpret it, you say if you think you agree or disagree with it, you find a book related to it, all done.

Finally, Dylan, whose first quarter English average was 85, describes the critical lens essay as typical of the writing he does in school. He expresses frustration with the prescriptive, formulaic nature of this type of writing.

JG: Tell me about the piece of writing that you selected as typical school writing. Did you bring one of those?

Dylan: Yeah. It's on Macbeth. We have this Regents exam we had a couple of weeks ago. Again, there's four types of essays you can write and what (the teacher) did was—all year until the Regents—he just made us write the same essay over and over again because it's the exact formula and this exact essay is what you'll get a hundred times.

JG: What do you mean?

Dylan: He'd write the notes, with blanks: "The literary element [blank] can be used to prove that [blank]; and the author [blank] used his [blank] to prove [blank]. This is seen in the scenes where the character [blanked]." He gave us the exact formula for this essay. I got probably 20 essays in my binder that are exactly pretty much the same as this—except (citing) different stories.

Dylan makes it clear that he did a great deal of writing during the nineteen weeks prior to the state examination. However, he questions quality of the literacy experiences these types of writing provided. Writing based strictly on fill-in-the-blanks examination tasks is not likely to foster the development of complex thinking skills. Newell (2005) explains that

Writing in and of itself may or may not serve as a tool to promote learning. Although writing may at least potentially serve as a means for the development of thought, it can only do so within the complex and rich social contexts that have been restructured according to teachers' conceptions of learning and the school's values. (p. 242)

If the writing experiences of students reflect the teachers' conceptions learning and the school's values, then it is evident that the examination serves as the basis for the structuralist epistemology of literacy in this school. Examination-based writing tasks dominate instruction, and the narrations of students reflect the powerful effect of state assessments on curricula and pedagogies and students' lived experience in this setting.

Scholars are clear in their assertion that students in poor and working-class schools are inordinately affected by the high-stakes standardized assessment-based reform. It is particularly interesting to note that *all* student participants were consistent in their narration of the powerful effects of the ELA commencement level assessment on the writing instruction they experience. Failing students as well as students who are enrolled in enriched English, a class intended to prepare them for AP English, are affected by the restricted approach to literacy defined by the state assessment. It is discouraging to see that even students who comply with academic norms—those who do *not* enact resistance—cannot escape the deleterious pedagogical effects that standardized assessments have on students in working-class schools. Compliant students may develop basic literacy skills, those consistent with domesticating writing and a structuralist approach to literacy but not with success in the new economy. Resistant students who refuse to participate in even basic writing activities are further disadvantaged.

Riley, who earned a 65 in English class during the first marking period, narrates faith in the instruction she is receiving. She describes the intensity of test preparation in both English and social studies classes. Her goal as a student writer connects explicitly to her performance on the written portion of the Regents examinations.

JG: What's your goal as a student writer, in school?
Riley: Basically my goal is to do good on my essays because for English or U.S. (history) or global, because you have to do them for exams. So my goal is to basically practice as much as I can so I can do good on the U.S. (History) Regents coming up in June. And, of course, I've been practicing for this English.
JG: So what kinds of things do you do to work toward that goal?
Riley: I basically practice. In our U.S. (History) books we have those practice Regents (examinations). I basically practice the essay parts because that will help me get an understanding of what

the Regents is asking and how to write it. And in English we've been practicing like two months, and that's just basically practice, and practice makes perfect. Essay writing is practicing because, for the Regents, it's New York State. You don't know how they think for their essays and I think practicing for them will give you an understanding of how they want you to write it and basically knowing more and more about what they're asking. I just think it's best to practice; that's why they prepare us with all these essays and stuff like that.

Riley alludes to the need to learn to think like "the state" in order to succeed on examinations. She expresses the need to practice so that she can understand "how they want you to write" and "know ... about what they're asking." Riley's words highlight the structuralist epistemology in that knowing and even thinking are defined through the hegemonic influence of state assessments.

Students describe perceptions of the ELA Regents examination as structured, formulaic, and limiting personal expression. They recount explicit instructions that resemble a "fill-in-the-blank" approach, as opposed to a recursive, reflective process of writing. Nelson (2001) asserts the fallacious nature of this approach.

Young people deserve writing classes with a vision that sees beyond tests, writing classes that do more than just teach skills and correctness and five-paragraph, write-by-the-numbers essays. In order to survive (physically, psychologically, spiritually) in the world of the twenty-first century, our students deserve and desperately need the power of the Word as an instrument of creation—a power that lies far beyond any instrument to measure standards. (p. 58)

Despite Nelson's claim, narrations of students at Pontiac High affirm the prevalence of "common sense" that reinforces structuralist epistemological approach toward learning and literacy. While this is not a new phenomenon—that is, schooling has traditionally been dominated by positivist notions of knowledge—high-stakes standards-based assessments have reinforced teaching as transmission and learning as passive. Students perceive school-based literacies as formulaic, alienating, and meaningless. Pedagogical approaches that involve self-expression, making sense, complex thinking—that is, empowering literacies—are imperceptible in this setting.

REDEFINING IDENTITIES

Good teaching comes from the identity and integrity of the teacher. (Palmer, 1997)

June Summers: We have the exam as a scale of us as a teacher and a scale that measures our students as well. So that's what we have to address. (Excerpt from interview with English Teacher June Summers)

If students are prepared to conform to a uniform standard, they're prepared to learn. (a Lakefront Public School science teacher quoted in The Lakefront News, October 3, 2007)

Identities of teachers and students are redefined through the disciplinary effects of high-stakes testing. The daily activities of teachers and students are deeply affected by state examinations, which have effectively established expectations for writing and, by extension, thinking. Englert, Mariage, and Dunsmore (2005) assert that "equating effective writing with performance in specific genres has had the impact of artificially narrowing 'what counts' as writing, literacy, and identity" (p. 218).

Students and teachers are consistent in their narrations of the powerful effect that state Regents examinations have on curriculum and the impact that has on who they are in school. Despite the uniformity of this perception, effects on curriculum are generally perceived by teachers to be negative. These teachers verify Macrine's (2003) assertion: "Teachers know that education is not just about taking tests" (p. 207). They are forced to either accept the hypocrisy of their decision to teach to the tests or redefine their professional identities to correspond with state requirements. Teachers at Pontiac High struggle with just this dilemma.

In the midst of enormous pressures related to the high-stakes tests, teachers are being forced to redefine their professional identities. Robertson (2000) describes the coercive possibilities of such redefinition: "Professionalism is a means of socializing an individual into a code of ethics and institutionally based social practises and therefore a mechanism for indirect control exercised by the state" (p. 155). The effects of high-stakes tests on teachers have been described as "deprofessionalization." However, as teachers accept and enact the characteristics of the culture of accountability, I argue that re-socialization is occurring. The identities of teachers who hope to survive and thrive in the environment created by

NCLB require such a redefinition and reconstruction of the professional identity.

Reinforcing the power of the examinations as a mechanism of control, math teacher Judy Hanley makes a direct link between herself as a teacher and the state assessment changes.

> **JG:** How have (New York State assessments) impacted the writing you do in your classroom?
>
> **Judy Hanley:** Well, we definitely are doing more so (students) can get used to it. So when they see "explain" on the exam they won't be completely lost. So I think that's why—because New York State has changed, I've changed.

Ms. Hanley's words illustrate the seamless nature of the effects of high-stakes examinations on curriculum, instruction, teachers and students. She describes making pedagogical changes that are based explicitly on the expectations of the state as manifest through examinations.

Another way professional identities are redefined relates to the purpose of education. Science teacher Michael Simon, during an in-depth interview, describes divergences in educational purpose that are reinforced by high stakes assessments.

> **JG:** Do you think the schools writing instructions fulfill the purpose for all students?
>
> **Michael Simon:** I don't know because, I find that with a lot of the kids,… We got everyone passing the exams. And I feel a lot of what our push is: "Let's get these numbers, let's get them to pass the exam. How many people are we going to get to pass the English exam? How many people are going to pass chemistry?" And we do that. And that's what we are good at that.

Mr. Simon raises the issue illuminated by Nichols and Berliner (2007), who state that

> educators largely acknowledge that the tests have severe limitations as indicators of what it means to be a successful student or a successful human being. Teachers know the test isn't worth that much. Students know it isn't worth that much. Yet educators are forced to try to sell it as best they can. (pp. 164-165)

In general, teachers opt to prepare students for examinations even though that option is contrary to their beliefs about what would be best for students. Underscoring this point, Mr. Simon indicates that what educators at Pontiac High are "good at" is getting students to pass the examinations. As Parker Palmer (1997). says, "Good teaching comes from the identity and integrity of the teacher" (p. 10). In this case, Mr. Simon feels pressured to enact a professional identity focused on getting students to pass examinations. The fact that he is conflicted about this choice is illustrated by his implementation of more frequent and more open-ended writing in classes he teaches that are not linked with Regents examinations.

Science teacher Miranda Schmidt emphasizes this point. When asked whether Pontiac High School fulfills its purpose in terms of educating students, Ms. Schmidt replies:

Miranda Schmidt: I would say yes in that it seems like that purpose is to get them through the exams....

When high-stakes tests set the purposes for teaching and learning, teachers and students are alienated from the process and possibilities for deep learning and critical thinking are diminished. Like Mr. Simon, Ms. Schmidt sees her professional identity as affected, reduced to getting students through the exams. Because identities are constructed through social interactions, it is likely that students are affected by their teachers' perceptions and expectations.

CONCLUSION

It is evident that teachers' and students' experiences of schooling—and writing in school—are profoundly affected by the high stakes standardized reform initiative adopted by New York State. Despite narrated flaws identified in the assessments, the consequences associated with them cause students and teachers to feel pressured to perform well. Teachers acknowledge that Pontiac High is "good at" getting students through mandated examinations, yet teachers question the validity or significance of these assessments. Narrations of students and teachers illustrate the prevalence of a structuralist epistemology in this working-class high school—an epistemology that does not support the types of curricula and pedagogies that will facilitate success in the twenty-first century.

High-stakes examinations have lessened the likelihood that social constructivist epistemologies which might offer access to powerful literacies and engaged experiences of writing can thrive. Curriculum and instruction are dominated by the discourse of high-stakes testing, which precludes dialogue that could lead to transformative pedagogies.

Teachers are re-socialized to emphasize assessment-based content and skills, and students' identities are normalized in accordance with state-prescribed definitions of what counts as knowledge. Moreover, the focus on test-preparatory instruction reinforces working-class norms consistent with old capitalism, undermining opportunities for students to succeed in the new economy. Both high-achieving, compliant students and failing, resistant students are subjected to writing instruction that reinforces domesticating rather than empowering literacies.

REFERENCES

Alsup, J., Emig, J., Pradl, G., Tremmel, R., Yagelski, R. P., Alvine, L., et al. (2006). The state of english education and a vision for its future: A call to arms. *English Education, 4*(38), 278-294.

Applebee, A. N. (1996). *Curriculum as conversation: Transforming traditions of teaching and learning*. Chicago, IL: University of Chicago Press.

Dorn, S. (2007). *Accountability Frankenstein: Understanding and taming the monster*. Charlotte, NC: Information Age.

Englert, C. S., Mariage, T. V., & Dunsmore, K. (2005). Tenets of sociocultural theory in writing instruction research. In C. A. MacArthur, S. Graham & J. Fitzgerald (Eds.), *Handbook of Writing Research* (pp. 208-221). New York, NY: The Guilford Press.

Finn, P. J. (1999). *Literacy with an attitude: Educating working-class children in their own self-interest*. Albany, NY: State University of New York Press.

Gunzenhauser, M. G. (2006). Normalizing the educated subject: A Foucaultian analysis of high-stakes accountability. *Educational Studies, 39*(3), 241-259.

Hillocks, G. J. (2002). *The testing trap: How state writing assessments control learning*. New York, NY: Teachers College Press.

Jackson, S. (2003). Commentary on the rhetoric of reform: A twenty-year retrospective. In K. J. Saltman & D. A. Gabbard (Eds.), *Education as enforcement: The militarization and corporatization of schools*. New York, NY: Routledge-Falmer.

Luna, C., & Turner, C. L. (2001). The impact of the MCAS: Teachers talk about high-stakes testing *The English Journal, 91*(1), 79-87.

Macrine, S. L. (2003). Imprisoning minds: The violence of neoliberal education or "I Am Not For Sale!" In K. J. Saltman & D. A. Gabbard (Eds.), *Education as enforcement: The militarization and corporatization of schools*. New York, NY: RoutledgeFalmer.

Mayher, J. (1990). *Uncommon Sense: Theoretical Practice in Language Education*. Portsmouth, NH: Boynton/Cook.

Miller, S., & Borowicz, S. (2005). *Why multimodal literacies? Designing digital bridges to 21st century teaching and learning*. Buffalo, NY: State University of New York Press.

Nelson, G. L. (2001). Writing beyond testing: The word as an instrument of creation. *English Journal, 91*(1), 57-61.

Newell, G. E. (2005). Writing to learn: How alternative theories of school writing account for student performance. In C. A. MacArthur, S. Graham & J. Fitzgerald (Ed.), *Handbook of Writing Research* (pp. 235-247). New York, NY: Gilford.

Nichols, S. L., & Berliner, D. C. (2007). *Collateral damage: How high-stakes testing undermines education*. Cambridge, MA: Harvard Education Press.

Palmer, P. J. (1997). The heart of a teacher: Identity and integrity in teaching [Electronic Version]. *New Horizons for Learning*. Retrieved from http://www.newhorizons.org/strategies/character/palmer.htm

Popham, W. J. (2001). *The truth about testing: An educators call to action*. Alexandria, VA: Association for Supervision and Curriculum Development.

Robertson, S. L. (2000). *A class act: Changing teachers' work, the state, and globalisation* (Vol. 8). New York, NY: Falmer Press.

PART II

RESISTANCE

CHAPTER 6

TEACHING OR SELLING OUT?

Although it might be in the public interest... to raise educational achievement and expand opportunities for the most disadvantaged students relative to the privileged ones, schools and school systems, fueled by a new era of federal intervention in their operation, seem instead to be adopting a plethora of strategies that, intentional or not, produce exactly the opposite outcome. (Sacks, 2007, p. 95)

"Reuse, recycle, regurgitate." (English teacher June Summers, during an in-depth interview, describes the axiom she uses to remind students of the strategies best suited for success on the state's commencement examination in English Language Arts.)

The epistemology of traditional schooling involves a structuralist approach exemplified by a transmission model of teaching and learning. Teachers and texts are the primary sources of knowledge and students are passive recipients of information. Hegemonic authority is not meant to be questioned, accepted truths are perceived to exist for transmission, and academic language is the privileged form of communication. Thinking is perceived as a linear process and assessments are primarily text-based and fact-oriented—not multimodal or performance-based. Miller and Borowicz (2005) argue that schools operating in a structuralist manner are preparing young people for a world that no longer exists.

Some scholars in New Literacy Studies (NLS) have characterized education "as the Institution of Old Learning (IOL), the historically situated routines, organizational structures and practices of schools" (O'Brien & Bauer 2005, as cited in Miller & Borowicz, 2005, p. 3) developed to

Power, Resistance, and Literacy: Writing for Social Justice, pp. 109–126
Copyright © 2011 by Information Age Publishing

prepare for work in the industrialized world of the eighteenth and nine-teenth centuries.

The epistemology of the school influences curricula and pedagogies that shape the experiences of students in all areas, including writing. Newell (2005) states that

> "Transmission" views of teaching and learning that emphasize memorization and recitation co-opted the more learner-centered underpinnings of writing for which theorists such as Janet Emig, James Britton, Donald Graves, and Nancy Martin had argued. (p. 235)

Although structuralist epistemology is dominant in schools, authentic literacies prevalent in the world outside of schools today require a multimodal, social constructivist embodied in a sociocultural pedagogical approach. Englert, Mariage, and Dunsmore (2005) elaborate on how a sociocultural approach differs from pedagogies centered in structuralism as well as the significance of the epistemological approach to literacy on the thought processes individuals develop:

> Rather than viewing knowledge as existing inside the heads of individual participants or in the external world, sociocultural theory views meaning as being negotiated at the intersection of individuals, culture, and activity. Higher psychological processes, such as writing and reading, have their origins in social processes that occur on an interpsychological plane, and that are mediated through language signs, symbols, actions, and objects (Vygotsky, 1978).... Through this mediated action, language begins to take on a unique role in psychological development as a mediator of cultural understanding and cognitive tools that can come under conscious realization to guide behavior (Bakhtin, 1986; Gee, 1996, p. 208)

Pontiac High, the working-class school which served as the research site of this study, embodies many characteristics representative of a structuralist epistemology. Data analysis reveals the prevalence of a structuralist approach to writing and learning. Structuralist, examination-oriented definitions of knowledge are evident in teachers' narrations of the narrowed curriculum, absence of critical thinking, and limited range of literacies. Knowledge is situated in authority; in fact, curriculum and assessment decisions for required courses are directly related to state examinations. Furthermore, "old literacy" i.e., "exclusively reading and writing the printed text" (Miller & Borowicz, 2005, p. 3) dominates instruction and assessment. There is little evidence of what Miller and Borowicz describe as the "total engagement in meaning making that we believe is the heart of literacy" (p. 3). Students are not perceived as active participants or coconstructors of meaning; instead, the epistemology of structuralism and the prevalence of old literacies persists.

In this educational setting, students—particularly those from poor and working-class backgrounds—are forced to make choices with respect to the construction of their identities. Language and literacy constitute an essential component of identity, and students whose language and literacy backgrounds are not congruent with academic language are disadvantaged because they must either assimilate or remain alienated—unless schools can provide ameliorating pedagogical approaches that allow students to construct identities that are integrated with rather than oppositional to schooling. Tests, by serving as the ultimate arbiter of what counts as knowledge and achievement, support a structuralist epistemology and do not support the implementation of social constructivist epistemologies.

Although research indicates that structuralism, domination, and alienation existed in working-class schools *prior* to standards-based reform and high-stakes testing (Anyon, 1981; Finn, 1999; Weis, 1990; Willis, 1977), the reform movement has certainly exacerbated these conditions (Dorn, 2003, 2007; Hillocks, 2003; Nichols & Berliner, 2007). Liberating, transformative pedagogies that incorporate the skills and experiences of Millennial learners are perceived to conflict with the goal of raising test scores on standardized assessments. In a culture of learning dominated by preparation for standardized assessments, writing based on student experience such as personal narratives has diminished almost to the point of omission.

Teachers face personal and professional conflicts as they teach to tests that they acknowledge are deficient. One effect of high-stakes standardized assessments is that they redefine many aspects of learning, narrowing curriculum and instruction to meet the demands of often flawed examination instruments. Teachers, even when they recognize this reality, typically accede to the constraints of assessments (Dorn, 2007; Nichols & Berliner, 2007; Popham, 2001). This illustrates structuralism in that the assessments assume a hegemonic role in the process of determining what counts as knowledge and what measures of knowledge are unquestioningly adopted vis-à-vis curriculum and instruction. Assessments thus control time, curricula, instructional practices, and definitions of knowledge, learning and literacies. In addition, standardized assessments are not designed to reinforce deep learning or critical thinking, yet, when high stakes are attached, these assessments provide the framework for instruction (Dorn, 2007; Nichols & Berliner, 2007; Popham, 2001). Therefore, the teaching-learning process is diminished with respect to cognitive engagement. High-stakes standardized assessments reinforce a structuralist epistemology as well as reliance on "old literacies."

High-stakes testing is a costly proposition. Tests must be developed, administered, and scored, all of which require the commitment of human and financial resources. Since educational resources are finite, decisions regarding allocation involve gains and losses; more time and money devoted to testing (and test-related activities) results in less time and money available for other endeavors. Besides these direct costs, Dorn (2007) identifies indirect costs of high stakes tests, expenses he defines as "opportunity costs." Among these are loss of instructional time and narrowed curricula. Since schools serving poor and working-class schools operate with fewer resources to begin with, educational inequities are exacerbated by high-stakes tests. Orfield and Kornhaber (2001) claim that "such reallocation of resources, along with the displacement of substantive curriculum, means that (high-stakes tests) may actually be widening the wedge" of educational opportunities (p. 11).

Teachers and students at Pontiac High are consistent in their narrations of the connections between high-stakes tests, assessment-associated pressures with respect to instructional time, and narrowing of curricula. Identity construction of students and teachers is influenced by these factors as well, since they are central to the nature of daily classroom interactions. Because high-stakes testing has more powerful negative effects on poor and working class schools, the loss of challenging curriculum and instruction contributes to the reproduction of social class. Furthermore, a structuralist epistemology reduces the likelihood that students will learn to challenge the status quo in ways that are constructive rather than in oppositional.

CONTROL OF INSTRUCTIONAL TIME

Instructional time is an essential component of schooling. Because classroom time is finite, teachers must make determinations about their use of time in every aspect of the instructional process. Concerns about available time influence what is taught, how it is taught, and how learning is assessed. Popham (2001) explains the effects of high-stakes tests on teachers' use of time, noting that, "As many beleaguered educators will comment, 'If our chief job is to raise test scores, why waste time teaching content that's not even tested?' " (p. 19).

Teachers in each core subject area, in separate interviews, assert that the demands of state assessments have powerful effects on decisions they make about the use of time in the classroom, and that these effects hinder effective instruction. The use of time in school is an example of how high-stakes tests contribute to the structuralist epistemology of learning in this school.

Time is a significant consideration for social studies teacher and department chairperson Linda Roberts. Ms. Roberts, who teaches both

Regents U.S. History and Advanced Placement (AP) U.S. History, states that the amount of time she spends on a topic is based primarily on how many topic-related questions appear on each respective examination.

> **JG:** Would you teach differently if there wasn't a test?
> **Linda Roberts:** Oh definitely.
> **JG:** How would it be different?
> **LR:** When I got to a topic I wouldn't be like, "That's a great topic but we don't have time." … I'm already two weeks behind (in Regents U.S. History) because we got into the constitution and we began talking about the Supreme Court nominees and all that, and we got behind. And it's easy to get behind. Like, this whole section that I'm teaching now, 1820 to 1860; some exams don't even ask a question about it. Unbelievable. So I will zip through it in a week, where in AP it'll take me three because it's on their exam, but it is not on the US…If it's on, it's one or two questions, tops.
> **JG:** Wow, my gosh. That's so specific….
> **LR:** It is. By now we are able to gauge it. Even someone teaching as long as Mr. Hoffman will say, "Why are you teaching that? It won't be on the exam." We have three (U. S. History exams) a year and he's been here six years so, he goes, "By now I know what's going to be on the exam." And you gotta get moving because so much is on the twentieth century, and we know it, so that's teaching to the exam. We do it because of the state report; everybody knows how we do, so we have to do it. And I would love to say that I'm being creative in the classroom but I gotta get through that exam and no one cares if I'm creative on the (state) report. They care if the kids passed, on the (state) report. That bothers me a lot. And now when they are going to do the (Grades) 3-8 testing, you know what's going to happen over there (in the elementary and middle schools). They are teaching to the exam.

This excerpt emphasizes Popham's (2001) assertion that, "A teacher who is constantly pummeled with score-boosting messages soon learns this lesson: *Teach what is tested; avoid what isn't*" (emphasis in original) (p. 20). Ms. Roberts states that class discussion of current topics in her field (e.g., supreme court candidates) has caused her to fall behind with respect to the assessment-based curriculum. Nichols and Berliner (2007) describe this as a common phenomenon, stating that teachers under the influence of high-stakes assessments "cannot often teach their favorite literature or spend time communicating their enthusiasm for certain curriculum topics, nor can they follow up on important current events because they are on tight schedules to cover only the content tested" (p. 168). Assessments control not only *what* is taught but also how time is allocated.

Ms. Roberts indicates that the concentration of examination items governs the amount of classroom time spent on particular topics. She also asserts that "teaching to the test" is a conventional, acceptable practice in this district given that the "state report," (where examination scores are published and schools are ranked according to these scores), is derived from test results.

Ms. Roberts and her colleagues spend hours analyzing state examinations, reviewing questions to determine how to organize their curriculum content and how to spend their class time. This content takes precedence over concepts and skills that she, as a professional, might prefer to spend class time on. The hegemonic influence of state assessments supersedes the professional expertise of educators as well as the needs of students who must function in the new economy.

While Nichols and Berliner (2007) acknowledge that some forms of test preparation, "such as reviewing content that is likely to be tested" (p. 122), are sensible, a key factor in determining whether or not test preparation is excessive involves time spent on activities related to test preparation. Since Ms. Roberts describes feeling rushed to "zip through" through material based on exam questions rather than ensure that students understand important concepts or develop significant skills, is evident that state assessments have undue influence on her use of instructional time. In addition, both students and teachers consistently refer to the prevalence of writing tasks that are modeled on assessments. Terms like "DBQ" and "critical lens" dominate the responses of students and teachers when they are asked about writing in school. In classes, students are provided with numerous graphic organizers and model outlines intended to serve as formulaic models for these assignments.

Another factor to consider in determining the effects of assessments on instructional time involves the quality of the assessments themselves, that is, are the content and skills being assessed significant and worth expending instructional time on? Nichols and Berliner (2007) state that "if we have a good test, then teaching to the test is appropriate" (p. 122). However, questions exist about the value of the standardized examinations. In general, high stakes tests emphasize rote memorization and low level cognitive tasks (Dorn, 2007; Jackson, 2003; Nichols & Berliner, 2007; Popham, 2001).

Gary Ventura, also a social studies teacher, questions whether content assessed on state examinations represents knowledges or skills that have significance beyond the assessments themselves. Mr. Ventura's concerns echo those of Miller (2005), who quotes quiz show performer Charles Van Doren: "True education does not mean the knowledge of facts exclusively" (p. 150). Mr. Ventura, citing the trivial, arbitrary nature of some of the content assessed on state social studies examinations, as well as the pressure to cover this content within the restrictions of instructional time, confirms this idea.

Gary Ventura: I'm no fan of standardized testing, I understand that you need it to measure accountability in some degree. You need it to measure one school versus another school, but there's gotta be alternative ways to do it that are more conducive to learning.... If you think big picture, the goal of high school is to prepare a student to go to college. But does knowing that George Washington set a proclamation of neutrality for the United States in 1796, is that going to help you in college? Is that going to help you get a job later on? No! Why can't we focus on the skills that these people need? At least one thing I'm trying to do is to try to teach skills in the course and just use the content as a guide to get through it. But the problem is these exams are so content driven that—and this has happened the last two years—you go through the skills throughout the year and you realize it's the first week in June and you've got 60 years of history to cover in a week and you say to yourself, "Holy shit!" (I mean you say to yourself, "Oh my god!") It's the last day of school, some people are out and about, and there you are teaching Ronald Reagan and the Cold War the last day of school! Because you've been stressing so many other things during the course of the year.... But then you say to yourself, "How's a kid gonna answer a question on Ronald Reagan if you haven't covered it?"

Mr. Ventura suggests a significant issue with respect to the political dynamics of high-stakes testing. He asserts that such assessments are practical for ranking schools, but are detrimental to teaching and learning. Consistent with a structuralist epistemology, only one definition of knowledge is deemed significant and this definition is based on state assessments. Despite his understanding of the inconsistency between political and educational purposes, Mr. Ventura continues to teach to the examination. It is evident that, in his case, the political purposes for high-stakes testing displace the needs of students. Jackson (2003) describes how the rhetoric of reform reinforces pressure to concentrate on improving scores on high-stakes examinations and argues that such examinations redefine the meaning of "achievement." She argues that the lofty claims of reformers conceal true political goals and obscure the negative instructional effects of high-stakes assessments.

> According to this version of achievement, teachers need to spend more time preparing students to take tests...That which is really promoted is a closer linkage between education and the needs of businesses, instead of a discussion of what we need for the twenty-first century in terms of communication and higher-level cognitive and problem-solving skills; scientific and technical literacy and thinking tools to understand the world order go unmentioned. (pp. 227-228)

Mr. Ventura stresses that the pressure to cover content is valued over skills that might benefit students beyond high school. Popham (2001), who argues that high-stakes assessments result in less challenging and less relevant instruction, expresses a similar perspective. Discussing the effect of high-stakes tests, he states that "the intellectual fabric of what's taught … tends to be dramatically distorted.… Thus, what's assessed in a high-stakes testing program … restricts the nature of the cognitive operations students face" (p. 20).

For Karen Sorenson, also a social studies teacher, even a question about student perceptions of her teaching style raises for her the issue of pressure to cover content. Like Mr. Ventura, she expresses doubt about the nature of the learning that is privileged by state examinations.

> **JG:** How do you think your students would describe you as a teacher?
>
> **Karen Sorenson:** Loud. I think they would probably describe me as being enthusiastic, but probably as placing too much importance on content. Especially in global, I'm just needing to get through the content. Sometimes I need to let go of that and I think that sometimes the student feel that push, feel my, "Oh my gosh, I'm getting behind" desperation….
>
> **JG:** Too much emphasis on content as opposed to what? Or in contrast with what?

KS: I suppose in contrast to just making sure...well, part of the content is making sure they get the big picture but I guess I feel that, as teachers, we have a responsibility that they're going sit down at these Regents exams and, gosh, if you haven't taught that one segment of history you're doing them this grave injustice. And sometimes we can get so bogged down in making sure they get that information that we forget how they're getting it and if they're getting it in a way that they're going to retain it as well. And I think that maybe if you let go of some of the content and focus on them retaining the big ideas I think, in the long run, they're probably going to benefit from it. But you still get that panicky feeling of "Oh my gosh, there's that decade in Russia that I forgot," or something like that.

Hillocks (2002) reinforces the negative aspects of time spent on test-preparation.

> Countless hours are spent on preparing for ... tests, often over several school years.... In many schools, ... time is ripped away to prepare for tests that do far more harm than good. This is a crucial time in American education. As a society, we cannot afford to spend valuable time on vacuous thinking and writing. (p. 207)

As mentioned earlier, the pressure from state tests coupled with the finite nature of resources—including time—creates unbearable dilemmas with respect to curricular and pedagogical decisions. Newell (2005) elaborates on the effect such dilemmas have on students.

> The teacher's dilemma lies in deciding not only which writing task to assign but also how to balance content coverage with students' efforts to make sense of the content. This becomes a very real and important practical problem when teaching is conceived as content coverage and learning, as absorbing information, a view that is a legacy of building-block and transmission notions of curriculum and instruction (Langer, as cited in Newell, 2005 p. 240)

Miranda Schmidt discusses this effect in her science classes. She describes being pressured by other teachers—who cite the time limitations–to focus instruction on the examination rather than on activities that would support pedagogical approaches that foster higher-level cognitive engagement.

Miranda Schmidt: It seems like, with the time, it's like no one really cares so much about (students' thinking). When I first started, there were things I wanted to do and was kind of told, "Well, that's all nice but we don't have time for that." So it's kind of like you're told that your focus is to get them to pass, to get them through the exam because that's what they need. We don't have time to do all the other ... (trails off)

JG: What kinds of things would you like to be doing?

MS: Like, I tried at the beginning of the one year. We were doing the life processes—living and non-living and that kind of thing—and I gave them this letter that said, "This sample came back from space and you have to design ways that you can figure out if it's living or non-living and so think about what goes into living and non-living, and what would you do?" You know, stuff like that, to make them investigate it and figure it ... but that kind of thing takes more time. So then it's like, "Am I wasting time here?" It's just discouraging in that it's not so much the focus....

JG: Where did you get the message not to do that kind of thing?

MS: From other teachers that are teaching the same thing, who are saying, "This is what we need to do." At least with the sciences, (the attitude is): "Know all this stuff, spit it back at me, you're great." ... So I think of that as how my students are. It's like they have been trained all the way. I mean, it's easier to just say, "Here it is, know this, this is what's going to be on the test." That's so much easier to teach that way and to get the result you want. "I know what's going to be on the test; here you go."

Ms. Schmidt perceives a division between test-preparatory instruction and effective instruction. She also asserts that a resistance to cognitive engagement and thinking is a result of institutional acculturation that can be traced back to pressure to prepare for assessments. She believes that a focus on the examination prevents her from spending time on activities that would enable students to develop relevant scientific skills such as investigation, and to apply constructivist, discovery-oriented strategies for learning.

Each of these teachers narrates reductive effects of state examinations, reinforcing Nichols and Berliner's (2007) perspective.

> Studies indicate that public testing encourages teachers and administrators to focus on test content, test format, and test preparation. Teachers tend to overemphasize the basic skills and underemphasize the problem-solving and complex thinking skills that are not well assessed on standardized tests. (p. 173)

Higher-level cognitive skills tend not to be assessed on standardized examinations (Dorn, 2003, 2007; Jackson, 2003; Nichols & Berliner, 2007; Popham, 2001); therefore, because preparation for these examinations consumes disproportionate quantities of instructional time, activities which might foster higher-level cognitive skills are neglected.

WRITING AND THINKING

> **JG:** Do you think this school's writing instruction fulfills its purpose for most of our students?
>
> **Stan Ryan:** Yeah, with the assigned purpose we are doing okay. Our students and their Regents exams, our writing tasks—their writing is okay.
>
> **JG:** How about if you defined the purpose?
>
> **SR:** Is it germane to their thinking, is it examples of their thinking, is it going to help them to do their thinking? No. I mean, if writing is a reflective activity, do they reflect on what they write? The answer is no. (Excerpt from interview with English teacher and department chairperson Stan Ryan)

At Pontiac High, purposes for writing in school are defined, as in many schools, according to the limited demands of high-stakes tests (Hillocks, 2002). This poses a significant dilemma for teachers who feel they must choose between providing effective instruction or test-based instruction. Supporting this point is a conversation following my observation of one of Blake Oliver's science classes. In our conversation, Mr. Oliver stated that he feels like a "sell-out" for allowing state examinations to limit his uses of writing in his Regents level classes. He claimed that he would "rather have students develop a deep and working understanding of science than to prepare them for a Regents exam" (Field notes). It is evident that, from Mr.

Oliver's point of view, the two purposes for writing are incompatible. Writing for examination preparation does not promote deep understanding.

Carla Cervi, the librarian, posits that the state examinations set the purposes for writing in school and that this results in lower standards.

> **JG:** How do you think this school does in preparing students to be writers? Does it fulfill its purpose for most students?
>
> **Carla Cervi:** I think so, if you're asking, "Are they able to write their Regents and pass their Regents for writing?"... I truly think with the exams that there is so much focus on the exams that we shortchange our kids in the ability to think. Because we have become so concerned about the testing. I think that's done very bad things to the whole education system. So, our kids are able, but we have to hand them things instead of teaching them to think. We teach them facts and things like that.... Why should we lower our standards from what I would think is an education - educating a whole child?

Ms. Cervi suggests that the high-stakes testing has compromised the educational system in that it is not serving the best interests of students. Roger Johnson, an English teacher, narrates a similar point of view by specifying the limitations of the ELA Regents examination. Mr. Johnson questions whether the examination represents "real" education as well as whether it promotes sound principles of writing instruction. Mr. Johnson articulates a point Miller (2005) raises about the writing in school and its relationship to potential (and actual) purposes of education: "When you teach composition, ... are you working for the system or against it?" (p. 138). Recognizing the structural limitations of educational institutions and the systems within which they operate, Miller asks, "Why prepare students to produce work that is valued by such a system? Why not teach them to resist, to intervene, to dismantle?" (p. 138). Mr. Johnson recognizes the dilemma reflected by these questions.

> **Roger Johnson:** I am up caught in this dilemma. I get these juniors. And I need to get them through. Not just through, we have to get them at a certain proficiency level. The dilemma is, do you teach to the test? I can do that. I think I have good proficiency results. I mean, teaching to the test, I have tricks, ... I can do that. The bigger question is: "Is it really helping them

> become better writers?" I probably would say no. So it is a dilemma.

JG: So you have the dilemma. What do you do?

RJ: Doing is, basically, teaching to the exam the first half (of the school year). I treat my junior year as two semesters. My first semester is getting them through the test. And I can do that. My scores are pretty good. Half my kids score eighty-five and above. But, it's a game. I did well on the Regents and I knew that it was a game and I figured out the game. Is that real education though? That's the thing. That's the dilemma.

Writing is an example of a process which, when practiced effectively, develops complex thinking skills. Hillocks (2002) elaborates on this contention.

> In the minds of some people, writing is one thing, but thinking is quite another. If they define writing as spelling, the production of sentences with random meanings, and punctuation, then they might have a case. But who would accept such a definition? Writing is the production of meaning. Writing *is* thinking (p. 198, emphasis in original).

A sociocultural epistemology connected to youth culture (as well as the new economy) would incorporate multimodal literacies, performances that involve more than textual representations of linear thinking. A structuralist epistemology (centered in a certainty regarding truth and knowledge) disregards new literacies that permeate the culture beyond school walls. Miller and Borowicz (2005) state that

> Our minds—and our students' minds especially—have been changed by such digital reading and thinking, changed by these digital ways of knowing.... A key distinction between traditional school learning and competence in such a domain is that instead of passively knowing facts, students learn through active performance, and competence is exhibited through understanding meanings and using tacit knowledge in the embodied experience of solving problems. (p. 9)

Effective uses of writing can enhance understanding of any topic, concept or issue (Russell, 2002). New York State Education Department officials, in an attempt to foster writing as a mode of learning, have incorporated some form of writing into examinations in all four core subject areas (Mathematics, 1999; "New York State Testing Program" Grade 3-8 Testing Program Mathematics/Scoring Training FAQ," n.d.). The notion that a sociocultural approach to writing (in contrast to a structuralist approach to writing) can develop discipline-specific ways of thinking is significant. The purposes for writing and the communities of practice in which writing skills are acquired have powerful effects on how people construct meanings about the world and how literacies function within it. The tools that equate with academic success can be made visible through the processes and products of writing. Newell (2005) states that

> one way to explain the differences in school success between working-class and middle-class children is that the latter have access to "ground rules" for what counts as academic success.... The conceptualization of the nature of academic learning in American schools is typically underconceptualized in that it fails to take the uniquely discipline-specific ways of reasoning and writing into account (Langer & Applebee, 1987). Although teachers may be completely aware of how particular content knowledge differs across content areas, they do not always know the ways of reasoning that are appropriate and necessary for learning and understanding within the particular field (Langer, 1991, p. 241)

Teachers at Pontiac High, however, perceive writing as a topic itself. They believe that developing students' writing ability would detract from instructional time necessary to cover their own curricular content. Therefore, teachers tend to focus only on the types of writing emphasized on their particular examinations.

Math teacher and department chairperson James Randall describes how state assessments drive his use of writing in his curriculum:

James Randall: I just think that if New York State told me that they wanted our students to be able to write more about how this math is applying to something in real life or applying to themselves, ... I would then be more encouraged to do that. But when I look at a test and I see that they really need to give a one sentence explanation then I don't feel I need to take a day out of my lesson planning or a day out of my lesson to say, "Here, we're going to write some paragraph stuff." I just don't see where I need it in there. Put the material in there that is required and I'll do that. I just don't want to take something that doesn't need to be explained too much and expand on it when they can get the concept and answer any questions that are being asked.

Mr. Randall's statements reinforce the assertion that assessment-based curriculum planning results in a reversion to "the basics," as predicted by

Gee (2004). He indicates that he will teach what is on the examination and does not intend to move beyond it. As the department leader, his beliefs are likely to have significant effects on curriculum and instruction.

When asked whether an in-service on writing instruction had affected science teacher Michael Simon's approach to teaching writing, he referred to the demands of his curriculum and the lack of time to include writing beyond what the examination requires.

JG:	Do you think that experience impacted the way you approach writing instruction?
Michael Simon:	No, because the Six-Plus-One (in-service) was really teaching the students to write, and that was essay writing and how to do an analysis of their own work. That's really not part of chemistry curriculum. Do I teach them how to balance equations or do I teach them this (writing)? We have such a short time to cover our material that I don't sit down and go through the process of writing. What I do is just try to encourage them to make complete sentences. "Follow the guidelines that we have. Everything has to be in complete sentences. You've got to make sense when you write." But I don't teach them the process of writing.

Despite assertions earlier in the interview about the importance of teaching the process of writing, Mr. Simon describes writing expectations that are in accordance with the expectations of the chemistry examination, a choice he makes based on the need to devote time to the curriculum content that will be assessed on the state examination. He perceives these options as mutually exclusive rather than perceiving the possibility that writing might be used in order to enhance students' understanding of chemistry.

English teacher Cindy Reynolds explains that the need to spend time practicing examination questions limits the writing students produce and the literature students read in her classes.

JG:	Where does writing fit into your curriculum?
Cindy Reynolds:	After reading a novel there's some writing. I don't do enough day to day as I should—because it would be beneficial—but there's just too much to do to spend that time. And this year I'm kind of throwing one book to the side because the juniors aren't able to answer the questions that they need to answer

for their test in January so we're not doing another novel. They are only going to do two or three.

Each of these teachers narrates how the pressure to prepare students for state examinations affects their approach to writing, limiting the possibility of using writing to foster higher-level cognitive skills. They express a fallacious, but common and historically prevalent, perspective regarding the potential for writing as a tool for learning. Russell (2002) explains.

> From very early in the history of mass education, writing was primarily thought of as a way to examine students, not to teach them, as a means of demonstrating knowledge rather than acquiring it. (pp. 5-6)

Even Ms. Reynolds, an English teacher, does not seem to recognize the possibility that she can use writing to cultivate thinking. And teachers like Mr. Ryan and Mr. Johnson, who recognize that possibility, acknowledge that it is not being enacted. Moreover, in describing her need to eliminate particular types of writing as well as at one novel, Ms. Reynolds suggests an additional result of the emphasis on examination preparation—that students will be exposed to a more narrowed curriculum as a result of high-stakes testing. Popham (2001) describes this effect as critical to students.

> The curricular content assessed by high-stakes tests tends to drive other subjects and other cognitive skills from teachers' classrooms. The erosion of a rich curriculum clearly robs our children of important things they should be learning. For them, the ultimate consequence of unsound high-stakes testing is a seriously diminished education. (p. 21)

Although the students at Pontiac High are part of a generation of students whose literacy experiences are deeply affected by digital technologies, there is no evidence of this reality in within school walls. Students are not provided with the opportunity to bring in skills they already have in these areas, much less develop them further. Furthermore, the old print-centric literacy privileged by standardized assessments has permeated writing and writing instruction to the extent that other possibilities are rendered insignificant and thus nonexistent.

REFERENCES

Anyon, J. (1981). Elementary schooling and the distinction of social class. *Interchange, 12*, 118-132.

Bakhtin, M. M. (1986). *Speech genres and other late essays* (V. W. McGee, Trans.). Austin, TX: University of Texas Press.

Dorn, S. (2003). High-stakes testing and the history of graduation. *Education Policy Analysis Archives, 11*(1). Retrieved http://epaa.asu.edu/epaa/v11n1

Dorn, S. (2007). *Accountability Frankenstein: Understanding and taming the monster.* Charlotte, NC: Information Age.

Englert, C. S., Mariage, T. V., & Dunsmore, K. (2005). Tenets of sociocultural theory in writing instruction research. In C. A. MacArthur, S. Graham & J. Fitzgerald (Eds.), *Handbook of Writing Research* (pp. 208-221). New York, NY: The Guilford Press.

Finn, P. J. (1999). *Literacy with an attitude: Educating working-class children in their own self-interest.* Albany, NY: State University of New York Press.

Gee, J. P. (1996). *Social linguistics and literacies: ideology in discourses.* Bristol, PA: Taylor and Francis.

Gee, J. P. (2004). *Situated language and learning: A critique of traditional schooling.* New York, NY: Routledge.

Hillocks, G. J. (2003). Fighting Back: Assessing the Assessments. *English Journal, 92*(4), 63-70.

Jackson, S. (2003). Commentary on the rhetoric of reform: A Twenty-year retrospective. In K. J. Saltman & D. A. Gabbard (Eds.), *Education as enforcement: The militarization and corporatization of schools.* New York, NY: Routledge-Falmer.

Langer, J. A. (1991). Speaking of knowing: Conceptions of understanding in academic disciplines. In A. Herrington & C. Moran (Eds.), *Writing, teaching, and learning in the disciplines* (pp. 69-85). New York, NY: Modern Language Association of America.

Langer, J., & Applebee, A. (1987). *How writing shapes thinking.* Urbana, OH: National Council of Teachers of English.

Mathematics, Science, and Technology Resource Guide. (1999). *Mathematics, science and technology assessment models.* Retrieved from www.emsc.nysed.gov/guides/mst/partIII2.pdf

Miller, R. E. (2005). *Writing at the end of the world.* Pittsburgh, PA: University of Pittsburgh Press.

Miller, S., & Borowicz, S. (2005). *Why multimodal literacies? Designing digital bridges to 21st century teaching and learning.* Buffalo, NY: State University of New York Press.

New York State Testing Program Grade 3-8 Testing Program Mathematics/Scoring Training FAQ. (n.d.). Retrieved from http://www.emsc.nysed.gov/3-8/faq/math-ttt.htm

Newell, G. E. (2005). Writing to learn: How alternative theories of school writing account for student performance. In C. A. MacArthur, S. Graham & J. Fitzgerald (Eds.), *Handbook of Writing Research* (pp. 235-247). New York, NY: Gilford.

Nichols, S. L., & Berliner, D. C. (2007). *Collateral damage: How high-stakes testing undermines education.* Cambridge, MA: Harvard Education Press.

O'Brien, D. G., & Bauer, E. B. (2005). New literacies and the institution of old learning. *Reading Research Quarterly, 40*(1), 120-131.

Orfield, G., & Kornhaber, M. L. (Eds.). (2001). *Raising standards or raising barriers*. New York, NY: The Century Foundation Press.

Popham, W. J. (2001). *The truth about testing: An educators call to action*. Alexandria, VA: Association for Supervision and Curriculum Development.

Russell, D. R. (2002). *Writing in the academic disciplines: A curricular history*. Carbondale, IL: Southern Illinois University Press.

Sacks, P. (2007). *Tearing down the gates: Confronting the class divide in American Education*. Berkeley, CA: University of California Press.

Vygotsky, L. (1978). Interaction between Learning and Development (pp. 79-91). In Mind in society. (M. Cole, Trans.). Cambridge, MA: Harvard University Press.

Weis, L. (1990). *Working class without work: High school students in a de-industrializing economy*. New York, NY: Routledge.

Willis, P. (1977). *Learning to labor: How working class kids get working class jobs*. New York, NY: Columbia University Press.

CHAPTER 7

WHAT "IS" AND WHAT "OUGHT TO BE"

INTRODUCTION

The connections among identity, language and schooling are multilayered and profound. Writers—active writers who use text confident of its vitality and their agency—are empowered by literacy. Writing hones their voices and authorship strengthens the meanings in their messages (Moffett, 1988). Writing reinscribes their humanity. Conversely, nonwriters are subjugated to the authority of sanctioned texts (Chomsky, 2003). This disparity between writers and nonwriters is significant since writing, an expressive component of literacy, can be an instrument of liberation or domestication (Finn, 1999). School experiences influence the development of young people as writers—or as nonwriters. If, in fact, writing "shapes thinking" (Langer & Applebee, 1987), then students' experiences with and practices of writing affect who they become and how they represent themselves and their cultures. Teachers, actors and agents who shape and are shaped by interrelations of structural factors such as social class, play a key role in the acquisition/transmission of literacy and whether it is an instrument of empowerment or domestication.

Classroom interactions help determine whether students develop their rights as genuine writers as well as the kinds of writing judged "right." In general, the discourse around writing instruction at Pontiac High is

Power, Resistance, and Literacy: Writing for Social Justice, pp. 127–159
Copyright © 2011 by Information Age Publishing

consistent with what Finn (1999) describes as "informational literacy," in which knowledge and literacy involve restating accepted facts in accepted formats without creativity, discovery, or real authorship. This conception of literacy leads to domestication rather than empowerment and undermines the ability to write for meaning in ways that promote critical thinking. Moffett (1988) describes this approach to teaching writing as formalism.

> Naturally allied to the emphasis on reading and general student passivity, formalism dominates the teaching of writing, by which I mean forming the language only without nearly sufficient concern for developing the thought. (p. 87)

Literacy, and by extension writing, involves more than the transmission of facts or skills. Serious writing, as noted by Moffett (1988), requires investment by the writer in developing thought, in "becoming" through language. The dominance of formalism in writing illustrates a phenomenon Weis (1990) described as a socially reproductive aspect of working-class schooling: a pedagogical emphasis of form over substance.

Chapters 7 and 8 will explore the contradictions between the "is" and the "ought" of students' and teachers' experiences of writing instruction at Pontiac High School. The "is" versus "ought" distinction will frame the discussion in two ways. The first, with respect to social class, involves the ability of dominant classes to impose their everyday activities—endeavors that reinscribe the status quo vis-à-vis social class stratification—on less powerful classes. Bourdieu (1987-1988) describes this as a struggle between and among "the plurality of visions" that serves to construct social class divisions. Class struggles play out through everyday practices that move from "what *is*" to "what *ought* to be" (the *is* to the *ought*) in the contexts of power dynamics. Noblit (2007) invokes Bourdieu in explicating this concept.

> (Class) struggle ... is one of symbolism aimed at "the definitions of boundaries between groups" which in turn imposes a vision of divisions that enables the constitution of "properly political collective struggles."... "In these struggles, ... agents ... struggle to impose representations which create the very things represented, which make them exist publicly, officially. Their goal is to turn their own vision of the social world, and the principles of division upon which it is based, into the official vision, into *nomos*, the official principle of vision and division." (Bourdieu, in Noblit, 2007, p. 325)

The perspectives of teachers and students at Pontiac High shed light on the ways in which everyday practices and uses of language reinscribe social class associations and divisions. Many teachers, most of whom were raised in working class communities and educated in public schools similar to

Pontiac High, narrate perspectives that indicate a sense of superiority to the students and their community. In addition, many aspects of schooling (for example, curricula—both hidden and overt) are not questioned, having already become part of the "ought" of daily interactions.

Another aspect of the "is" versus "ought" frame for this chapter involves pedagogies and curricula in practice. As with many schools, there is a significant gap between what "is" happening and what historical research and current scholarship claims "ought" to occur in classrooms. Sperling (2004) notes that theoretical contradictions, that is, incongruities between stated beliefs and existent practices, are ubiquitous in education. She does not, however, depict this as negative. Instead, Sperling observes the need for deep investigation of salient contradictions, noting that these contradictions reflect and are caused by the "contradictory environments in which teachers live and work." She further posits that, "Perhaps that condition is our greatest consistency" (p. 250). It is important to consider the experiences and practices of teachers and students as reflecting and shaping the contradictions inherent in their shared and separate environments.

SOCIAL CLASS AND TEACHERS

The relationships between students and teachers within educational structures are deeply affected by social class. In the first-ring suburban school where this study took place, teachers were raised and schooled in local communities very similar to the one in which they teach. However, teachers now associate with the middle class and narrate a sense of disconnection, even superiority, with respect to the working-class culture of Pontiac High's students, their parents, and the community. This is consistent with Robertson's (2000) analysis of the social class experiences of teachers. She notes that teachers "labour on the curriculum in particular settings, which reinforce and reward particular types of linguistic competence, authority relations, and curricular knowledge" (p. 28). That is, even if teachers' cultural origins were grounded in the working class, becoming teachers has resulted in the development and assumption of a different set of cultural assets. Robertson explains:

> There are two crucial points here in respect of teachers' cultural assets. First, teachers as an occupational group possess a particular level of cultural capital, largely as this capital has been objectified as a form of academic qualification which they have been able to convert into some form of economic capital (through the monetary value of given academic capital). This enables teachers to use this cultural capital as an immediate form of exchange, ... to use that knowledge to further their own social projects as a form of class

legitimacy as well as to derive the material or economic benefits (state-employed professionals).... Second, by actively or uncritically participating in a system that privileges and legitimates particular knowledge forms and practices, teachers engage in what Bourdieu calls *symbolic violence*. (p. 28, emphasis in original)

Symbolic violence can be enacted through various means. These include curricula, pedagogies, and definitions of what counts as learning, knowledge, the "right" language and "good" writing. Every interaction in school involves dynamics of power that produce and are derived from the structural conditions that surround and permeate—that form, reform, and transform—the institution itself.

REVEALING WHAT "IS"

Filling Empty Vessels

Approaches to writing and thinking in school are affected by teachers' impressions of the teaching-learning process. At its extremes, schooling can be seen as either a means of sociocultural indoctrination or a process of sociocultural transformation and thereby a catalyst for change. Whichever extreme the experiences of schooling are perceived to represent, formal education is a key mechanism in the process of what Bakhtin termed "ideological becoming" and, therefore, identity construction.

In Bakhtinian writings, *ideological becoming* (emphasis in original) refers to how we develop our way of viewing the world, our system of ideas, what Bakhtin calls an ideological self.... Language use and literate abilities provide ways for people to establish a social place and ways for others to judge them. The choices learners make about what types of language to acquire and use are political just as the decisions teachers make about what types of language to promote and accept in the classroom are political. (Freedman & Ball, 2004, p. 5)

To apply liberating, transformative, progressive pedagogies, teachers must perceive learners as active participants in the process of education. Students must be understood as whole, complete people who bring sets of knowledges and experiences to the classroom, and learning must be understood as a dialogic process—one in which authoritative perspectives are continuously revealed, questioned and challenged. Essential to dialogism in the classroom is the belief that students possess valid ideas of their own, whether or not these ideas reflect those of school authorities.

Bakhtin's conception of true dialogue involves the convergence and exploration of perspectives—none of which are perceived as a "truth" that cannot be challenged. Each participant in a dialogic interaction benefits from a deeper understanding of the perspectives of the other. The "dialogic sphere" in which such a culture of learning exists requires embracing opposition and consciously testing one's own beliefs against those of others. This sphere represents a contrast to the more oppressive, monologic approach in which information is transferred from an authority to a passive "learner." Morson (2004) clarifies this contrast.

> The point of (a non-dialogic) exchange is to destroy the other's point of view and convert him or her ... to ours. However, in dialogue, the destruction of the opponent destroys the very dialogic sphere in which the word lives. One wants not to destroy but to learn from an opponent, to enrich one's own perspective by the exchange. (pp. 323-324)

A dialogic approach to learning, literacy, and writing, then, requires that teachers see students' perspectives as legitimate and worthy of attention. Teachers must recognize that students' cultural backgrounds, while not necessarily middle class, have value. However, narrations of many teachers at Pontiac High reveal a different viewpoint, one in which students are perceived as "blank slates" or "empty vessels," who quietly (or perhaps resistantly) wait for knowledge to be transmitted from teachers and texts.

Judy Hanley, a math teacher in her 10th year at Pontiac High, ascribes the poor performance of her low achieving students to their "weak background." Students who have the most difficulty, she believes, enter her classroom with cognitive and psychological deficits.

> **JG:** What kinds of students have the most difficulty?
>
> **Judy Hanley:** I think those students that have maybe a weak background and that feel insecure about themselves as math students. I spend a lot of time building them up, letting them know that they can do it. If I can convince them of it, maybe I'm successful. If not, I'm not.... Students that maybe have a weaker background are not successful.

Presumably, time that might have been spent on math instruction is, to some extent, consumed by building confidence and remediating content. Therefore, with respect to Ms. Hanley's expectations, students who begin the year with "weak backgrounds" are likely to have ongoing difficulties and perpetuate teachers' perceptions of deficits.

Amy Wells, a math teacher in her seventh year at Pontiac High, describes the challenge of teaching students whose background knowledge and skills make them unable to progress adequately in her classes.

> **JG:** What kinds of students have the most difficulty?
>
> **Amy Wells:** I think … the students that are coming up without the background. I think that's the biggest thing. I get a lot of students that come up here and they don't know how to do the basic skills. So the stuff that I'm teaching them is past that already, and so when they come up from the middle school or elementary school or wherever, they were lacking, and it's hard for them to move on because they don't know the basics.

Ms. Wells describes students as lacking "background" and implicates their prior school experiences as faulty. Moreover, she narrates a perception of curricula as particular sets of content to be delivered sequentially by teachers ("stuff that I'm teaching them is past already"), not a recursive process of discovery in which students exert agency in constructing meaning. Ms. Wells situates the knowledge ("stuff") students need as instantiated in the institution of schooling. Curricula are not described as fluid or potentially student-centered; they are established and unchanging ("the basics"). For a math teacher to narrate this perspective is intriguing, since state mathematics standards and assessments (and the resulting scope and sequence of curricula) have undergone significant changes over the past 10 years, requiring teachers to struggle to adapt to modifications. Instead of perceiving students as partners in a learning process, Ms. Hanley and Ms. Wells describe students who have difficulty in mathematics as lacking "background." Extending the focus beyond the low-achieving students described by Ms. Wells and Ms. Hanley, Mr. Ventura discusses students in general.

Gary Ventura, a social studies teacher in his fourth year at Pontiac High, is candid about treating students as "blank slates." One benefit he ascribes to this perspective is that it provides a means of avoiding the institutional blame narrated by Ms. Wells ("when they come up from the middle school or elementary school or wherever, they were lacking").

> **Gary Ventura:** There are some people in this department that will complain about the middle school, "Oh what are they doing in the middle school?" And then the finger pointing game starts. "Well you guys aren't doing

> this." "Well, you guys aren't doing this!" And then it
> turns into a big problem. You gotta think of a kid as
> almost like a blank slate, to use the Lockeian term the
> "tabula rasa." A kid comes to you as a blank slate. If
> you treat 'em that way, you'll have all the kids on the
> same page, at least.

The belief that students are "blank slates" centers teachers and texts as the source of all the knowledge and skills students need. Although Mr. Ventura does not explicitly identify students as deficient, neither does he attribute them with having background knowledge. To facilitate delivery of content, he chooses to presume that students arrive as "blank slates" and that he will provide what they need to "fill the page." A dialogic approach would involve discerning the social and cultural knowledge that students bring to class as a foundation to build on, rather than assuming they bring none. His "tabula rasa" perception of students is somewhat disconcerting, since a key aspect of the social studies curriculum concerns cultural awareness.

Stan Ryan is chairperson of the English department and has been teaching at Pontiac High for 37 years. He narrates a slight variation of the theme that students are "empty vessels" who come to school to be filled with knowledge.

Stan Ryan: I used to talk about filling buckets. Okay? You come to
me and have buckets that need to be filled so that you
can now leave me and go on. This is an empty bucket.
And, fill it.... But until you've read it, you don't get it....
We're not a reading society at this point, at least in this
place. If you don't put the stuff in—it's that "stuff in, stuff
out" (idea). If you don't put enough different stuff in,
you're not going to get very much different stuff out....
I'm looking at my kids and saying, "They don't have
much stuff coming in."

Mr. Ryan situates knowledge in reading ("until you've read it, you don't get it"), clearly narrating a deficiency in students' knowledge from this perspective ("they don't have much stuff coming in"). It is evident that Mr. Ryan does not consider the texts people in this community *do* read as adequate or valuable. By focusing on reading certain texts as the central means of learning, Mr. Ryan reinscribes a limited, academic perception of knowledge (and language), one that does not consider the sociocultural realities of learning and schooling (Gee, 2004). Mr. Ryan characterizes the community as "not a reading society," a perspective that does not consider the varieties of literacies in which people might demonstrate proficiency. Since Mr. Ryan narrates knowledge as situated in particular texts (ones he presumes that students do not read), he perceives students as deficient.

The ideas narrated by these teachers are consistent with the "banking" model of education as described by Friere (2003), in which education is reduced to a one-way transmission of information from teacher to student. In this model, critical inquiry is not encouraged, compliance is rewarded, and knowledge—including skills related to language and literacy are reduced to the kind of superficial meanings that lend themselves to memorization, not exploration or discovery. Friere elaborates on the characteristics of this approach to teaching and learning.

> The teacher talks about reality as if it were motionless, static, compartmentalized, and predictable. Or else he expounds on a topic completely alien to the existential experience of the students. His task is to "fill" the students with the contents of his narration—contents which are detached from reality, disconnected from the totality that engendered them and could give them significance. Words are emptied of their concreteness and become a hollow, alienated, and alienating verbosity.
>
> Narration (with the teacher as narrator) leads the students to memorize mechanically the narrated account. Worse yet, it turns them into "containers," into "receptacles" to be "filled" by the teachers. The more completely she fills the receptacles, the better a teacher she is. The more meekly the receptacles permit themselves to be filled, the better students they are. (pp. 71-72)

Ms. Hanley and Ms. Wells ascribe students' difficulty to their deficient backgrounds. Mr. Ventura and Mr. Ryan describe students as "blank slates" or "empty buckets"—receptacles needing to be filled with information. None of these teachers describes students as agents of their own learning, or even as possessing (much less constructing) "information" that is meaningful to them.

Students at Pontiac High are not typically credited with possessing valuable knowledge, skills, or experiences. At the May, 2006 meeting of the English department, a teacher in her second year at Pontiac High expressed frustration with her students by saying: "They have no knowledge." When I challenged this statement, contending that perhaps their background knowledge was just different from our expectations, she clarified her assertion, saying that students' background knowledge is not entirely absent; however, it is insufficient for them to make essential curricular connections. This teacher's narration of the discourse regarding students at Pontiac High is reinforced by field notes written in early June, close to the completion of the study. These notes indicate that English department meeting rhetoric repeatedly represents students as deficient in both language and knowledge. These deficiencies are perceived as rooted in the community.

> Our students and our community were consistently denigrated at department meetings. At every meeting, Pontiac High students were described, by my department head, as illiterate. At every meeting, student lack of achievement was blamed on the ignorant, ill-bred community. (Field Notes, June department meeting)

Teachers at these meetings narrated a perspective indicative of their sense of superiority over the students and community served by Pontiac High. These narrations indicate that teachers do not themselves identify with the community or their students, nor do they recognize or validate the experiences (or achievements) of students or community members as culturally relevant. Depicting students as empty or blank nullifies their knowledge and reifies the academic skills and information possessed by teachers. Students are perceived as having nothing to "say" until they are exposed to and interact with appropriate "texts."

At Pontiac High, the teachers' narrations indicate that they perceive themselves and their experiences as valid, whereas students' experiences are negated. As the keepers and disseminators of knowledge in school, teachers become agents of legitimation whose authority is reinscribed by state standards and assessments. Noblit (2007) elaborates on the processes through which everyday activities construct and reconstruct social class stratification:

> With reification, ... ideas and practices take on a life of their own. People begin to organize their lives with them moving literally from "is" in a specific time and space, to "ought" in a wider set of spaces.... This move is often then coupled to power legitimation, creating a fortification around what was once simply a seemingly good idea about the particular into the "right" way to think and act.
>
> Legitimation becomes fortified when it is embedded in a set of practices all seen as the right way to believe, act and ultimately when the power at play in everyday interaction to enforce an "ought" is coupled with the state. (p. 325)

Teachers who narrate perceptions of students as unfilled vessels show their "acceptance of the given order of things," their movement toward the "ought" of class stratification which justifies their relative privilege. Ignoring, or unaware of, students' "practical knowledge of the social world that can be a truly creative power" (Noblit, 2007, p. 325), these teachers narrate a perspective that limits both their students and themselves.

Accepting the status quo as natural and inevitable inhibits collective action that might result in social justice, resulting in schools that "inscribe differences as deficits so that inequalities are both created and reproduced" (p. 338). In this case, the culture of working class students is reinscribed as deficient and state-sanctioned bodies of information, delivered by teachers, are reinscribed as significant. If students are perceived as empty vessels and the teacher's role is to fill them, it is important to consider the content, that is, what sources count as knowledge.

Just the Facts

> **JG:** What do you think it takes to be a good writer?
>
> **Patricia Brown:** I think that … you really need to know something about what you're going to say. I see in kids that they don't have any clue so, if they don't know the facts, no matter how they construct it, there's nothing there.

Anyon (1981), in exploring the differences in educational experiences of students in schools of varied social classes, found that in working-class schools knowledge is perceived as emanating from "an authority." Meanings are not "constructed" by students; meanings are gathered from authoritative sources like teachers and textbooks. Finn (1999) applied this conception of knowledge and learning to literacy, describing the type of literacy in working-class schools as informational literacy. Proficiency in this kind of literacy involves repeating facts as presented by authoritative texts and reflects a lack of understanding that "in making sense the writer is making knowledge" (Moffett, 1988, p. 148). Many students, in describing their school experiences with literacy and writing, emphasize the notion that writing involves restating commonly accepted facts.

A nontransformative, text-based orientation toward writing is prevalent at Pontiac High. Chloe, whose overall average hovers near 90, describes learning as finding meanings in books. The writing experiences she enjoys most involve rewording information from texts. Moreover, she narrates a belief that the content of the written product is separate from the quality of the written form. In her description of writing, the meaning and development of an essay are reduced to details, and including "facts" that are "true" is the principal requirement.

> **JG:** Do you think your experiences in school have affected you as a writer?

Chloe:	Yeah…. You learn things from reading books in school and finding out what they mean and writing them down…. I like the writing for DBQs and history and stuff because they're really easy because the information is all right there for you and you just have to put it into your own words, and that's easy.
JG:	How do teachers grade your writing?
Chloe:	Actually, they base it on the purpose, like the whole meaning of the essay—the development, which is basically the details and stuff…. Depending on the class they'll be like, "It's just an essay. I'm grading it on the quality of it, not writing or grammar."
JG:	The quality of what?
Chloe:	What you have in it—your facts, if they're true.

Evan, whose English class average is in the high 60s, writes in a variety of contexts outside of school. He publishes poems on the internet and plays a fantasy game in which writing is critical for creating characters and effecting strategies. However, like Chloe, Evan appreciates writing in social studies because it is relatively effortless for him. Once again, reiterating established facts is the primary task.

| Evan: | I like writing the essays for global…. Because you have all the facts in front of you. I can just look at the facts and I can think of the whole essay in my head and just write it down. |

When Evan writes in social studies classes, he simply "looks at the facts" so he can "think of the whole essay" and "write it down." This simplistic conception of writing does not involve grappling with meaning. "Thinking," in this case, seems to require only a rather low level organizational skill, since he can do it all "in his head." The ease with which Chloe and Evan write in social studies classes invalidates the value of the activity itself. According to the report by the National Writing Project (2006), meaningful writing is essentially difficult.

> The very difficulty of writing is its virtue: it requires that students move beyond rote learning and simply reproducing information, facts, dates, and formulae. Students must also learn to question their own assumptions and reflect critically on an alternative or opposing viewpoint. (pp. 22-23)

In general, students describe being encouraged to memorize and restate information, not to synthesize or question it. Students and teachers describe writing as a process of getting information and meanings from established sources and then rephrasing and sometimes reorganizing it. These activities require only minimal textual engagement, not analysis, synthesis, or transformation (National Writing Project & Nagin, 2006).

Outside of school, Emma, whose English grades are in the mid-80s, has written several short stories which have moved her friends and family to tears. Yet, in discussing how teachers might help her improve as a writer, Emma wishes that her teachers would provide more facts so that essays would be easier to write. Echoing Friere's (2003) perception that in the hegemonic institution of schooling teachers bestow knowledge on students, Emma wants her teacher to "give" more details to fill in her essay.

> **JG:** How could your teachers help make you a better writer?
>
> **Emma:** For my English class, … she doesn't give us as much detail as she wants us to put in the essays. Maybe if she gave us more details and stuff like that it would be a little easier to write essays.

Emma believes she would be a "better writer" if her teachers provided the details necessary to correspond with what the teacher "wants." Connor, who is barely passing English and writes only when he is required to, repeats this idea. He describes himself as a good writer because he rarely "gets" errors and he knows how to "use information." He does not describe himself as "making" errors; as a student writer he passively reiterates information and errors are ascribed to the product of his writing. Like Emma, he states that his writing would improve if teachers would "give" more information.

> **JG:** How do you think your teachers would describe you as a writer?
>
> **Connor:** Pretty good writer. I don't get any spelling errors or punctuation errors. I use information.
>
> **JG:** How would you change this school to make writing instruction better?
>
> **Connor:** Probably give more examples or details, give information to use instead of finding it somewhere else and put it in. Just more details I guess. Explain it better.

Connor believes writing instruction would be improved if teachers gave him more information. He resists even the low level of engagement that "finding" information requires. Connor accepts the premise, his reality, that the school provides information, details, and explanations for student writers and the way to improve writing instruction is to intensify these procedures.

Dylan, on the other hand, narrates frustration with his experiences of writing in school. He senses that school experiences inhibit expression and independent thought. A resistant student whose grades vary widely according to his effort, he resents having to subjugate his identity to authority and authoritative texts in order to get good grades.

> **JG:** What kinds of writing do you dislike doing?
>
> **Dylan:** I guess the ones with the strict guidelines, the ones where they kind of put words in your mouth. We have the ones that are based on a quote and the quote will be like, "All literature is awesome," and that will be the quote and you have to write this essay that says, "Oh, I agree. Literature is awesome." Pretty much, you have to lie because you have to agree with the quote and you can't really disagree because they'll give you a bad grade on the essay because you have to follow the guidelines strictly. So those ones are always annoying.

A top student whose parents have advanced degrees (her father has a PhD and her mother has two masters degrees), Alexis experiments with composing a variety of forms of poetry and fiction outside of school. However, her description of the writing she does in school is exclusively text-based, an approach consistent with informational literacy. Speaking rapidly and confidently, Alexis demonstrates discursive fluency with the norms of school-based writing across disciplines.

> **JG:** What kinds of classroom activities are associated with writing?
>
> **Alexis:** For English you read a book. You take your own notes on it, then you go over the notes on it in class. Then you ... are given one or two ... topics for your essay. You can choose one, and then you write it. For History you just you study one or two articles. Then you are given a multiple choice test and then you're given a thesis. Usually you take notes on that too but you go over it much faster and ... only focus on the most important points.... In Biology you learn a topic, you read a chapter, ... you fill out some sort of notes.... And you might be given one topic with, like, three bullets beneath it and you have to include all those points in your essay.

Applebee (2000), having analyzed writing instruction in American schools, describes this type of writing as decomposition, which he defines as writing without composing: fill in the blank and completion exercises, direct translation, or other seat work in which the text was instructed by the teacher or textbook and the student supplied missing information that was, typically, judged as right or wrong. (p. 91)

Alexis describes reading, note-taking and testing as integral to school-based writing. Writing is explicitly text-based, time-oriented, and alienating. Furthermore, Alexis states that she is "given a thesis" by her social studies teacher. Flower and Hayes (1981) explain the flaw in this approach. They note that writers

typically *don't* (all emphases in original) start with a thesis or well-focused body of ideas. Instead, they start with a body of knowledge and set of goals, and they *create* their focus by such complex actions as drawing inferences, creating relationships, or abstracting large bodies of knowledge down to *what I really mean*. (as cited in Hillocks, 1986, p. 45)

In Alexis's case, the prescriptive nature of the content prevents the possibility of writing to learn what she really means. Instead, she is expected to *know* what is meant prior to writing. Writing is narrated as demonstrating awareness of information, not a process of constructing meaning.

Ms. Brown, a science teacher and department chairperson, narrates a perspective that echoes the notion of decomposition. She states that she already knows what students need to know and she uses writing to assess whether they have "learned" the information that she (and perhaps the state) have determined they need.

>   **JG:** Where does writing fit into your curriculum?
> **Patricia Brown:** I do have things where I've come up with worksheets where I've asked them to respond to questions. I think it's a challenge to make them more than just the recall type thing but … you just know what they need to know so you make up questions.
>   **JG:** And how do you assess their writing?
>   **PB:** Generally for content…. Is the answer right or wrong?

Mr. Ventura, a social studies teacher, reinforces the prevalence of form over substance in writing instruction. From his perspective, writing instruction involves providing the facts and the structure. Students must simply fill in the frame.

>   **JG:** What's the biggest challenge about writing instruction?

> **GV:** You give the kids the pieces, you give 'em the foundation, you give 'em the structure, that's the ultimate format—and they don't fill it in! They don't do it. I think that's the hardest part.

In Anyon's (1981) working class school, knowledge was perceived as oriented toward experts or authorities. In Freire's (2003) banking model, teachers, as experts, give knowledge to students. The discourse around writing at Pontiac High indicates that the prevalence of this perception of learning is extended to the writing instruction: Teachers pass along authoritative, unquestioned knowledge (facts/content) to students who pass along knowledge (facts/content) to their papers.

Hillocks (1986), in his comprehensive meta-analysis of writing instruction, reveals the complexity of the idea of writing as a "process of discovery" (p. 7). There is a tension between the extremes of a writer who knows too little to begin writing and a writer who knows exactly what will be on the page. Like most contradictions in education, its benefits are derived from exploration, not resolution (Sperling, 2004). Hillocks invites Perl to clarify:

> Composing always involves some measure of both construction and discovery. Writers construct their discourse inasmuch as they begin with a sense of what they want to write. This sense, as it remains implicit, is not equivalent to the explicit form it gives rise to. Thus, a process of constructing meaning is required...Constructing simultaneously affords discovery. Writers know more fully what they mean only after having written it. (as cited in Hillocks, 1986, p. 7)

"Good" Writing and Inner Speech

Teachers and students at Pontiac High narrate a discourse that closely resembles a monologic, banking approach to learning and literacy. Writing instruction "is" focused on facts and formats. Teaching writing, however, "ought" to involve more than simply repeating and reorganizing information. Providing instruction that relates to authentic authorship, according to Moffett (1988), requires association with inner speech. Moffett elaborates on the origination and extensions of this idea:

> Whatever eventuates as a piece of writing can begin only as some focusing on, narrowing of, tapping off of, and editing of that great ongoing inner panorama that William James dubbed the "stream of consciousness." What I call here "inner speech" is a version of that stream which has been more

verbally distilled and which can hence more directly serve as the wellspring of writing.... So we must understand "inner speech" as referring to an uncertain level of consciousness where material may not be so much verbalized as verbalizable, that is, at least potentially available to consciousness if some stimulus directs attention there and potentially capable of being put into words because it is language-congenial thought. (p. 135)

Moffett (1988), invoking the concept of multivoicedness (or heteroglossia) described by Bakhtin (1981), notes that one's inner speech is really distilled from a "confluence of streams" (p. 136) created and influenced by numerous circumstances. The inner speech that accompanies our everyday activities shapes and is shaped by our sociocultural experiences. As social beings, humans are acculturated in and through language, and it is through social and cultural experiences that people learn to distinguish between public and private speech. Moffett describes as "momentous" the shift that a child makes from continuously voicing thoughts externally to editing and revising thoughts silently before allowing them to become public or "voiced." And while this child's thoughts may seem private and individual, they are, of course, constructed from the multivoiced community of which he is a part.

> Internalizing languages and acquiring discourses are part of one's ideological becoming: identities are shaped by these experiences. Individuals, within (and outside of) the institutions that compose and are constructed by their cultures, use language and are disciplined by norms of language.
> Individuals are in a sense "bugged" by institutions, implanted with an invisible transmitter in the form of a discursive system that structures their own nervous system so that they are in some degree participating in group think whether they know it or not or like it or not. Language works by resonance, between sender and receiver, and this requires tuning all circuits to the same frequency. (p. 138)

In this school, the "frequency," with respect to writing instruction, is that students use writing to organize facts. Good writers are perceived as those who gather and assemble facts. Writing is reduced to a transcript of external speech which does not require explicit engagement with or interaction between inner and outer speech (Although the terms "inner speech" and "outer speech" imply a distinction, the delineation is a rhetorical convenience. Inner and outer speech are mutually constructed and constructive of one another.) Students and teachers serve as recorders of socially acceptable curricula rather than communicators. This, according to Moffett (1988), is contrary to authentic writing and even good education.

> Probably nothing is so important to education as this circularity of inner and outer speech, mind and society. By external speech, individuals com-

municate to each other, and by inner speech each informs itself. (Moffett, 1988, p. 139)

If students are not attuned to their own inner speech, they will be unable to inform themselves and must depend on authorities to provide the information they need. Real authorship is more than organizing information; it requires tapping into inner speech, itself a process of discovery, and engaging with content deeply. A product of authentic writing process is never entirely predictable. At Pontiac High, however, writing is frequently perceived as accessing and organizing information.

Patricia Brown, who is the chairperson of the science department, notes that for students to be good writers they should know what they are going to say before they begin to write. Discovery is precluded by the primacy of facts.

Patricia Brown: You really have to have information that you're clear about in your head before you can put it down in writing. So I think you need to have something to say, I think you need to know where you want to go with it and I think that you have to have a good vocabulary because the more words you have to use the more nuances you can convey in your writing.

Bill Hoffman, a social studies teacher, describes a "good writer" as someone who is willing to collect information and practice putting it on paper.

JG: What do you think it takes to be a good writer?

Bill Hoffman: I think you have to have a lot of dedication to gather the knowledge of whatever topic you're looking to write about. Commitment to, at least, have information to write about.... In the elective I teach,... I do two to three essays every semester. Basically we'll give them the facts... They take a topic and, we always say, "The more information about the topic, the better you explain it, the better your grade."

Mr. Hoffman's conception of good writing focuses on facts and information. Writing primarily demands superficial manipulation of language associated with external speech; students gather information and repeat it in writing to better understand it, not to construct meaning from/with it.

Mr. Hoffman and Ms. Cervi, the librarian, whose comments follow, express the idea that the role of student writers is to find, organize and restate information. Ms. Cervi echoes Mr. Hoffman's perspectives, asserting that writing amounts to sifting and organizing information and that practicing this process is the primary vehicle for improvement.

> **JG:** What are the biggest challenges that student writers face?
>
> **Carla Cervi:** I think the hardest thing they have to do is organizing, learning how to extract relevant information. Not have too much. Not have too little. Not have too much, or any irrelevant information to the task. Sifting through the tons and tons – there's way too much information out sometimes.

Ms. Cervi's description of the main challenge facing student writers is quite different from that described by Moffett (1988), who argues that authentic writing must start by recognizing and engaging inner speech, not external information.

> Paradoxically, writing does not become an instrument of investigation and discovery of external things until it is acknowledged to be grounded in inner speech, because only when the individual brings some consciousness to the monitoring of the stream of experience does he start to become the master instead of the dupe of that awesome symbolic apparatus that, ill or well, creates his cosmos. (p. 148)

Students describe the challenges of writing as unrelated to thinking or engagement with ideas. Chloe, an honor student, asserts that the most difficult aspect of writing involves providing an acceptable concentration of detail.

> **Chloe:** You can't give too much detail, you can't give a plot summary of the book, but you have to have enough detail where you prove your literary element.
>
> **JG:** That's a tough balance.
>
> **Chloe:** It is, because you can't get too in-depth. That's another thing I don't like, because you have to write what they say.

Chloe does not write what she really means; she writes "what they say." "What I really mean," deemed by Flowers and Hayes (1981) as essential to writing, is absent from this process. Chloe's experiences of writing at Pontiac High involve putting the right number of "true facts" or details on paper. She describes being discouraged from getting "too in-depth," a perception which seems to signify a superficial approach to writing.

> **JG:** What factors impact your ability to help students be-
> come better writers?
>
> **MS:** I don't know that it makes them better. I try to make
> them more comfortable just by getting them to think
> it's not such a big deal: "Writing is how you are showing
> me what you know, so it's not the writing that you have
> to get hung up on. Just tell me what you know, and
> you're telling me with words on paper."

It is encouraging that Ms. Schmidt's reply indicates the potential for
critique of her practice ("I don't know that it makes them better."). According to Moffett (1988), "Teaching writing is teaching *how* to manifest
thought into language" (p. 141). Therefore, Ms. Schmidt seems to be on
the right track in trying to get her students to use writing to demonstrate
what they know. One problem, however, is that Ms. Schmidt is acting intu-
itively; she believes that writing should facilitate understanding, but isn't
sure how to make that happen. A bigger issue affecting Ms. Schmidt's
ability to ameliorate this deficiency is that the culture of writing instruction at Pontiac High does not, in general, engage students' thoughts at
all. Writing serves primarily to answer questions, to repeat facts, to describe procedures, and to demonstrate knowledge.

Likewise, when asked how students use writing in school, the librarian
responds:

> **Carla Cervi:** They use writing to answer assignments. They use writ-
> ing to communicate and they use writing as a tool to
> get their feeling or opinion out, if that is the require-
> ment of the assignment. They use writing to show what
> they know. Like in an assessment, teachers look at what
> (students) know and understand if they really know
> what they are talking about.

"Knowing," as in Anyon's working class schools, involves repeating
facts. For Ms. Schmidt, writing strictly involves putting words on paper;
it is neither a means of learning nor a process of discovery. It is a way of
assessing the knowledge one already possesses. This perspective is prevalent in the discourse around writing at Pontiac High.

Facts Versus Feelings

Teachers and students at Pontiac High narrate a division between
facts and feelings. They perceive facts and information as being utterly

separate from their own thoughts and feelings. This perception incorporates neither the sociocultural nature of language and learning nor the relationship between language, discourse and identity. Moffett (1988) explains the connection between inner speech, identity, and culture.

> The idea that most thinking, the discursive part, derives from internalized speech seems rather universally agreed on by specialists in cognition.... Society peoples the head of the individual via speech, which is learned from and for others but in shifting inward merges with universal inborn logical faculties, biologically given, and with idiosyncratic penchants of mind to result in thinking that is at once personal and cultural. (p. 137)

One's identity cannot be separated from one's language any more than experiences can be separated from knowledge. A division between fact and opinion, in the realms of thinking and writing, is fallacious. Belief in such a division reinforces the notion that knowledge exists outside the self, and is imposed on students by teachers and texts.

James Randall, a math teacher and chairperson of the department, narrates a distinction between students' inner selves and the writing they are expected to do in mathematics. When asked to describe how writing is used in his classroom, he depicts writing as answering questions—an experience he sees as patently detached from "emotions or feelings." He narrates a perspective of learning in which students are essentially alienated from both the content and process of the activity.

James Randall: The only thing that we really don't do much of in our writing is saying how this makes them feel or how this really relates to them. It's a lot of just, kind of, reading a problem, solving it, reading a problem and explaining how you used this estimation to get this answer and where it came from and your thought process. But we don't really put any emotions or feelings in that stuff.

Mr. Randall's description of writing indicates that he does not consider the viability of writing to learn deeply in math class. Writing about math is perceived as external—explaining a procedure—and is utterly disconnected from thinking or feeling (types of writing which might, in this teacher's mind, be more likely to occur in English classes). Ms. Hanley, also a math teacher, narrates a similar perspective.

JG: How do you develop your writing assignments?
JH: You know what? They really don't have to be developed because they're more of explaining their

> thinking. So we're not into the creative, "What did
> you think of when I said this?" Or "If you were a tree
> what would you be?" It's not anything like that. It's
> more technical.

Ms. Hanley dismisses an approach to writing that has its orientation in personal experience, writing which she describes as "creative." However, to foster critical literacy, writing assignments should incorporate meaning-making that is not alienated from students' experiences. Boyd et al. (2006) describe the role of literacy in mastering content.

> Educators must provide meaningful learning experiences to introduce content, while at the same time providing students with the skills and strategies that will allow them to create their own meaningful learning experiences that promote mastery of content. (p. 343)

Mr. Randall and Ms. Hanley describe a distinction between personal experience (perceived as the province of English teachers, not math teachers) and writing in math class. Such a perspective negates the possibility of writing to learn mathematics or writing in order to develop dialogic interplay (between inner and outer speech) that could enhance the understanding of mathematics. Later in the interview, Mr. Randall expresses a perceived distinction between fact and opinion:

James Randall: Even research is changing now because I used to go
             and pick up an encyclopedia or pick up a book and
             now it's all on the Internet. One of the things that I
             tell kids, too, is, "Don't believe everything you read
             on the Internet." It could be some jerk that goes
             and puts something on there and say that it's fact.
             And they (students) believe everything they read. So
             that's the other thing, I wish I had some guidelines,
             too, on how (to help students) take information
             that's being given to them and determine whether
             this is fact or just opinion.

Mr. Randall's description of students' interacting with information is consistent with the acquisition metaphor of learning as well as Friere's (2003) description of the banking model. Mr. Randall describes students as "taking" information that is "given" to them and accepting it uncritically. Their primary task as learners in this model, then, is to categorize information as fact or opinion. Absent from this discourse is the idea that students make sense of information or construct opinions using facts/experiences that bombard them daily. Also missing is the possibility that writing might provide an avenue for making sense of information. Furthermore, Mr. Randall indicates that texts like books or encyclopedias do not require the same level of critique or skepticism as "the internet." His acceptance of these tests as authoritative beyond critique demonstrates his acceptance of established curricula and materials (the "is").

Social studies teacher Karen Sorenson also narrates a division between fact and opinion in student writing. She describes a paper that students write in her sociology elective class, indicating that students can select a topic of interest to research, but can integrate their opinion only in the last paragraph.

> **Karen Sorenson:**   Part of (this class) is a research paper. They write just a four-page research paper on their topic using a bibliography and in-text citations, and can take any perspective they want, really, as long as it's sociological.... Some of the topics are very broad so they can take what they find in the research that interests them. They can take any angle they want in the paper, but it has to be a research paper. They can't integrate their opinion until the final paragraph, in which case they can talk about where they stand on an issue or whatever.

Ms. Sorenson offers a range of topics from which students can choose, indicating an awareness of the need for students to forge a connection to their writing. On the other hand, she indicates that the facts of the research precede students' ability to form and express an opinion. This perspective violates the recursive nature of authentic writing and reinforces a formulaic approach to writing process: first the facts, then your opinion. The mandated delineation of facts prior to students' statements of opinion reinforces a perceived division between facts and thoughts.

Moffett (1988) critiques the approach to writing conveyed by Ms. Sorenson's research paper.

> All this traditional school and college writing only *looks* (all emphases in original) mature because it is laced with generalizations of a high abstraction level—quotations from the greats, current formulations of issues, and other ideas received from books or teachers. Such haste to score, to make a quick intellectual killing, merely retards learning, because those kids have not worked up to those generalizations themselves. This short-circuits the natural circularity between thought and society, bypasses any true mediation by minds, and results in a simply more insidious form of inculcation, less honest than straight formula feeding because book criticism, research

papers, and essay exams make students *appear* to be more the authors of the ideas than they really are. Consider too what a deceptive view this conveys to youngsters of both writing and themselves. (pp. 140-141)

Students rarely describe opportunities to inject their opinions into the writing they do in school. Their narrations about writing indicate that information is perceived as entirely separate from thoughts and feelings. This indicates that the contents of schooling are not likely to be integrated into their inner speech, a condition which limits learning. Learning consists of facts being memorized primarily in preparation for their eventual transfer to paper at assessment time.

Olivia, who is failing English, discusses the difficulty of trying to incorporate her opinion into the content of written products.

> **Olivia:** I think that (teachers) don't always understand the way I go about my writing. A lot of the time I put a little bit too much into the content than ... into the task. I'm just trying to get my opinion across.

Olivia's statement indicates that her desire to get her "opinion across" inhibits her teachers' ability to understand her process of writing. The emphasis on the *form* of writing ("the task") hinders Olivia's ability to include her thoughts. Olivia believes that she includes "too much" of her *own* content, thus not performing as well as she might otherwise.

Bailey, who describes herself as a lazy student despite an overall average in the 80s, reports school writing as fact-based and different from personal writing that allows her to be expressive.

> **JG:** How is (school) writing different from the poetry that you ... like writing?
>
> **Bailey:** You're not really expressing yourself, I feel. In poetry you can express yourself. I just like expressing myself and when you write an essay you're just trying to state facts and get a point down.

She also believes that having teachers "explain more" would improve her writing. She perceives essays as stating facts, supporting a thesis that she does not seem to perceive as her own – it is just "a point." This implies that the argument she makes in her essays is not her own; it is determined by the authority of texts, tests, or teachers.

> **JG:** How could your teachers help make you become a better writer?

> **Bailey:** Explain what you want more in detail—what you're asking us
> to write.

Paralleling the idea that schooling involves teachers' filling students with knowledge, teachers and students narrate a description of writing as filling papers with information. "Good" writing means the right quantity of correct facts presented in precisely the right order. Although students recognize this tendency in school, most are not satisfied with it. Many students echo Bailey's desire for more self-expression in their writing. Grace, whose English average is 70, notes that school requires text-based writing, but she wishes that there were more room for her own thoughts and feelings.

> **JG:** How could your teachers make you want to write?
> **Grace:** They could give us more—I know, obviously, the require-
> ments are that we have to read books, but they could give us
> more essays on how we have feelings toward (a topic).

There is little opportunity in school-based writing for students to express their own thoughts or ideas. The prospect of constructing knowledge by integrating inner speech dialogically with external speech/information seems to be beyond their range of experiences, or at least their ability to articulate.

Taylor, whose English class average is in the high 90s, also expresses a desire to write about meaningful, as opposed to always focusing on facts.

> **JG:** How could your teachers help make you a better writer?
> **Taylor:** They could probably give you more stuff that you want to
> write about. Everything else that they give us is just facts.
> Maybe every once in a while just throw in an essay that you
> could write yourself...We got an essay for entrance into
> college where you had to write about yourself, and that was
> more interesting for me because I got to evaluate how I
> wanted to write and what I wanted to write about myself.

Once again, "facts" and "books"—not thinking or learning—are prevalent in the writing students do in school. Taylor notes her lack of interest in the writing she does; she states that teachers just "give" facts for them to write about. She describes one anomalous assignment in which she felt she was able to express herself, as well as make some decisions about "how" she wrote.

Dylan, who resists formulaic writing, responds to the same question in a similar manner.

JG: How could your teachers help make you a better writer?

Dylan: Personally, I think, in general ... just kind of let us go, give us creative writing and just let us write free, or give us subject matters that have a little more meaning to them. They do those kinds of things occasionally, and sometimes you'll get a teacher that likes that kind of thing, but usually it's just "Read Macbeth, write about Macbeth," and that kind of stuff. It would be nice if we could get an opportunity to say what we want ... I just wish they'd hear us out more. I guess that would be a nice thing.... Whenever we read a book and finish it they don't ask us what we thought of it, they tell us what we thought of it. They say, "This was brilliant. There was conflict," and we just nod our heads. It would be nice if we could say, "I think 1984 was stupid. I don't think people would go along with a government like that anyway. I think it was wrong." And they don't let us do that kind of thing.

Dylan critiques both the text-based nature of writing at Pontiac High as well as the way that texts and teachers' interpretations of texts are presented as unquestioned, unquestionable truths. He asserts that the writing he is asked to do in school does not require, or even allow for, critical engagement. Moreover, he articulates the teacher-centered nature of knowledge in this setting ("they tell us what we thought of it"). Moffett (1988) condemns this phenomenon for its effect on student writing, invoking the sense of filling vessels or "stuff in, stuff out" described earlier in this chapter by Mr. Ryan.

> So much of the dullness, awkwardness, shallowness, and opacity that teachers object to in student writing owes to skimming along in the froth instead of plunging into the current, where intuition lines up with intelligence and particularities of experience correct for cliché. Seldom has anyone shown them how to work their way down.... Most discourse in society today follows the now notorious circuit of the computer, "garbage in, garbage out." Something really significant has to happen inside—mediation by minds. If "output" differs from "input" mainly in being more amateurishly put together, then subjectivity has little meaning, and objectivity cannot be an authentic enough issue to be dealt with. (p. 140)

Dylan's description of his experiences of writing indicates his belief that teachers want him to repeat what they tell him is "right." His own

thoughts are silenced, and he feels that he must either be silent and compliant or strident and defiant.

Alexis, a very high achieving, motivated, and involved student, describes the most challenging aspect of composition as its alienation from
herself and her interests.

> **JG:** What would you say is your biggest challenge as a writer?
> **Alexis:** Maybe, writing about something that you don't have any pas-
> sion about. Like something factual and writing with a time
> limit, under pressure.... If you have forty-five minutes to
> write a two-page essay on the twenty years between 1800 and
> 1820s then it's not easy.

This approach to writing alienates students from school and from
learning, a situation which Gee, Hull, and Lankshear (1996) note as
detrimental to their futures. Gee (2004) states that "learning is based
in situated practice, ... a form of extended engagement of self as an
extension of an identity to which the (learner) is committed" (p. 108). He
asserts that learning is essentially experiential: "People primarily reason,
not by logical computations and on the basis of abstract generalizations,
but by manipulating records of their actual experiences.... You are what
you have experienced" (p. 109). Gee designates the experiences that
shape one's identity, including one's social class status, as a "portfolio,"
and the people who can effectively construct portfolios for use in the new
capitalism as "shape-shifting portfolio people." From Gee's perspective, a
person's experiences—which are necessarily coconstructed (because they
are experiences, not mere "facts") are then included in a person's portfolio
(of "marketable" skills, talents, knowledge, and abilities). This model
is not dehumanizing in the way that the banking model is because the
portfolio is not the *person*; it is an *asset*, perhaps, in that it is a reflexively
developed reflection of the person to be used *by* the person at his or her
will. The model of the shape-shifting portfolio person privileges agency
over subjugation and experiences over facts.

In contrast, Friere (2003) describes the limitations of the banking
approach:

> This is the "banking" concept of education, in which the scope of action
> allowed to the students extends only as far as receiving, filing, and storing
> the deposits. They do, it is true, have the opportunity to become collectors
> or cataloguers of the things they store. But in the last analysis, it is the people
> themselves who are filed away through the lack of creativity, transformation,
> and knowledge in this (at best) misguided system. For apart from inquiry,
> apart from the praxis, individuals cannot be truly human. Knowledge
> emerges only through invention and re-invention, through the restless,

impatient continuing, hopeful inquiry human beings pursue in the world, with the world, and with each other. (p. 72)

When knowledge is perceived as being established within the authority of teachers and texts, there is little for students, as learners, to do besides restate and reorganize information.

Confidence: Do I Have the Right to Write?

A perceived division between fact and opinion inhibits the development of empowering literacies. Miller (2005) asserts that it is essential to explore "the interplay between personal experience and academic training," further noting that academic training is "also part of personal experience" (p. 31). At Pontiac High, the dearth of experiences using writing in empowering ways has significant effects on the self-confidence with which students approach writing.

Miranda Schmidt, a science teacher, describes students as quick to "give up" and lists lack of confidence as the biggest challenge for student writers.

> **JG:** What's the biggest challenge for your student writers?
> **MS:** I think the kinds of questions I have them write, … or answers I have them give: you know, "Describe this to me, explain this to me." I think it's that they have to pull this from someplace. And I think it scares them that they have to come up with stuff or find the information. So then they're just, "I don't know the answer," and they'll give up.

Mr. Ventura, a social studies teacher, echoes this perspective.

> **JG:** What's the biggest challenge that student writers face?
> **Gary Ventura:** For some kids, they just don't feel confident enough in what they're trying to put down on paper, what they're writing.

Stan Ryan has taught English at Pontiac High for 38 years and he considers students' lack of confidence to be prevalent and significant.

> **JG:** In general, how would you describe the students at Pontiac High?

Stan Ryan: (long pause) Oh, gee whiz. Let's pick this one right up. (laughs) Cowardly. Cowardly, which has been ingrained in some ways and has been pushed on them long before—as soon as they come here.... They have little esteem and they have little certainty of their abilities and are quite ready and willing to abandon them on a moment's notice. Abandon that sense of confidence that's necessary. Unconfident? And that's not really a word, but ... nonconfident.

The idea that writers need to know what they are going to say and be certain that it is "right" *before* they write it down is prevalent at Pontiac High, and it is detrimental to the ability to conceive of or use writing as a means of thinking. Imagine censoring thoughts for "correctness" prior to thinking them. The notion is paradoxical. Thoughts—even misconceptions—must be permitted in order for understanding to be constructed. The possibility of using writing to construct understanding is eliminated if potentially inaccurate thoughts are silenced/erased prior to being written. Instead of a means of constructing meaning, writing is perceived as a product with which to demonstrate awareness of acceptable information or knowledge. Judy Hanley, a math teacher, notes the effect of this kind of thinking on her own writing, as well as on the writing of her students.

JG: What factors impact your ability to help students become better writers?

JH: It's just my confidence level, I believe. I second-guess myself, "Is that right? Is that wrong?"

JG: So you think that if you were more confident you would be better able to help your students?

JH: I think so, yes.

Ms. Hanley notes that her students show the same inclination she does, that is, they feel that the answer needs to be right before they are willing to write it down. The authority of texts as sources of knowledge has a powerful impact on the ability to perceive oneself as a writer. Written text is not seen as constructed; it is viewed as a product derived from an objective authority.

During an in-depth interview, Ms. Hanley reveals an approach to teaching writing that differs from her approach to teaching math—which she perceives as a process of discovery. She notes that her own writing, admittedly minimal, has shifted over time to represent a more discovery-oriented process.

JG: How would you describe your processes of writing?

JH: I think it's laborsome. I have a difficult time. I guess I'm also a procrastinator. I wait and I wait until I have to do it and then I do it. As far as the process, what I'm starting to do now that I'm getting older and a little bit smarter, I'll collect my thoughts on paper first and then group them into categories and then I'm finding myself doing it a little bit better. I'm approaching it more like a math problem than I am actually something creative and something "English."

JG: You know what's interesting is that I tell my students, when I try to get them to write and they feel like they have to know everything they are going to say before they write, I tell them to approach it like a math problem.

JH: Really?

JG: I do. I tell them when you look at a math problem that's hard you don't know where it's going to go, but you just start it anyway.

JH: That's very interesting… I wish someone would have told me that sooner, th ough. Because I thought I had to know everything in the beginning. And I often tell my math students, you don't know where this math problem is going, just take it easy and just do one step at a time, and I should take my own advice, I guess (in approaching writing).

Our dialogue reveals a shift in her approach to writing. It is noteworthy that teachers do not perceive writing as inquiry-based. They use writing to set down the right information. The "is" of this approach to writing is so prevalent that an alternate perspective seems almost unimagined.

Ms. Hanley narrates a perception of writing as established and authoritative. A writer is perceived as already knowing what to say, and the writing process is perceived as mere transference or, at best, reorganization, of facts.

JG: What do you think is the biggest challenge for student writers?

JH: Probably my challenge, being able to get what they're thinking down on paper. I think a lot of them question whether or not they're right, so they just don't write it down or they don't write it down the way they are thinking about it.

JG: So your sense is that the thoughts are there but—

JH: they can't pull it out…. But then if you speak to them and you ask them a question they can definitely answer it. So why aren't they writing it down? …They're afraid of it, they don't think that they're right, maybe, I'm not quite sure why they're not writing it down.

JG: From your experiences what factors help them improve? You described an improvement from ninth (grade), to tenth, eleventh … why do you think they're getting better?

JH: Experience, feedback from the teacher—whether or not they are doing it right, skill level. I think just when you get a little older you're just a little more bold, you just write it down. Put something down, at least. I think when you are younger you're afraid to, "Well, if it's not right, I don't want to write it down." But when you're older you're not quite as intimidated by putting something down that's wrong.

Because writing and thinking are intertwined, each affected by the other, it is conceivable that Ms. Hanley is describing a phenomenon that relates directly to her own, and her students', confidence as *thinkers*. Since writing derives from inner speech, the block that prevents students from putting "what they're thinking down on paper" may also affect their ability to learn by thinking deeply about and interacting with ideas. If one's writing, and by extension one's thinking, must be correct before it is written, then writing (and perhaps by extension thinking) cannot result in discovery. "Wrong" or inaccurate perceptions must be understood as part of the process of learning. According to Moffett (1988), disorder is a necessary precursor of order.

> What really teaches composition—"putting together"—is disorder. Clarity and objectivity become learning challenges only when content and form are *not* given to the learner but when he must find and forge his own from his inchoate thought. Now, *that's* hard, not the gloried book-reporting or the filling in of instances to fit some else's generalization (topic). (p. 140)

Having the right answer prior to beginning to write negates the higher levels of thinking and discovery that writing can facilitate. At Pontiac High, few teachers and students narrate engagement with writing as inquiry. Newell (2005) cites Langer in asserting the connection between students' conceptions of writing and their teachers' experiences of writing: "Students are unlikely to be learning how to gather evidence and develop effective arguments when their teachers (and the field in general) have not articulated such concerns to themselves" (Langer, 1992 as cited in Newell, 2005, p. 242)

CONCLUSION

To become empowered as critical thinkers, students must become empowered as users of critical literacy. Such empowerment, if it is to be fostered in schools, requires that their own thoughts and their own language norms be acknowledged and valued in school settings. Boyd et al. (2006) reinforce the significance of critical literacy in the context of social justice.

> All students need to be taught mainstream power codes/discourses and become critical users of language while also having their home and street codes honored.... Difficult though this dilemma may appear, English language arts teachers have a further, absolute responsibility to help students master ... mainstream power codes in order to become truly critical users (and creators) of language, not passive consumers of others' language. Indeed, too often passive consumption of others' language is at the heart of race-based inequality, socio-economic inequity, and oppression. (p. 344)

The current system of schooling is an inadequate means of social mobility for working-class students. Van Galen and Noblit (2007) admit that "social mobility through schooling is very much the exception rather than the norm" (p. 7) and note that "We simply do not see students making it through the complicated social structures of school on their own merit alone" (p. 7). It is clear that, at Pontiac High, the norms of writing instruction so not foster critical literacy. However, Pontiac High is part of a larger hegemonic structure. Van Galen and Noblit elaborate about working class communities and how schooling serves to perpetuate privilege:

> the social cohesion and relative homogeneity of these community may simultaneously mask their relative disadvantage while also narrowing the range of possible futures to which they might aspire. (p. 6)

> The "game" (of schooling) itself continues as privilege defends itself. The rules still favor more privileged students, and the costs of the game are still extraordinarily high for poor and working-class students. (p. 8)

Writing in this school reinforces domesticating, not empowering, uses of literacy. It is evident that, in general, the "ought" that is consistent with the norms of social stratification wherein teachers maintain hegemonic domination over students supersedes the "ought" of what should be happening in transformative classrooms. Writing instruction tends to reinforce informational language and writing for domestication, not empowerment or transformation.

Finn (1999) describes the possibilities for change:

> The status quo is the status quo because people who have power to make changes are comfortable with the way things are. It takes energy to make changes, and the energy must come from the people who will benefit from the change. But the working class does not get powerful literacy, and powerful literacy is necessary for the struggle. How can the cycle be broken?
>
> Teachers who see themselves as allies of their working-class students can help their students see that literacy and school knowledge could be potent weapons in their struggle for a better deal by connecting school knowledge with the reality of working-class students' lives. (p. xi)

Spaces for hope exist in the narrations of students and teachers who express resistance to literacy practices that compromise the potential for empowering literacies. This image does not, however, represent the whole picture. Paralleling Foucault's (1993) assertion that resistance is a fundamental component of power relations, some teachers and students narrate recognition and critique of current practices—an awareness that what "is" may not correspond to ideal conditions. This awareness, which will be explored in the following chapter, is a crucial first step toward challenging the status quo.

REFERENCES

Anyon, J. (1981). Elementary schooling and the distinction of social class. *Interchange, 12*, 118-132.

Applebee, A. N. (2000). Alternative models of writing development. In R. Indrisano & J. R. Squire (Eds.), *Perspectives on writing: Research, theory, and practice*. Newark, DE: International Reading Association.

Bakhtin, M. M. (1981). The dialogic imaginatiion (C. Emerson & M. Ho

Bourdieu, P. (1987-1988). What makes a social class? On the theoretical and practical existence of groups. *Berkeley Journal of Sociology, 32-33*, 1-17.

Boyd, F. B., Ariail, M., Williams, R., Jocson, K., Sachs, G. T., McNeal, K., et al. (2006). Real teaching for real diversity: Preparing English language arts teachers for 21st century classrooms. *English Education, 38*(4), 329-369.

Chomsky, N. (2003). The function of schools: Subtler and cruder methods of control. In K. J. Saltman, & Gabbard, D. A. (Ed.), *Education as enforcement: The militarization and corporatization of schools* (pp. 25-35). New York, NY: Routledge-Farmer.

Finn, P. J. (1999). *Literacy with an Attitude: Educating working-class children in their own self-interest*. Albany, NY: State University of New York Press.

Flowers, L. S., & Hayes, J. R. (1981). The dynamics of composing: Making plans and juggling constraints. In L. W. Gregg & E. R. Steinberg (Eds.), *Cognitive processes in writing* (pp. 31-50). Hillsdale, NJ: Erlbaum.

Freedman, S. W., & Ball, A. F. (2004). Ideological becoming: Bakhtinian concepts to guide the study of language, literacy, and learning. In S. W. Freedman & A. F. Ball (Eds.), *Bakhtinian perspectives on language, literacy, and learning* (pp. 3-33). Cambridge, England: Cambridge University Press.

Friere, P. (2003). *Pedagogy of the oppressed* (M. B. Romos, Trans. 30th anniversary ed.). New York, NY: Continuum International.

Gee, J. P. (2004). *Situated language and learning: A critique of traditional schooling*. New York, NY: Routledge.

Gee, J. P., Hull, G., & Lankshear, C. (1996). *The work order: Behind the language of New Capitalism.* Sydney, Australia: Westview Press.

Hillocks, G. J. (1986). *Research on written composition: New directions for teaching*. Chicago, IL: ERIC Clearinghouse on Reading and Communication Skills: National Institute of Education.

Langer, J., & Applebee, A. (1987). *How writing shapes thinking*. Urbana, OH: National Council of Teachers of English.

Moffett, J. (1988). *Coming on center* (2nd ed.). Portsmouth, England: Boynton/Cook.

Morson, G. S. (2004). The process of ideological becoming. In A. F. Ball & S. W. Freedman (Eds.), *Bakhtinian perspectives on language, literacy, and learning* (pp. 315-332). Cambridge, England: Cambridge University Press.

National Writing Project, & Nagin, C. (2006). *Because writing matters: Improving student writing in our schools*. San Francisco, CA: Jossey-Bass.

Newell, G. E. (2005). Writing to learn: How alternative theories of school writing account for student performance. In C. A. MacArthur, S. Graham & J. Fitzgerald (Eds.), *Handbook of Writing Research* (pp. 235-247). New York, NY: Gilford.

Noblit, G. W. (2007). Class-Déclassé. In J. A. Van Galen & G. W. Noblit (Eds.), *Late to class* (pp. 313-346). Albany, NY: State University of New York Press.

Robertson, S. L. (2000). *A Class act: Changing teachers' work, the state, and globalisation* (Vol. 8). New York, NY: Falmer Press.

Sperling, M. (2004). Is contradiction contrary? In A. F. Ball & S. W. Freedman (Eds.), *Bakhtinian perspectives on language and literacy* (pp. 232-251). Cambridge, England: Cambridge University Press.

Van Galen, J. A., & Noblit, G. W. (Eds.). (2007). *Late to class: Social class and schooling in the new economy*. Albany, NY: State University of New York Press.

Weis, L. (1990). *Working class without work: High school students in a de-industrializing economy*. New York, NY: Routledge.

CHAPTER 8

HINTS AT HOPE, GLIMMERS OF RESISTANCE

I don't want to be a product of my environment—I want my environment to be a product of me. (Protagonist Frank Costello in *The Departed* [Scorsese, 2006])

In order to employ effective practices of writing instruction, it is necessary to engage students as authentic writers—as creators of meaningful texts. Working-class students whose experiences of language may not parallel academic language norms ought to be exposed to explicit language through direct methods that respect their own experiences (Finn, 1999). Effective implementation of these methods is grounded in the kind of socioculturally-based pedagogies encouraged by the New Literacy Studies. Critical pedagogical approaches seek to make the "invisible visible by examining the ways in which well-meaning educators attempt to silence diverse languages" (Alim, 2005, p. 28). Critical pedagogies attend to the relations of power that obtain through and with language use, and focus on questions like the following: "How can language be used to maintain, reinforce, and perpetuate existing power relations?" And, conversely, "How can language be used to resist, redefine, and possibly reverse these relations?" (p. 28).

In order to interrupt the reproduction of social stratification, students and teachers must become conscious of their own "position in the world"

Power, Resistance, and Literacy: Writing for Social Justice, pp. 161–193
Copyright © 2011 by Information Age Publishing
161

and they must consider "what to do about it" (Alim, 2005, p. 28). The possibilities for social justice will be enhanced when "students become more conscious of their communicative behavior and the ways by which they can transform the conditions under which they live" (p. 28).

However, at Pontiac High, writing instruction typically consists of the transmission of terminology and conventions without explanation—an approach that implicitly establishes teacher superiority and undermines student agency. Students are not taught to value their own thoughts, nor are they taught strategies for exploring or expressing them (Hillocks, 1986). Instead, class distinctions are reinscribed through discourses that signify differential power relations (Finn, 1999; Lareau, 2003; Van Galen & Noblit, 2007). Writing is understood to be a way of thinking; as such, it shapes and is shaped by culture. As an aspect of culture and an instrument of discourse, language reveals and reinscribes social class in ways that are invisible to those whose norms are dominant. Making these norms visible is an essential first step toward transformation, towards critical literacy. Shor (1997) explains.

> We are what we say and do. The ways we speak and are spoken to help shape us into the people we become. Through words and other actions, we build ourselves in a world that is building us. That world addresses us to produce the different identities we carry forward in life: men are addressed differently than are women, people of color differently than whites, elite students differently than those from working families. Yet, though language is fateful in teaching us what kind of people to become and what kind of society to make, discourse is not destiny. We can redefine ourselves and remake society, if we choose, through alternative rhetoric and dissident projects. This is where critical literacy begins, for questioning power relations, discourses, and identities in a world not yet finished, just, or humane. Critical literacy thus challenges the status quo in an effort to discover alternative paths for self and social development. This kind of literacy—words rethinking worlds, self dissenting in society—connects the political and the personal, the public and the private, the global and the local, the economic and the pedagogical, for rethinking our lives and for promoting justice in place of inequity. (Introduction, para. 1, 2)

The inception of critical literacy, according to Shor, occurs when power relations, discourses, and identities are questioned instead of accepted as the natural order of things: the way things "ought to be." This chapter explores the movements of teachers and students toward writing instruction and uses of language that reflect principles of critical literacy.

CRITICAL INQUIRY

Change, positive movement toward effective transformational writing instruction, requires a capacity for critical inquiry (Shor, 1997). To progress
from "is" to "ought" in terms of best practice, teachers and students must
first recognize flaws in the current state of affairs. Sean Thomas, a social
studies teacher, narrates awareness that current practices in school-based
writing do not coincide with what it takes to help students become good
writers.

> **Sean Thomas:** In social studies, with the thematic and the DBQ,
> it's totally content driven. So are we fulfilling the
> purpose of them being good writers? Not necessar-
> ily. We just want 'em to spew facts back at us. Any
> way that they can.

Mr. Thomas understands that the approach to writing that is prevalent in social studies classes is not consistent with the broader purpose of
helping students become good writers. Gary Ventura, also a social studies
teacher, agrees that writing instruction—particularly as it is geared toward
high stakes state assessments—is less than ideal.

> **JG:** Does this school's writing instruction fulfill its pur-
> pose for most students?
> **Gary Ventura:** The way we do it here? In our department I'm
> gonna say for the Regents exam, yes. Past the Re-
> gents exam, no.

Social studies teacher Karen Sorenson critiques the rigid prescriptions
on writing in her content area. She notes the importance of student investment in the task of writing. When asked how improve writing instruction, she states:

> **Karen Sorenson:** If writing could be approached less as, "This is the
> way you have to do it and this is the way you have
> to set it up" and more as, "Just write, don't worry
> about those things, just write." And maybe inte-
> grate some of the more mechanical things later on.
> But I think we have to get positive attitudes about
> writing. How are kids going to be motivated to

> do well in writing if they don't see any interest or value?

Like Mr. Ventura and Mr. Thomas, Ms. Sorenson doubts the quality of writing instruction beyond the requirements of state assessments.

> **JG:** Does this school's writing instruction fulfill its purpose for most of our students?
>
> **KS:** I would say probably not, and I don't know that it's exclusive to this school. I think that it's the state; it's the mandates by the state. I would say that what we really, what we all—if you sat every teacher, every parent, everyone down and said, "What do you want our kids to get out of writing? What are the most important things about it?" We're probably not going about it the right way in that we aren't achieving those things. We're achieving results on the maybe on a state-mandated test. Maybe we're getting kids to think, "Okay, this is how I write a DBQ, this is how you write a thematic essay." But as far as long term changing attitudes about writing and really helping them in so many different situations in life, I don't think we're achieving that.

Ms. Sorenson not only critiques the writing instruction for its lack of application beyond state assessments, she also credits teachers and parents with having an untapped appreciation of the important aspects of writing. This is a significant departure from other teachers' perceptions of the community as illiterate and lacking background.

Ms. Schmidt, a science teacher, acknowledges her own lack of expertise in facilitating writing, noting that what she is currently doing does not seem effective:

> **JG:** What factors impact your ability to help students become better writers?
>
> **Miranda Schmidt:** Hmmm ... I don't know. I don't really know that I do anything. Um, I mean, like I said, I correct stuff that they do wrong, but do they actually learn from that? Probably not. They probably don't look at it. So, um, I don't know. I really don't know.

Without exempting themselves from critique, these teachers problematize the "is" that represents the current state of writing instruction.

Although Ms. Schmidt might be criticized for her deficiency as a writing teacher, Freire (2004) would applaud her willingness to face and state what she doesn't know.

> Education makes sense because women and men are able to take responsibility for themselves as beings capable of knowing—of knowing what they know and of knowing that they don't. They are able to know what they already know better and come to know what they do not yet know. (p. 15)

Awareness, reflection, and critique of deficiency are necessary elements of change. Mr. Thomas, Mr. Ventura, Ms. Sorenson, and Ms. Schmidt hint at deficiencies in the writing instruction at Pontiac High. In the next section, a more direct critique of the writing instruction at Pontiac High is narrated by Roger Johnson, an English teacher who is also a published poet.

TEACHERS AS NONWRITERS

The following excerpt begins with a startling statement: that students at Pontiac High are not "ever taught how to write." Mr. Johnson's experiences have led him to hypothesize that English teachers choose their field based more on their interest in literature than in writing. This contention is upheld in research about teaching composition (Hawkes, 1999). The fact that few English teachers at Pontiac High are practitioners of writing, Johnson argues, makes writing instruction uncomfortable for teachers and unfair to students.

JG: What is the biggest challenge students' writers face?

Roger Johnson: In the classroom? ... I think, a challenge that faces them is probably not being—in the classroom—ever taught how to write. The emphasis is not on writing. It's on just talking about reading. And if the teachers started to switch those emphases a little bit, I think it probably would change. Although, will that change? I don't know. I can imagine, but I don't know. I can imagine why, if someone doesn't write at all or doesn't like writing, why (teaching writing) would be hard for them. I can imagine that, for a person who doesn't write, teaching writing would be very hard. They wouldn't want to do it or wouldn't find satisfaction in it. They might find it difficult. Whereas, being a writer, the type of thing I most enjoy doing is teaching writing because I am a writer. My own personal belief is that if you have experience of writing, if you know what it involves, then I think you end up being a better teacher of writing. I think that's just a natural progression.

Mr. Johnson narrates an issue that is essential to the implementation of the sociocultural approach to writing promoted by Englert, Mariage, & Dunsmore (2005), who emphasize the importance of teacher experts facilitating the process of student writing.

> Sociocultural theory is replete with references to the role of adults, experts and agents who provide access to strategies and tools through instruction, explanations, modeling, and think-alouds (Baker, Gersten, & Graham, 2003; Daniels, 2001; Scribner, 1997; Wells, 1999). Research supports a prominent view of teacher agency in the sharing of expertise in the teaching-learning process. Otherwise, students gain no insight into the way experts write and think. (p. 2)

Mr. Johnson continues, discussing how nonwriting teachers affect the writing experiences of students.

RJ: I have never taken a poll or anything, but I imagine English teachers go into English because they like to teach reading, and writing is just this other thing they have to do. Whereas me, I prefer teaching writing all of the time. Because I am a writer, and that's the big difference.

A lot of teachers aren't writers and that is not in their comfort zone. And so when they even teach it, probably, it's like this weird thing that they're almost trying to teach. It's like someone who has never driven a car trying to tell someone how to drive a car. We all write, obviously, but to be an effective writer is different...
In other words, I couldn't imagine if I was never really a writer, without all of those hours upon hours of the writing process, that I would know how to teach it. I wouldn't probably like it.

When I started teaching here we had a creative writing elective. And I am not giving any names, but the woman who had taught that class had never done any creative writing. And I thought that was really odd. And I thought to myself, how can someone that has not done any creative writing teach a creative writing class? And I thought to myself, isn't that the same thing as if

> I'd never done photography at all and then someone
> said, "You get to teach photography"? I don't do pho-
> tography. I've never taken photographs. So how would
> I even know how to do it? It would be really kind of
> dishonest to the kids. And I don't think it would be very
> effective.

Once again, Englert et al. (2005) reinforce Mr. Johnson's perspective,
highlighting the notion that writing, an inherently social endeavor, requires expert facilitation in order to be effective.

> Although writing seems to be a solitary discipline, the roots of writing com-
> petence are developed in social interaction with teachers who can dramatize
> the thoughts, words, dilemmas, and actions in highly visible ways. Effective
> teachers create spaces to make available to students the full range of semiotic
> tools and discourse in constructing written texts. By forging concrete links
> among specific thoughts, words, and actions, teachers bring the relationship
> between "knowing and doing" into a plane of more active consciousness
> within an individual (Shotter, 1995, p. 209)

Teachers in each of the four core subject areas narrate agreement with
Mr. Johnson's assertion that they are not really writers. Mr. Randall, a
math teacher and chairperson of the math department, is candid about
his own lack of experience as a writer.

James Randall: I guess for myself, I was always trained in writing as
a student and I was always trained in high school
and college but I was never really encouraged to
improve my writing when I got out of college. As a
matter of fact, I was never really encouraged to improve my writing past my freshman year of college
when I took a writing course. ... I've never sharpened
my skills since, and you lose some of that over time.
So I think the fact that I just haven't been trained
more in writing has impacted my ability to teach my
students to become better writers. I think for me to
give my students the best explanation on how to do
some kind of writing it would probably be best if I
was trained every now and then.

Ms. Hanley, also a math teacher, admits to doing little writing. Like
Mr. Randall, she believes that her writing ability may have declined since
college. She reflects on her own skills and hints at recognition of the interplay between writing and thinking.

JG: How would you describe yourself as a writer?

Judy Hanley: Well, I often joke with my (own) kids and I tell them that I can help them with their papers up until, say, 9th or 10th grade and after that I struggle. I find it difficult to collect my thoughts. I have good ideas but as far as how to organize them and put them down, I find that is probably my weakest skill. My ideas are okay, I think my vocabulary is adequate, but definitely organizational skills are difficult.

JG: What kinds of writing do you do?

JH: Unfortunately, not enough. As far as being a teacher having to write, I'll do a little bit with the lesson planning but it's the same vocabulary, it's the same set up all the time so I don't stray as far as creativity and having to do different things. So I would say not a lot. So practice is minimal.

JG: How about outside of the school setting?

JH: Probably hardly at all unless I'm helping my children. So not at all.

JG: Does your writing impact your teaching?

JH: I think I'm finding, now that I'm getting older, that it's starting to impact. Not because it's the writing process, because I think it's more of the thinking process and how I speak, my patterns of speech. I find that since my writing is starting to decline because I'm not doing it quite as much, that I have to read a little bit more to keep my thoughts flowing and the words that I want to use there. Otherwise, I'm tending to forget what I want to say and how I want to say it. So I think that the reading/writing component, because I'm not doing a lot of that in my life, is affecting how well I can communicate, finding my words. Is that possible?

JG: Sure. But I'm not sure I understand.

JH: Because I'm not writing as much and not formalizing my thoughts and steps that way and I feel like it's affecting how I communicate.... I feel that it's not quite as clear, not to the point. So I'm finding my language to be suffering because I'm not writing quite as much. My communication skills are declining.

JG: So you used to write more than you do now?

JH: Absolutely, sure. Through college and graduate school, yes. You could think more about your philosophies and how you speak to people and how you commu-

nicate and I'm just not doing that quite as much. So
maybe it's even more than the writing process that I'm
not doing. I'm not doing the reflection that goes with
the whole thing.

JG: What do you think it takes to be a good writer?

JH: Something I don't have.... Well perhaps because I'm
having such a tough time answering, it explains why
I'm not such a good writer. I'm not sure what it takes
to be a good writer. Probably confidence. If you're not
confident in it, you're always questioning the words
that you're choosing and writing down when confidence is low.

Ms. Hanley is candid about her lack of writing experience. She describes the effect of the absence of writing (since graduate school, which
is probably about a decade) on her language use, communication skills,
thinking, and level of confidence. Moreover, questioning—critical inquiry
—is perceived as a weakness in the writing process rather than in integral component of meaning construction. Since teachers are considered
to be experts vis-à-vis student writing, the fact that teachers are not experienced writers is detrimental to the effective development of literacies in
this school. As a sociocultural process, writing instruction requires a community of practice that includes proficient teachers who can articulate,
explicitly, their performances of literacies. Englert et al. (2005) explain
the benefits of communities of practice:

In these contexts, students experience legitimate reasons to communicate
their knowledge, express their uncertainties, reveal their confusions, and
request information or explanations from others who are more knowledgeable (Mercer, 2002). In such classrooms, students also learn to use texts and
ideas as thinking devices that can be questioned and extended to create an
elaborated knowledge reflective of the contributions of the group. In fact,
Alvermann (2002) suggests that participatory approaches that actively engage students in their own learning, and that treat texts as tools for thought
and reflection, are more likely to promote higher order thinking and critical
literacy. (p. 214)

As a writer, Ms. Hanley narrates a fear of making mistakes and a lack
of confidence in her own skills. Without expanding her conception of discourse and literacies, she will be unable to assist her students in becoming

proficient writers. Again, the deficiency she narrates is troubling, but her recognition of the situation and her own role in it is encouraging.

Social studies teacher and department chairperson Linda Roberts narrates a similar lack of confidence in herself as a writer. She depends on her English teacher colleague to "correct" her writing.

> **JG:** How would you describe yourself as a writer?
> **Linda Roberts:** I'd like to think I'm good but I know I'm not because whenever I do a written thing I give it to Hillary Lawrence to correct and she corrects it and then I know how bad a writer I am. Because, you know what? I write the way I talk and I'm not concerned with grammar. I just write and then I have to read it over and it only makes sense to me. That's why I give to Hillary, like, students' (recommendation) letters and stuff.

Ms. Roberts makes an implicit connection between inner speech and the written product she creates ("I write the way I talk"). However, the *revision* of inner speech presents an impediment for her. Ms. Roberts notes that her image of herself as a writer is diminished by Ms. Lawrence's correction ("she corrects it and then I know how bad a writer I am"). Once her initial "stream of consciousness" is on paper, Ms. Roberts cedes agency and expertise as a writer to her English department colleague. Deservedly or not, English teachers are purported to be experts in writing and writing instruction.

Science teacher Miranda Schmidt does not perceive herself as a writer. Her description of herself in this role denotes a deficit model belief: she says she is "not horrible."

> **JG:** How would you describe yourself as a writer?
> **Miranda Schmidt:** I would not think of myself as a writer. I'm apparently not horrible at writing, since I made it through grad school and that kind of thing and never had any problems when we had writing assignments. I took a class in writing about nature, which was really interesting. We just kind of went on hikes and took notes and then we had to write stories or papers about what we experienced in nature to kind of tie in a little bit of science. So that was kind of hard for me because I don't think of myself as a writer and it was (taught by)

an English professor who likes science so I was
nervous.

Ms. Hanley, Ms. Roberts, and Ms. Schmidt (teachers of math, social
studies, and science, respectively) evoke self-image as a key component
of their writing experiences. The connection between identity and written expression is evident, as is the ability of English teachers/professors to
affect the self-perception of writers. Not being empowered, transformative writers themselves, it would be difficult for these teachers to provide
pedagogical experiences that enable students to overcome structural inequities inherent in domesticating writing instruction.

While it may not be surprising that teachers in disciplines outside of
English language arts do not perceive themselves as writers, even English
teachers narrate spotty experience as writers. Stan Ryan has been an English teacher for thirty-eight years and is in his second year as chairman of
the department. Mr. Ryan narrates a variety of writing experiences, albeit
acquired over a decade ago, yet still describes himself as a "novice."

> **JG:** How would you describe yourself as a writer?
> **SR:** As a writer, okay, I have done everything short
> of a novel, I guess. I guess I would say that prob-
> ably short stories would be stronger than my
> poetry. I've done adaptations of Shakespeare. And
> we've performed them here at Pontiac High. So
> I guess... I'm still a novice, apprentice, whatever,
> beginner. I've only had two things published and
> those were many years ago.
> **JG:** What were they?
> **SR:** Poems.
> **JG:** Where were they published?
> **SR:** Lakefront News—no actually it was the City Ex-
> press (both are local daily newspapers).
> **JG:** Do you still write poetry?
> **SR:** Honestly, no. I don't have the time or the interest
> to devote to it as what I once did.
> **JG:** How about the short stories, adaptations, things
> like that?
> **SR:** I haven't done any of those in ten years.

Hillary Lawrence, who has been teaching English at Pontiac High for
35 years, narrates a rather limited range of writing experiences as well:

> **JG:** What kind of writing do you do?

Hillary Lawrence: Most of the time I spend creating parallel assessments (writing assignments that correspond to state assessment questions) for my classes. I have a journal that I keep for my daughter about my thoughts since she's been away. And I've been keeping that up and I will give that to her when she graduates.

Cindy Reynolds, in her third year of teaching English, has difficulty even describing herself as a writer. She narrates minimal writing experience beyond her own schooling.

JG: How would you describe yourself as a writer?
CR: Meaning?
JG: If I said to you, "Describe yourself as a writer?" what would you say?
CR: (long pause) More … not creative, more expository type.
JG: What kinds of writing do you do?
CR: Lesson plans, letters, things like that now. No papers for school, nothing like that.
JG: And what kinds of feedback have you received on the writing you've done?
CR: None. Since I've been teaching, nothing. I haven't submitted anything that would provide feedback.

English teacher June Summers, in her seventh year at Pontiac High, states a desire to be more accomplished as a writer than she is. Ms. Summers wishes she could *present* herself as a writer, but she does not describe the writing process as meaningful to her. In addition, she states that the realities of her classroom present obstacles to her development as a writer.

JG: How would you describe yourself as a writer?
June Summers: Probably not as developed as you probably might want to say that you are. I guess what I mean by that is, you might want to say that you write more often than you actually do. I think as a teacher, we spend so much time critiquing others' writing, and teaching, and trying to critique our style of teaching that we don't spend time maybe reading as much as we would like, or actually writing. I know in our minds we're always, like, "Oh, maybe

I'll write a children's book" or "Maybe I'll write this," But you don't really write.

JG: What kinds of writing do you do, or have you done?

JS: I've done a lot of descriptive writing, I've done expository writing, I've done, the business letter, the friendly letter. Obviously Regents style writing.... I guess I write letters of recommendation for students. I write letters to parents. I write letters for whatever administrative purposes we need to. I guess the writing I do is more organizational than it is leisure. I guess I could categorize it that way.

Essentially, Mr. Johnson's (the English teacher and poet) perception of teachers at Pontiac High as nonwriters is accurate. This is problematic for effective writing instruction, since decades of scholarship have established the essential link between being a habitual practitioner of writing and an effective teacher of writing. Moffett (1988) asserts that "a major reason that many teachers ignore, slight, or mangle the teaching of writing is that they lack direct experience with the learning issues entailed in writing" (p. 81). He summarizes the grounding principle of the Bay Area Writing Project, founded in the 1960s: "If teachers are ever going to teach writing more and teach it better, they will have to practice writing more themselves" (p. 81). Identification of this issue, that is, the need for teachers to employ critical literacies themselves in order to use them in the classroom, illuminates the possibility of the development of transformative pedagogies that promote, critical literacy.

DIALOGISM

> Throughout the instructional process, the heart of writing development is the dialogue in which teachers and students collaborate, inform, question, think aloud, self-correct, challenge and construct meaning together. (Englert et al., 2005, p. 211)

Dialogism involves the multivoiced nature of individuals and as well as "discursive interactions with others" (Englert et al., 2005, p. 211). Librarian Carla Cervi describes students who perform best as those who can integrate their inner and outer selves. She introduces the idea that students might *interact* with knowledge, rather than merely access and then report it. Her rhetoric suggests a complex approach to language and literacy, an approach more nuanced than the monologic, authoritarian perspective in which knowledge exists outside the self and is acquired by the learner. Instead, students are perceived as participants in learning, constructors of knowledge and meaning in which their own experiences figure prominently. This is a constructive approach, since Gee (2004) asserts that

> People learn (academic or non-academic) specialist languages and their concomitant ways of thinking best when they can tie the words and structures of those languages to experiences they have had. (p. 4)

Ms. Cervi hints at a dialogical perspective reminiscent of Gee's (2004) assertions about the connections between language learning and personal experiences that coalesce to construct identity.

JG: What kinds of students perform best (in school)?

Carla Cervi: Students who are willing to read. Students who are willing to research. Students who are willing to work at what they are doing and try to find the answer outside of themselves, find the answer within themselves with the knowledge they've got.

Ms. Cervi describes high performing students as those who construct knowledge by integrating what they already "know" with information that is outside their experiences. In this response, she does not dismiss the experiences of students; she sees students as potentially active participants in the expansion of their "portfolios" of knowledge. In narrating this point of view, Ms. Cervi depicts a model of learning that is participatory rather than acquisitional. Drawing on the work of Sfard (1998) and Rogoff (1990), Sperling (2004) describes these apparently contradictory approaches.

> In a reflection on two metaphors for learning, what she calls the "acquisition metaphor" (learning as accumulation of goods) vs. the "participation metaphor" (learning as apprenticeship in thinking, a concept drawn from Rogoff, 1990), Sfard (1998) argues that "different metaphors may lead to different ways of thinking and to different activities in the classroom. Surely, thinking about the learning of reading and writing as the acquisition of something (information, skills, and so on) inspires different types of teaching and assessment than does thinking about such learning as ongoing participation in a broader social or cultural system. (p. 237)

Ms. Cervi's description of high performing students refers to disposition (willingness to work) as well as active participation in a process of discovery (*finding* answers by integrating their inner selves with outside "knowledge"). This is a departure from the descriptions of literacy as an acquisitional process, wherein teachers transmit information and skills to students. The participation metaphor also encompasses the aspect of critical literacy that involves social change, as discussed by Shor (1997).

> The position taken by critical literacy advocates is that no pedagogy is neutral, no learning process is value-free, no curriculum avoids ideology and power relations. To teach is to encourage human beings to develop in one direction or another. In fostering student development, every teacher chooses some subject matters, some ways of knowing, some ways of speaking and relating, instead of others. These choices orient students to map the world and their relation to it. (para. 7)

The approach to writing instruction narrated by students and teachers in this school illustrates an epistemology of structuralism in which authority, situated first in the state, then in school administrators, then in teachers, determines what counts as knowledge and literacy. This stance reaffirms a working-class approach to schooling wherein students are alienated from the labor of their learning (and their writing). Echoing Weis' (1990) conclusions, these "students are not involved in the process of learning. They are involved in the *form* of schooling, but not is substance" (p. 30). Literacies valued by students' (youth and working-class) culture are not part of the curricula, so students must choose to adopt academic literacies, despite their lack of authenticity, or to resist. Unfortunately, neither path leads toward success in the twenty-first century economy, so students in this setting are not positioned for upward mobility.

Although most of the teachers and students interviewed accept the status quo, some express doubt about the effectiveness of prevalent practices. Shor (1997) explains that

> Many teachers reject authoritarian education. Many strive against fitting students quietly into the status quo. Many share the democratic goals of critical literacy. This educational work means, finally, inventing what Richard Ohmann (1987) referred to as a "literacy-from-below" that questions the way things are and imagines alternatives, so that the word and the world may meet in history for a dream of social justice. (para. 11)

The teachers excerpted in this chapter indicate their willingness to question the status quo, at least in terms of the quality of writing instruction. Their words evoke a sense of the agency that learners possess and the need to activate such agency in order to generate participation rather than a replicate the passive model of acquisition. These teachers hint at a sociocultural approach to learning and literacy that involves consideration of how writing "can offer new ways of knowing and doing" (Newell, 2005, p. 236).

Like Ms. Cervi, math teacher Amy Wells shifts in her narration of student learning from acquisition to participation. She describes students as needing to find their own thoughts, and then discusses the challenge of integrating outside information with students' "own ideas." Ms. Wells notes that large volumes of information should be accessed ("read a million things") in order to facilitate expression of ideas, but she is explicit about the distinction between students' own ideas and those belonging to an authority ("someone else").

> **JG:**   What's the biggest challenge for student writers?
> **Amy Wells:**   Probably finding their own thoughts to write about. I see a lot of the taking pieces of the internet and just, like, throwing them all together. I think sometimes that's why they don't make sense, because they're taking little bits and pieces from everything and trying not to plagiarize it so they're just switching things around.... That'd probably be it: having them be able to take their own information and get it out ... being able to say what they wanna say—read a million things and just being able to say what they wanna say with all this, like, vast stuff around them—like, information that they get. So, I guess, putting things into their own words, and getting their own ideas out instead of somebody else's.

Ms. Cervi and Ms. Wells narrate the need for integration between outside information and students' thinking. This assertion echoes the sociocultural perception of writing described by Englert et. al. (2005), who state that

> writing is an inherently social and multivoiced activity, with text construction being distributed and negotiated among writers and readers. Dialogic and symbolic interactions fill the writer's page with words. (p. 211)

Likewise, science teacher Blake Oliver expresses the desire for students to integrate information into their experiences; he narrates an understanding that each is affected by the other (Bakhtin, 1973; Gee, 2004). Mr. Oliver describes the way he tries to help students realize that information is *related* to feelings and opinions. He wants students to be able to interpret facts in order to form opinions that they can express, whether verbally or in writing:

BO: I feel like, for my kids—the topics that we choose, the discussion that we have or the way that they present it and the discussion that we have that follows—that we are promoting literacy. Does that mean that they can sit down and write to the editor of a paper and influence them about a recycling program? I don't know. I don't care. Because they may be at a bar someday talking about their tax dollars or whatever and ... I want them to be aware of the facts and to be able to speak scientifically and accurately about it. And it's based on their research. So maybe they can't write it out the best way, but can they present themselves in a way to interpret the facts and hopefully formulate an educated opinion about something.

Mr. Oliver's goal is for his students to demonstrate understandings of scientific concepts, understandings that can be expressed through various literacies. His view of the application of students' learning to their lives beyond school reflects what Gee, Hull, and Lankshear (1996) call "strategic intelligence" (p. 58), in which the emphasis is not so much on the knowledge itself, but on what people can *do* with their knowledge.

MISCONCEPTIONS, THINKING, AND WRITING

Affirming a dialogic approach, Mr. Oliver notes how student perspectives —even those he describes as "misconceptions"—affect his teaching. Using errors as evidence of student *thinking* as opposed to accepting (or expecting) the parroted texts of authorities, he narrates an appreciation of the role that contradiction can play in the learning process. Mr. Oliver's perspective indicates application of the Bakhtinian idea that

> discourse and thought are born of multiple and sometimes opposing forces. For Bakhtin, discourse and thought are always in a process of becoming, in the interactive, dialogic contexts that give them shape and meaning. In this respect, ... discourse and thought exist in the "tension-filled interaction" of the living moment. (Sperling, 2004, p. 233)

Narrations around writing at Pontiac High reveal a sense that student writers, particularly those who earn good grades, are more inclined to repeat information than they are to think. Gee et. al (1996), discussing conceptions of knowledge and understanding in traditional schools and how these conceptions lead to deficiencies in meeting the demands of New Capitalism, note that

> Even (students) with good grades do not "really understand" what they are learning. Students in traditional schools, it is claimed, master only basic, rote, low-level skills, at best. While such students may be able to pass tests and carry out basic computations, they really do not understand, in any deep way, what they are doing. (p. 55)

Mr. Oliver describes such a phenomenon with his student writers, particularly those with good grades, who tend to repeat what they think he wants to hear.

BO: For my good kids, them saying things back is disappointing to me, to have kids that have been on a Regents track, in essence writing, like, "Dear Mr. O, this is a great course," and not giving me—actually, not thinking. I'm more impressed by a kid who's a poor writer —you know, grammatically, whatever, structurally—as long as they have a well formed opinion on the facts— even if it's not the same one that I have. Then I have some of my smart, (I'm using my finger quotes here) my "cookie cutter" kids that are giving the response that they think that I want to hear. So when they come into a science course they automatically—I'll go back to the recycling. They automatically think that I should be an advocate of recycling so they should be an advocate of recycling even if they don't feel that way based on the facts that I was giving them.

Instead of seeing students' opposing thoughts, that is, mistaken interpretations or perspectives of science concepts, as merely mistakes to be corrected, Mr. Oliver perceives misconceptions (generated more often by weaker students than "good" ones) as evidence of thinking. Instead of silencing misunderstandings, he chooses to draw on them to enhance student interest and thinking.

Blake Oliver: As far as the kids, their writing sometimes will get me back on track. I will look at the misconceptions that they have and think "All right, now that's something I can run with and they'll really enjoy." Like, it seemed that they had an interest in it when we did it at the time. Sometimes, the moment passes, and this is the other part of the summary writing that I actually like.

It's that when they do it by themselves, even if they have a really structured outline, there's interest. That's the best teaching...

It's my second year of teaching the upper class for the applied course. And I thought, based on my own views, that I had a specific direction that I would take the kids, not try to influence how you feel about recycling, or "You should feel like I feel," but I thought there were things I had learned—like I had the facts and I was going to present them in a certain way. And they would come up with the understanding that I had. And, in fact, that's not what happened. In fact, it's good; it's what I love about teaching. It's that their opinions taught me different things. I never would have charted it this way, thinking that high school kids could teach me—I know it's supposed to happen, or we say it's going to happen, but I never really truly believed in it. That, through their writing and their research and the articles that they presented, that they influenced the way I thought, but it did.

JG: How?

BO: On recycling, was one of the ways. You know, I became an earth science teacher and I really believed in (recycling), but when you sit down and you respect the opinions of the kids—and their parents would feel the same way. And now that I'm a little bit older and I pay more attention to my own tax bills, those things too—not to say that I'm throwing plastic items out of my truck as I'm driving down the road or anything. But yeah, it's just one of those things.... I thought I knew where I stood, and it changed.

JG: Influenced by some of the kids....

BO: And by their research. I'm influenced not only by what their opinions are, which sometimes are very misguided, but I'm influenced at least by their factual research, even if they didn't completely understand it.

Mr. Oliver describes experiencing a shift in his approach to teaching, narrating a previous contradiction between what was "supposed to happen" and what he was "supposed to say" and what he really believed. Prior to teaching the Applied Science elective, which he designed with emphases on student-centeredness and writing, Mr. Oliver experienced a contradiction between what he was "supposed to believe" and what he

believed. Explaining his willingness to learn from students, Mr. Oliver expresses a perspective in opposition to the banking model and narrates
movement toward dialogism. Sperling (2004), extending Bakhtin's notion
of multiple voices enacting various social perspectives (heteroglossia), describes the existence of such contradictions as not problematic, but simply
"the way things are" (p. 234). She calls for "unpacking the multiple points
of view that inform teachers at given moments" (p. 234) as an alternative
to censuring or silencing them. Contradiction, from this perspective, is
not "a temporary condition that should be resolved" (p. 235); it is, instead, a way of deepening understandings. Mr. Oliver narrates his hope
that students will be able to integrate facts and feelings – to be able to
trust themselves as thinkers and learners. At the same time, he understands the role of schooling, and his own structured approach to instruction, as hindering that aim.

> **JG:** What do you think is the biggest challenge for student
> writers?
>
> **BO:** I think there are a lot of challenges. The one that I
> think I have the biggest hang up on is to trust them-
> selves and to say something about how they feel based
> on the facts, if they've taken the time to read the facts.
> Sometimes it's tough for them to get that…. But again,
> when I think about it, maybe this is my fault in some
> ways, that I'm so structured and from the classroom end
> of it, when I do my normal instruction, I'm very about
> the facts and everything's black and white. And now I'm
> telling them to trust themselves with the opinion that
> maybe they don't agree with the science.

By inviting student voices into the curricular conversation of his
science classes, Mr. Oliver is challenging the status quo of the structuralist
epistemology. His interest in listening to students and valuing their ideas
has to potential to go beyond motivation and engagement (which are, of
course, significant) and move into the realm of scientific discourse. As he
facilitates the integration of students' experiences, thinking, and writing,
Mr. Oliver seems to be engaging in "practices that make the writing
apprenticeships within a sociocultural perspective a reality" (Englert et
al., 2005, p. 211). However, Mr. Oliver also describes a contradiction
in his own practice. The class in which he facilitates students' trusting
themselves to question "the science" is an elective entitled Applied
Science, a course generally taken by students in the lower academic
tracks. In his "normal" teaching, that is, courses driven by New York
State standards and assessments (in this case, earth science), Mr. Oliver's

instruction focuses on "the facts" which he describes as "black and white," indicative of the authoritative position content-oriented information has in this setting.

English teacher Hillary Lawrence describes how an in-service session about higher order thinking skills made her aware that students were parroting her words instead of thinking. She states that this awareness—essential to any change—caused her to reorient her teaching.

> **JG:** Thinking of the (in-service classes), how have these, if they have, affected you as a writer … and/or as a teacher?
>
> **Hillary Lawrence:** I think they made me look at what I am saying to the class as being a little bit more important than I had thought it was. I didn't think what I said about a piece of writing or a piece of literature was meaningful, because they should be able to do this on their own. When I realized that what they were doing was parroting what I was saying I had to tailor my instruction, giving them more of a chance to think about their responses. As opposed to parroting what I said.
>
> **JG:** That's interesting. Can you say more about that?
>
> **HL:** Well, I watched as students picked up on the comments that I was making about a piece of writing. And I would read an essay that I was correcting and I thought that was odd that they would say that when I had said that. I realized that what they were doing was simply giving me what they thought I wanted and not thinking about it on their own. So I have a tendency to do less explicit instruction with them and have them do more in terms of their own thoughts, but still giving them the information that they needed to be supported with something from the literature.

Ms. Lawrence's narration echoes many of the themes in this chapter, some of which are contradictory. She talks about obtaining a balance between what she gives students and what they give her. She would prefer that they not simply repeat what she has told them, but she does refer to giving them "information they need."

> **HL:** They do look at the facts. But I don't think they think about the facts. They don't imagine the

feeling. They don't see—they don't actually see it. And you need to be able to visualize it. We talked at the beginning of the year about students who either run track, or snowboard, or ski or swim and if they had any competitive sports there is that visualization where you see yourself going down the hill. And you imagine the mogul. And you see yourself making the turn and they teach you how to do that. And I don't know we don't really do that with kids. So by the time we see them, their capacity to visualize has really been limited.

In this excerpt, she seems to be attempting to scaffold students toward thinking more about the texts that they read. Ms. Lawrence mentions this adjustment to her teaching in the context of a school-wide initiative regarding higher order thinking skills. (Visualization is one of the six skills being emphasized.) Finally, at the end of this excerpt, Ms. Lawrence's words are reminiscent of the notion that students' deficient backgrounds will limit their opportunities for success.

These teachers narrate a perspective that illuminates the possibility of positive change. Freire (2004) argues that education represents a point of opportunity for becoming through change, and that awareness is an essential component of that change. Education makes sense because the world is not necessarily this or that, because human beings are as much *projects* (emphasis in original) themselves as they may have projects, or a vision, for the world. Education makes sense because women and men learn that through learning they can make and remake themselves...

> Awareness of the world, which makes awareness of myself viable, makes inviable the immutability of the world.... It makes me capable of intervening in the world and not only of adapting to it. (p. 15)

The shifts in awareness, contradictions, and critiques narrated by these teachers provides evidence that the possibility for change exists. The status quo is not immutable; as long as awareness exists, critical inquiry and dialogism are possible.

GLIMPSES OF STUDENT RESISTANCE

At Pontiac High, writing is rarely used as a means of critical thinking. This reality is significant because student identities are affected by their uses of language, whether they accept the principles and effects of academic writing or resist them. Shor elaborates, beginning with Kenneth Dowst's definition of composition as "the activity of making some sense out of an extremely complex set of personal perceptions and experiences of an infinitely complex world.... A writer (or other language-user), in a sense, composes the world in which he or she lives" (Dowst, 1980, p. 66). Shor (1997) asserts that the implications of critical literacy for student writers are profound.

> Because there are multiple ideologies at the root of the social experiences which make us into who we are (for example, male supremacy, white supremacy, corporate supremacy, heterosexism), the positions or identities for contesting the status quo also need to be appropriately multiple. Critical literacy thus crosses identity boundaries because it is a discourse and pedagogy for counter-hegemonic resistance. This resistance occasionally becomes a common cause against dominant culture when diverse insurgent groups coalesce, but much stands in the way of coalitions in a society where *every difference is used against us* (emphasis in original) by an elite minority maintaining power by divide-and-conquer among other mechanisms. (p. 16)

While their ability to effect change may be limited, a few students narrate resistance to the norms of writing instruction at Pontiac High. Samuel, who writes poetry for a personal blog and is heavily involved in an online game which requires creative writing, relies on himself rather than the school to improve his writing. He seems to have managed to fulfill the school's writing expectations (albeit barely, with grades in the 60s) without compromising his own thought processes. However, he is not confident that his own written products will be taken seriously by teachers.

> **Samuel:** That's where writing comes in handy...being able to think outside the box.
>
> **JG:** How does writing help you do that?
>
> **Samuel:** It's actually myself who helps me do that for writing. If you can think outside the box, you can read a task and know what it's looking for and not follow the straight path, to kind of swerve around and use different ideas.
>
> **JG:** What is your goal as a student writer?
>
> **Samuel:** I don't know. There've been times where they do that poetry or story submission (for the school's literary magazine). There've been times when I've had, like, ten pages of poems to hand in and I just never got the guts to do it because I feel it would be taken advantage of. Like, people would overlook the fact of how it actually meant. They would read it and just be, like, "Oh, that's

good," and just keep going. I would want somebody to actually think about it and not just read it and be done with it.

Despite his extensive use of writing outside school, Samuel is barely passing English. Although his personal experience has taught him that writing equates with thinking, he narrates a lack of trust in the school's commitment to appreciate the meanings in his poetry. He perceives the school's approach to writing as cursory and superficial, not worthy of his own work. The institutional forces that affect academic writing, however, have not prevented Samuel from maintaining his own identity as a writer outside the academic arena.

An outspoken student athlete, Grace challenges the status quo in a few areas. First, she flouts the "empty vessel" viewpoint by recommending that teachers ask students for input with respect to curriculum and instruction. Second, despite admittedly exerting minimal effort, she calls for more and more challenging writing assignments. Grace notes that students' first reactions are likely to be negative, acknowledging that if *she* were asked what she wants to read or write, would probably say "nothing." However, she narrates a belief that more, and more challenging, writing would ultimately be beneficial for students.

> **JG:** What most needs to be changed to make writing in school better?
>
> **Grace:** Probably the input that we need to give to the teachers. I think that they need to ask – well, I don't know if I was a teacher if I would really like this, because if a teacher asked me, "What do you think we should do?" I would probably be, like, "Nothing." But even so, I think that maybe they should ask us, like, give us a choice of novels, or give (students) a summary of the books: "This one's about high school," or "This one's about math." Obviously we're going to pick the one about high school because we're in high school. They should give us a choice of the novels and give (assign) us a well thought out essay on our feelings or what we think about the good novel that we pick.

It is interesting to note that Grace, who is from a working-class background, exhibits a sense of negotiated curriculum that is typically associated with middle-class norms (Finn, 1999). Her indication of a willingness to employ the skill of negotiation illustrates the possibility of constructive resistance by employing the tactics of the professional elite.

> **JG:** Do you think this school's writing instruction fulfills
> its purpose for most of its students? Are we giving you
> what you need?
>
> **Grace:** I think that they are but, again, I think that the teach-
> ers should require more. Yeah, the students are going
> to complain and moan and groan, but I think that if
> we boosted up the writing a little bit then I think that
> people would become better writers and grades would
> increase because then we would do more work, but it
> would help us. It wouldn't be a negative thing for us, it
> would be positive. So I think that if they increased what
> we need to do then I think it would be better.

Grace's critique is on target, since the effectiveness of the combination
of choice and challenge is well-documented in scholarship about writing
instruction. Moffett (1998) explains why Grace's perspective is accurate.

> Personal choice is at the center (of language learning), not only so that the
> learner cares about what he is doing, but so that good judgment will devel-
> op.... The wisest decision for educators to make is to stock a classroom with
> as many things as possible to *choose among* (all emphases in original). The
> traditional classroom has not had *enough* structures. This is one way in which
> it has been overcontrolled. One lesson plan for all each day, one sequence
> for the year – that is not to structure *more*, it is simply to let a single structure
> monopolize the learning field. This monopoly rules out any real possibility
> of learning to develop judgment, which requires that the learner be struc-
> tur*ing* in school, not structur*ed* by the school. Structuring is choosing. Com-
> prehending, composing, making sense of the world—these are structuring.
> School should be harder and more fun. (p. 24)

Olivia had English grades in the high 80s last year but is barely passing
this year. She attributes the change in achievement to conflicts with her
current teacher, whom Olivia states, she doesn't "get along with." Olivia
believes that exercising choice as a writer will irritate her teacher, yet she
is willing to risk displeasing her teacher in order to experiment with a
form that she thinks might please her audience. Comments just prior to
this excerpt indicate that Olivia believes that her teachers don't always understand or appreciate her writing because she puts too much of herself
into the task.

> **JG:** Can you explain what you mean by that, you do more
> with the content than with addressing the task?
>
> **Olivia:** Well, if the task is to write an application, a college
> application essay like what we're doing in English now,

> what I did instead, was that I decided to do something
> different. Instead of an essay I wrote a funny little poem
> for it. Because nobody wants—they don't want millions
> and millions of essays. Who wants to read a bunch of
> essays? I think they'd like to see something a little bit
> different.

JG: And how did your teacher react to that?

Olivia: I'm not so sure because I haven't handed it in yet, but I
don't think she's going to like it. I don't think it totally
addresses the task good enough.

JG: If you think she's not going to take it well, why would
you do it?

Olivia: I started it and at first it was just something I was play-
ing around with and then I really liked it. It does address the task; it's just not an essay.

Writing that is grounded in inner speech is inextricably intertwined
with students' identities. The self cannot be separated from the written
product, much as content cannot be divided from composition nor form
torn from function. For this assignment, Olivia chose to use a different
form for the function of presenting herself, employing a bit of self-cre-
ation that positions her differently from the working-class norm of those
who just follow the rules. However, many students at Pontiac High describe writing as separate from self. Olivia reinforces the presence of this
discourse because she expects that writing she feels connected to and that
she believes will engage her audience is likely to be unacceptable to her
English teacher.

Moffett (1988) explains why disconnecting writing from the author's
"self" is misguided.

> However personal or impersonal the subject matter, *all* writing as authoring
> must be some revision of inner speech for a purpose and an audience. To
> say this is not at all to say that writing is solipsistic thinking about narcissistic
> content or even that it favors "personal experience." Because of the circular-
> ity (between inner and outer speech), one's revised inner speech may reflect
> convention so much as to hardly bear a personal mark. (p. 140)

Dylan, an avid reader with a 70 average in English, narrates a scathing
critique of writing instruction at Pontiac High as well as the Regents examination that drives this instruction.

JG: How would your teachers describe you as a writer?

Dylan: All my teachers would probably say "good." "Very good
but could be better if he tried" is what I usually get....
It's … because a lot of times I won't follow the guide-

lines as good as they hope, or I'll make changes in the
essay because I think it sounds better that way. But
that'll be a bad thing, because it's supposed to be exactly like they wrote it…. They'll say, "four paragraphs,"
and I'll do five because it needed it. Just bend the rules.

Like Olivia, Dylan refers to the rule-following behavior typical of working-class schools and he resists the strict prescriptions of his writing assignments. In addition, he ascribes the writing process and product with
having agency ("I'll do five because *it* needed it"). As writers, Olivia and
Dylan feel capable of making authorial decisions, particularly regarding
form and structure, but the discourse around writing at Pontiac High dis-
courages them from doing so. Questioning the status quo becomes an act
of resistance.

Dylan narrates strong animosity towards the school's approach to writing. He is critical of English classes, condemning both the content and
pedagogy as dull, repetitive, and mind deadening.

> **JG:** What kinds of classroom activities go along with writ-
> ing?
>
> **Dylan:** I can run you through it. In the class I'm in, like I said,
> up until Regents (examination) was finally over, we
> just did the same thing. I realized after watching this
> class for so long, (that) he (the English teacher) only
> had three lesson plans and he'd just circulate them.
> One day he'd give us all these notes and tell us how
> to write that one essay there, and the next day we'd
> write that essay, and the third day he'd hand us back
> all the essays saying they were terrible and tell us to
> rewrite. And then the next day, he'd come in and say
> the rewrite essays were terrible so we're going to take
> more notes. So then we'd write notes, the next day he'd
> say it's terrible and just keep going on every day. He'd
> give us the notes and instructions on exactly how to
> write it and then he'd give us the piece of paper that
> tells us the exact guideline and then write our essay. I
> have one of those pages with the exact guidelines for an
> essay. Here's one (pointing to a document he brought
> to the interview). They give you … the critical lens: "All
> literature is protest." You can't name a single literary
> work that isn't protest? It's okay, but I don't think it's
> entirely true. Maybe it is, when you think about it, but,
> again, when I'm writing an essay of that kind—it's not

really what matters. Saying all the right things and trying to get examples that match it is what matters.... That's an okay quote, but it seems awfully specific. The critical lens quotes always annoy me because sometimes it'll be a half a sentence and it'll be like, "All literature is bad," or there'll be a quote and I'm positive that it was taken out of a book and they (the writers) see what their context is, and the quotes are completely nonsensical because it'll say, "Muhad maghandi" is the quote, or "I don't like cats." But where was he (the author) going with that? And how can I write an essay on that if I don't actually know what he meant by that?

Dylan states that what matters is "saying all the right things." He asserts the importance of context in his ability to construct meaning from text. When asked about the feedback he gets from teachers on his writing, Dylan describes an act of resistance on his part: writing what he was thinking.

JG: So what kinds of feedback do you get on the things that you're writing?

Dylan: I had a teacher that I really didn't like a year ago and she made us write this essay. And it was after we did ten of these (types of) essays and I just got so sick of the format that I was really annoyed with it. So I just wrote this essay that was exactly how I'm talking now. It was in a conversational tone with that whole dry humor thing and I was being really, really sarcastic. I knew I'd get an F on it. It was actually an important grade so it was a dumb idea to do it, but I passed (the course) so I don't care. But I just got so sick of it, I just wrote completely how I—what I—was actually thinking. I remember kind of getting mad about it. I went to the principal about it but he didn't really care. It was this big essay and we had the standard rules of written English which it was graded by and I admit the essay was not a traditional essay and I understood I'd get a bad grade, but it was a big grade—out a hundred—and she gave me a zero on it. And it was like a three page essay, too. I knew I was going to get a terrible grade on it, but she gave me a zero on it and it annoyed me because I wrote it at least. That should be one point right there.

JG: So what are your teachers' expectations about writing?

Dylan: It's mostly just follow the format, agree with everything, agree with all the quotes and again a lot of repetitive stuff like that. They tell you what to write and you copy it down exactly. The only difference between your essay and the guy next to you is the name on top of the essay.

I try to write creatively when I can but after years of going through English I've got their expectations figured out: to write what they, to say what they want to hear. And I can accept that. I usually know what it is they want us to write so I'll just forego creativity and just give them that. But again sometimes I'll just go off on my own or I'll get creative with it a little. I do one of those quote papers and actually try disagreeing with it instead, because it says you can agree or disagree. But the problem is, they give us this long format and tell us how to agree and you're not allowed (to disagree)…. Our teacher actually tells us you're not allowed to disagree. You'll get a zero on the essay if you disagree. So they (state examination directions) say "or disagree" but they really don't mean it. Occasionally I'll try to do that but I'll just end up getting in trouble or getting a bad grade because all of those essays are agree with the quote and then use proofs from two books we read in class. So basically the quote they pick has to do with the books, obviously. But that's the thing, it's impossible to disagree with one of their critical lens quotes because if you disagree with it there's nothing to cite. So you can't do that.

Dylan's narration reveals a sense of being silenced through academic writing. He feels that his authorial agency is stifled by the school's approach to writing. He describes being told what to write and how to write it, depicting his teachers as authoritarian and the state examination as hypocritical. He states that he has been told that he cannot disagree with the powerful, hegemonic expectations of this educational institution, and reports being punished by teachers and stifled by the state examination. Although many students elect either to comply enough to earn good grades or to shirk their work and earn zeros, Dylan enacts resistance through his writing. This act is punished with a zero as though it is equal to nothing. Dylan has learned that writing what he thinks, for example, by disagreeing with a critical lens quote, is equivalent to a zero.

Dylan is openly critical of his teachers, narrating a strong sense of resistance to what he perceives as an oppressive environment, one which promotes neither creative nor critical thought. Although Dylan has not yet been successful in his challenges to authority, his willingness and ability to articulate critique represent a step toward critical literacy. Shor (1997) explains the connection between literacy and critical literacy.

> *literacy* is understood as social action through language use that develops us as agents inside a larger culture, while *critical literacy* is understood as "learning to read and write as part of the process of becoming conscious of one's experience as historically constructed within specific power relations" (Anderson & Irvine, 1993, p. 82). Consequently, my opening question, "What is critical literacy?," leads me to ask, "How have we been shaped by the words we use and encounter? If language use is one social force constructing us ('symbolic action' as Kenneth Burke, 1966, argued), how can we use and teach oppositional discourses so as to remake ourselves and our culture?" (Introduction, para. 3)

> Essentially, then, critical literacy is language use that questions the social construction of the self. When we are critically literate, we examine our ongoing development, to reveal the subjective positions from which we make sense of the world and act in it. (Introduction, para. 4)

Courtney and Olivia critique the writing instruction at Pontiac High. Samuel doubts that his writing would be taken seriously by school personnel, so he maintains and nurtures his identity as a writer outside of school. Dylan does not allow himself to be a passive language user in school. He maintains the right to use language to critique and resist, even when his efforts are punished.

CONCLUSION

> My interest is in language use and thinking, how they are defined and assessed, and how they are opened up or shut down by social circumstances (Rose, 2006, p. 1)

Overall, the discourse around writing at Pontiac High is consistent with a structuralist epistemology and domesticating literacy. Students and teachers describe knowledge as rooted in authority figures and authoritative texts. Facts subjugate opportunities to construct opinions, and, since knowledge is seen as prescriptive, the possibility of integration or synthesis of facts and opinions, that is, constructed knowledge, is rarely narrated. The type of writing instruction described has been critiqued for decades, and is not likely to prepare students to participate actively in the New Capitalism.

Rare as they are, however, critique and resistance are present. Although teachers have an immediate stake in the preservation of the status quo, both teachers and students affirm the gap between what is happening and what ought to be happening. This awareness is the first step toward transformation. Moffett's (1988) words are ideal to end this chapter. In discussing the effects of the "educational-industrial complex," he is reminded of the agency that learners bring to classrooms—agency that is typically neither recognized nor nurtured in working class schools. Teachers are also part of the educational culture, and teachers in this high school were educated in working-class schools. It is likely, then, that their own experiences of literacy were domesticating rather than transformative. Furthermore, as actors in the educational-industrial complex, teachers "feel powerless and don't trust their perceptions" (p. 9). To inspire teachers, Moffett (1998) reminds them of the agency learners possess. They are not "blank slates" or "empty vessels." Education ought to be an awakening of what we know, a construction of identity that includes the awareness of our continuous state of becoming.

> I remember a dedication in a book I have forgotten. It read: "To So-and so, who taught me what I know." No, no, it didn't read that; my cliché-ridden mind read that. I looked again: "who taught me *that* I know." Who taught me that I know. What I know that's of use to you is that you know. Sweeping aside the intervening clutter, recall yourself as a young learner, then review those learners in front of you. You know. But you must assume the power to do what you know. (p. 9)

The teachers and students who are hinting at resistance know that the current state of affairs is not working, and they are not afraid to say so. Their critiques represent the power of possibility.

REFERENCES

Alim, H. S. (2005, October). Critical language awareness in the United States: Revisiting issues and revising pedagogies in a resegregated Society. *Educational Researcher*, 24-31.

Alvermann, D. E. (2002). Effective literacy instruction for adolescents. *Journal of Literacy Research, 34*, 189-208.

Anderson, G. L., & Irvine, P. (1993). Informing critical literacy with ethnography. In C. Lankshear & P. L. McLaren (Eds.), *Critical literacy: Politics, praxis, and the postmodern* (pp. 81-104). Albany, NY: State University of New York.

Baker, S., Gersten, R., & Graham, S. (2003). Teaching expressive writing to students with learning disabilities: Research-based applications and examples. *Journal of Learning Disabilities, 36*(2), 109-123.

Bakhtin, M. M. (1973). *Marxism and the philosophy of language* (L. Matejka & I. R. Titunik, Trans.). New York, NY: Seminar.

Burke, K. (1969). *Language as symbolic action*. Berkeley, CA: University of California Press.

Daniels, H. (2001). *Vygotsky and pedagogy*. New York, NY: Routledge.

Dowst, K. (1980). The epistemic approach: Writing, knowing and learning. In T. R. D. & B. W. McClelland (Eds.), *Eight approaches to teaching composition* (pp. 65-85). Urbana, IL: NCTE.

Englert, C. S., Mariage, T. V., & Dunsmore, K. (2005). Tenets of sociocultural theory in writing instruction research. In C. A. MacArthur, S. Graham, & J. Fitzgerald (Eds.), *Handbook of Writing Research* (pp. 208-221). New York, NY: The Guilford Press.

Finn, P. J. (1999). *Literacy with an attitude: Educating working-class children in their own self-interest*. Albany, NY: State University of New York Press.

Freire, P. (2004). *Pedagogy of indignation*. Boulder, CO: Paradigm.

Gee, J. P. (2004). *Situated language and learning: A critique of traditional schooling*. New York, NY: Routledge.

Gee, J. P., Hull, G., & Lankshear, C. (1996). *The new work order: Behind the language of new capitalism*. Sydney, Australia: Westview Press.

Hawkes, D. (1999). Composition, capitalism and the new technology [Electronic Version]. *Bad Subjects, 44*. Retrieved from http://bad.eserver.org/issues/1999/44/hawkes.html

Hillocks, G. J. (1986). *Research on written composition: New directions for teaching*. Chicago, IL: ERIC Clearinghouse on Reading and Communication Skills: National Institute of Education.

Lareau, A. (2003). *Unequal childhoods: Class, race, and family life*. Berkeley, NY: University of California Press.

Mercer, N. (2002). Developing Dialogues. In G. Wells & G. Claxton (Eds.), *Learning for life in the 21st Century: Sociocultural perspectives on the future of education* (pp. 141-153). Malden, MA: Blackwell.

Moffett, J. (1988). *Coming on center* (2nd ed.). Portsmouth, England: Boynton/Cook.

Newell, G. E. (2005). Writing to learn: How alternative theories of school writing account for student performance. In C. A. MacArthur, S. Graham & J. Fitzgerald (Eds.), *Handbook of Writing Research* (pp. 235-247). New York, NY: Gilford.

Ohmann, R. (1987). *Politics of letters*. Middletown, CT.: Wesleyan University Press.

Rogoff, B. (1990). *Apprenticeship in thinking: Cognitive development in social context*. Oxford, England: Oxford University Press.

Rose, M. (2006). *An open language: Selected writing on literacy, learning, and opportunity*. Los Angeles, CA: Bedford/St. Martin's Press.

Scribner, S. (1997). The cognitive consequences of literacy. In E. Tobach, R. J. Falmagne, M. B. Parlee, L. M. W. Martin, & A. S. Kapelman (Eds.), *Mind and social practice: Selected writings of Sylvia Scribner* (pp. 160-189). New York, NY: Cambridge University Press.

Sfard, A. (1998). On two metaphors for learning and the dangers of choosing just one. *Educational Researcher, 27*(2), 4-13.

Shor, I. (1997). What is critical literacy? *Journal for Pedagogy, Pluralism & Practice, 1*(4), 1-26.

Shotter, J. (1995). In dialogue: Social constructionism and radical constructivism. In L. P. Steffe & J. Gale (Eds.), *Constructivism in education* (pp. 41-56). Hillsdale, NJ: Erlbaum.

Sperling, M. (2004). Is contradiction contrary? In A. F. Ball & S. W. Freedman (Eds.), *Bakhtinian perspectives on language and literacy* (pp. 232-251). Cambridge, England: Cambridge University Press.

Van Galen, J. A., & Noblit, G. W. (Eds.). (2007). *Late to class: Social class and schooling in the new economy*. Albany, NY: State University of New York Press.

Weis, L. (1990). *Working class without work: High school students in a de-industrializing economy*. New York, NY: Routledge.

Wells, G. (Ed.). (1999). *Dialogic Inquiry: Toward a sociocultural practice and theory of education*. New York, NY: Cambridge University Press.

CHAPTER 9

RESISTANCE LITERACY

Two Approaches

ROOTS OF RESISTANCE

In order to fulfill the potential of empowerment for students with respect to literacy and learning, it is essential to understand the significance and complexities of relations of power that are present in schools.

According to Michel Foucault (1975, 1983, 1993), power is not a tool; it is a relation. The condition of freedom (which can be realized as relative empowerment), therefore is directly connected to existing relations of power. It is also important to recognize that power is distinct from domination. Using Foucault's conception of the term, power is not possessed; it is exercised. And where there is power, there is always also resistance.

Schools, like any social institutions, are overflowing with interactions in which power is present. Power is exercised continuously through countless interactions. Sometimes power relations are obvious, other times all but invisible. Explicit, yet sometimes overlooked, representations of power include daily schedules, mandated curricula and assessments,

Parts of this chapter have appeared previously in in Porfilio and Carr's (2010) *Youth, Culture, Education and Resistance*.

Power, Resistance, and Literacy: Writing for Social Justice, pp. 195–209

and principal-student interactions. More subtle and shifting relations of power involve interactions among parents and teachers, teachers and support staff, students and support staff, and contacts among various peer groups (for example, teacher-teacher and student-student). All of these relations are realized through concrete and cultural phenomena, such as patterns of movement and seating within the building, expressions that are allowed and suppressed, and behaviors that are punished and rewarded—beginning as early as enrollment (for students) and hiring (for personnel). Power, it is evident, is incessantly exercised in schools.

Therefore, according to Foucault, resistance (as a corollary component of power) is also ever-present. Circumstances certainly bear this out. If compulsory attendance is an exercise of power, skipping classes is an obvious example of resistance. A less obvious example, however, is arriving late or refusing to engage in the work of class. All participants in schooling exercise the power/resistance dynamic; that is, anyone who is subject to someone else's exercise of power has the capacity to comply or resist. And these exercises of power and resistance occur continuously through the daily actions and decisions of students, teachers, administrators, and support staff—as well as parents, board members, and political officials at all levels. It is clear, then, that power and resistance coexist. But, in general, they do not coexist as equals. Consider the fact that acts of resistance tend to result in an institutional response, as represented in Table 9.1. The examples presented in Table 9.1 indicate the disparate ways in which power and resistance tend to be exercised in institutional settings such as schools. Those in authority generally exercise greater power when faced with resistance, expecting that acts of resistance will be minimized as a result. The problem with this scenario, this sequence of cause/effect encounters, is that in *schools*, resistance to the engagement of learning results in limitations with respect to students' future life chances. If an adolescent exercises resistance to authority at her part-time job, she might be fired—and even forego the possibility of a reference on her next application. But this resistance will probably not restrict her long-term ability to succeed. If, however, student resistance leads to disengagement from learning—from the curiosity, confidence, and critical thought necessary to be a full participant in a democratic society—then that young person suffers significant disadvantages.

In this vein, let's consider how which institutional power limits the freedom of those within it, particularly students, by considering the ways in

Table 9.1. Examples of Power, Resistance, and Institutional Responses

POWER	*RESISTANCE*	*INSTITUTIONAL RESPONSE*
Teacher assigns homework	Student does not do homework	Low grade/possible start of discipline cycle
Teacher reports suspected abuse	Child/family denies allegation	Investigation ensues
Principal disciplines student for insubordination	Student vandalizes school property	Student is arrested
Staff development activity is mandated by administration	Teacher does not attend	Teacher is written up; letter placed in file
Attendance is compulsory	Student skips school	Student enters discipline cycle/is potentially dropped from school

which power is exercised over students in schools. How much control over their own achievement do students have?

It is widely believed that students control their achievement in school. The prevailing myth looks something like Figure 9.1

The notion behind this myth is that all students have educational opportunities and, therefore, each student has an equal choice: to (comply and) succeed, or to (resist and) fail. There are three major (and myriad minor) flaws with this notion. First, students do not have equal educational opportunities. This phenomenon is widely documented and, in general, relates to the socioeconomic status of the families and the communities in which schools are situated. Second, compliance—as has been argued throughout this book with respect to literacy, in particular—does not necessarily correspond to success. Compliance in public schools serving poor and working-class communities may not provide access to critical literacies or to the types of skills needed to thrive in college or university settings. And third, the graphic illustrating the extent of control students exert over their success or failure is more accurately portrayed as something like Figure 9.2:

Since resistance is an integral component of power, levels of resistance can be linked to the levels of power being exercised over various participants in the process of schooling. Students, then, over whom such significant levels and forms of are power being exerted, can be expected to resist. The system of schooling itself virtually guarantees it.

We know that, generally speaking, student resistance inhibits achievement. What can teachers, as part of the institution of schooling, do to reduce the negative effects of student resistance? The first step, of course,

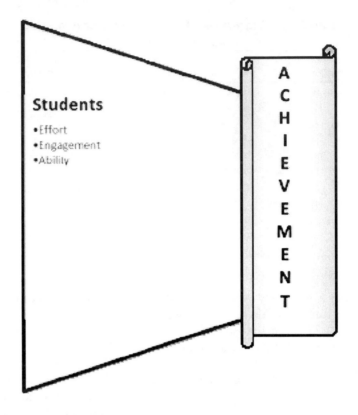

Figure 9.1.   The myth of student achievement.

is to understand the nature of resistance, as well as its relations to power and agency. Lois McNay (2000) defines agency as the "ability to act in an unexpected fashion or to institute new and unanticipated modes of behavior." This conception of agency fits well with the skills and dispositions of critical literacy, in that educators hope to foster students who are creative thinkers capable of constructing and critiquing knowledge. Resistance literacy expands on critical literacy by deliberately capitalizing on the existence of student resistance in ways that foster empowerment. According to the National Council of Teachers of English (NCTE, 2004), "Literacy's link to community and identity means that it can be a site of resistance for adolescents. When students are not recognized for bringing valuable, multiple-literacy practices to school, they can become resistant to school-based literacy."

Relative to power and literacy, then, it is important to ask two questions: What opportunities, in school, do students have to exercise agency

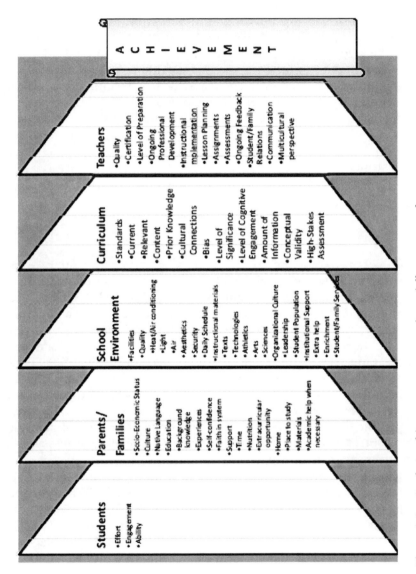

Students
- Effort
- Engagement
- Ability

Parents/ Families
- Socio-Economic Status
- Culture
- Native Language
- Education
- Background knowledge
- Experiences
- Self-confidence
- Faith in system
- Support
- Time
- Nutrition
- Extracurricular opportunity
- Home
- Place to study
- Materials
- Academic help when necessary

School Environment
- Facilities
- Quality
- Heat/Air conditioning
- Light
- Air
- Aesthetics
- Security
- Daily Schedule
- Instructional materials
- Texts
- Technologies
- Athletics
- Arts
- Sciences
- Organizational Culture
- Leadership
- Student Population
- Institutional Support
- Extra help
- Enrichment
- Student/Family Services

Curriculum
- Standards
- Current
- Relevant
- Content
- Prior Knowledge
- Cultural Connections
- Bias
- Level of Significance
- Level of Cognitive Engagement
- Amount of Information
- Conceptual Validity
- High-Stakes Assessment

Teachers
- Quality
- Certification
- Level of Preparation
- Ongoing Professional Development
- Instructional implementation
- Lesson Planning
- Assignments
- Assessments
- Ongoing Feedback
- Student/Family Relations
- Communication
- Multicultural perspective

ACHIEVEMENT

Figure 9.2.   Student achievement as a systemic, socially constructed process.

in ways that are productive and do not inhibit learning? And how can educators not only minimize the negative effects of resistance, but also exploit resistance to benefit students.

I believe there are two possibilities of accomplishing this goal: first, students can be provided with increased controls over their own choices vis-à-vis literacy to minimize their desire to resist school and schooling in ways that inhibit potential empowerment. That is, we can increase students' opportunity to exercise freedom and agency. Second, educators can capitalize on resistance that does emerge in order to develop instructional activities that build on the critique and critical thinking that resistance expresses. That is, tap into resistance as a means of engaging students and enhancing literacy proficiency. "Resistance literacy" encompasses both of these concepts.

EXERCISING AGENCY

Recent work has examined the role of writing classes as a site of social change for working-class students in postsecondary educational institutions (Bizzell, Cooper, Okawa, Malinowitz, & Cushman, 1998; Gos, 1995; Grimm, 1998; Mitchell, 1994). Writing well commands power and Grimm notes that writing well "means projecting certainty, confidence, and clarity" (p. 1). She asserts that composition instruction serves to regulate identity, and argues that "learning literacy is not necessarily liberating" (p. 2) because of class-based inequalities. In composition classrooms, middle-class definitions of what is "normal" become the basis for instruction and assessment. This type of coercive symbolic violence perpetuates the privileging/problematizing of the individual and simultaneously maintains the myth that literacy is inherently transformational. In reality, Grimm argues, "class forms the basis of composition" (p. 5).

In considering the cultural struggles of working class adult students in postsecondary academies, Livingston and Sawchuck (2000) argue that working-class students frequently and invisibly enact agency through creative cultural practices, including writing. Echoing the work by Collins (1993) on writing instruction and the work of Willis (1977) and MacLeod (1995) on working-class identity formation, Livingston and Sawchuck describe the phenomenon of "discursive penetration," a practice through which working-class students exercise agency by constructing oppositional cultures through and in written discourse. Christopher and Whitson (1999), in arguing for a theory of working-class literature, elaborate on the nature of working-class identity as it relates to literacy development. They note that working-class discursive identities are constructed against the "other" of the middle class, and that working-class discourse is perceived as a "subspecies" of bourgeois literacy, a resistance culture that is perceived to be in binary opposition to the dominant culture. In exploring the characteristics of working-class literacies, Christopher and Whitson begin by considering the written representations of the working class. Cultural characteristics of working-class literature uncovered include suppression of individuality, waiting for change rather than effecting it, distrust of authority, and orientation toward communal rather than individual development. Composition and literature in schooling privilege middle-class values like individualism, upward mobility and glorification of authority. Christopher and Whitson argue that these elements work against the cultural orientation of working-class students as writers in the academy. They explain the effect of teachers who uncritically promote middle-class discourse in writing classrooms:

> Such teachers may think they're generously helping a "poor kid" succeed, but what they are actually doing is erasing the idea that working-class culture has its own exceptional people who do not choose to leave their culture.
>
> The idea that any exceptional person will leave the working class and want to become middle class represents a facile acceptance of the myth of the American dream—that upward mobility and "success" are available to anyone deserving. What is actually at work here, in the propagation of this myth, is something not at all innocuous—the demand that working-class students see their culture of origin through the eyes of the middle class, as something to be abandoned in order to join the intellectual world. (p. 79)

Grimm (1998) describes college composition classes as a "repeated regulated performance of a required subjectivity for students" (p. 13). She asserts that uncritical views of composition work do not promote student agency; in fact, she encourages ambivalence as essential to the development of empowering written discourse. After describing ambivalence as "at the heart of agency" (p. 19), Grimm elaborates: "Appropriately mobilized, a sense of ambivalence might be put to constructive uses in writing" (p. 14). She then connects this idea to the nature of writing instruction in college composition classrooms, noting how agency is undermined through academic applications of written discourse: "It is irrational to believe that in matching the specifications of the assignment, students are learning to exercise agency in writing or taking ownership of texts" (p. 19).

Despite of wealth of current research about working-class student writers in post-secondary educational settings, research exploring how students and teachers in a working-class high school experience academic practices of writing is limited to practitioner-oriented work—texts that tend to identify problems and then pose solutions. Finn's (1999) work provides a theoretical and pedagogical framework for empowering working class students through literacy. This work, while providing invaluable contributions to the field of writing pedagogy, does not address the deep influences of written discourse on the identities of students and teachers. This study builds on that work explored how students and teachers experience writing in their daily school activities. Discourse and literacy are integral to identity, and, in academic institutions, working-class identities are marginalized. MacKenzie (1998) explains the ideology that working-class students experience in school: "The message is this: Working-class students must remediate their identities, and most them will receive little or no respect until they do" (as cited in Van Galen & Noblit, 2007, p. 11).

It can be difficult for educators in public schools serving poor and working-class communities to develop and implement practices that embody the notion of increasing student agency. What do these ideas look like and how do they apply "on the ground" with real students and real teachers in real classrooms? The answer is both simple and impossible complex, because it involves the establishment and promotion of a critical stance. One example from the high school where the study was conducted illustrates this idea.

CHALLENGING TEXTS

In my ninth grade English classes in the school where the study was conducted, I liked to start the year with short stories that are engaging, timely, and provocative. One recent fall, a review of our anthology revealed an ideal choice: Liam O'Flaherty's "The Sniper" (1923). The story relates closely to the author's experience as a soldier in the Irish Civil War. It describes an encounter between a sniper and his target in a brief, descriptive, suspenseful vignette. With the sniper fire in the Iraq war dominating the news, the story's plot was current and had a natural authenticity.

To make it easy for students to read the story, even without carrying home our unwieldy, anthology (it weighs over five pounds), I found free online access to the short story. As I read through the online version and compared it to the one in our text, I noticed that there were discrepancies. One involves a point in the story where the sniper is hit in the arm by a bullet. The two versions are listed in Figure 9.3.

Considering the cultural milieu of the author which is clearly relevant in these references (this civil war did involve religion, after all), the editorial omissions seemed disingenuous and offensive.

After a day or so of cathartic seething, it occurred to me that this incident offered a possibility to engage students in a multicultural endeavor.

Original Story	Anthology
"His forearm was dead. 'Christ,' he muttered, 'I'm hit.'"	"His forearm was dead. . . . He muttered, 'I'm hit.'"
"his right arm was paining him like a thousand devils."	"his right arm was paining him..."

Figure 9.3.   Original and edited versions of "The Sniper."

What if *they* challenged the authority of our text by evaluating its editorial choices? The opportunity seemed perfect; I began to compose the lesson.

The ellipses in the anthology made it easy for students to discover the omitted words. We talked at length about literature and textbooks, especially issues such as who decides what to include and how and why such decisions are made. Discussions involved power, money, and political influence. Students researched textbook policies and considered their reactions to the edited words in the original as well as their elimination from the anthology. Finally, students composed letters to the editors of the anthology, indicating whether or not they agreed with the editorial decisions and providing reasons for their positions.

In their letters, about two-thirds of the students criticized the editors for censorship. They asserted that, as teenagers, they had the capacity to understand the words in context and to evaluate potentially offensive language without being influenced or upset. A handful of students praised the editors for being sensitive to people who might be offended for religious reasons. And the rest of the students answered with ambivalence; they explained that they both agreed and disagreed with the editorial decision. They understood the complexity of the editors' task and expressed multifaceted insights. I was pleased that the students had drawn conclusions and that they could see the text as a human construction with which they might engage, rather than a rigid source of authority. Satisfied with our efforts, I composed a cover letter to the editors and sent the package to the publisher.

Exactly 2 weeks later, we received a response. The vice president and editorial director sent my students a marvelous letter in which she acknowledged their correspondence, commending my students for their thoughtful presentation of both sides of the issue. In addition, she specifically addressed power relations with regard to the changes to "The Sniper." She explained that editors do not have complete autonomy regarding editing decisions, and that school districts or state school boards in some regions where their books are used have restrictions about using God's name, profanity, or references to the occult. She also noted that changes are never made without the permission of the author or other copyright holder.

I copied the letter and distributed it to my students, who read it with delight. The editor had taken their responses seriously, and had replied with gratitude for their input. My working class students, who are schooled to resist authority even as they accept the immutability of the status quo, had a sense of how to use language for their own empowerment. I felt that I had begun to approach Sleeter's (1996) standards for multicultural teacher activism.

Based on her research, Sleeter (1996) delineates four tenets for teachers: First, a teacher must "recognize the ethical dimensions of teaching other people's children" (p. 246). As the parent of children who attend my school, this precept was effortless. I could teach these children as if they were my own because I could envision my own children in my classroom. Her second principle involves initiating constructive dialogue with students and community members. It is essential to understand the culture of a community without perceiving it as deficient, and to be sensitive to disparities in power. Educators can be critical of families without appreciating cultural differences; this approach is detrimental to the teaching-learning process. Third, Sleeter requires teachers to become advocates for marginalized groups, promoting political action that advances social justice. Fostering a school culture of support rather than blame is vital for student success. Fourth, Sleeter asserts that:

> a teacher who takes the social movement metaphor seriously teaches children and youth to act politically, to advocate both individually and collectively for themselves and for other marginalized people. Young people can learn to affect their social world quite powerfully....
>
> Children and youth who learn to use the democratic process effectively to advance ideals of social justice can become adults who are able to actualize the ideals of justice and equality through the political process. (p. 247)

Although we hadn't engaged in civic action per se, I did feel that this activity had made my students feel more capable of challenging textual authority. They had used language as a source of empowerment by critiquing a symbol of authority, and the human representative of that symbol had validated their assertions. These students, who tend to resist authority even as they accept the immutability of the status quo, had a sense of how to use language for empowerment.

Moreover, this endeavor required less *curricular* revision than it did a shift in perspective. I did not abandon any of the traditional objectives connected with teaching short stories in a ninth grade English class; I simply added a critical stance designed to enable students to begin to understand that texts are social constructions and that their experiences and opinions matter.

Our goal, then, as teachers who embrace the first tenet of resistance literacy (enhancing opportunities for students to exercise agency) it so provide opportunities for students to have both choice and voice in their school-based literacy experiences.

TAPPING INTO RESISTANCE

The second facet of resistance literacy involves accepting genuine expressions of resistance as an opportunity to establish dialogue and to reinforce a dialogic pedagogical approach. By listening, respecting, and responding to cultural norms without judgment, teachers can seek to coconstruct a classroom where transformations can occur and where resistance can signify the initiation of dialogue and a struggle that results in mutual learning and movement toward liberatory learning and social justice (Freire, 1968/2007). Again, implementation is both deceptively simple and incredibly challenging, since it involves a conscious shift in perspective. This example also involves my work with Grade 11 students in the school where the study on which this book is based was conducted.

Tapping into student resistance requires the deliberate creation of a caring, responsive classroom because "Caring, responsive classroom environments enable students to take ownership of literacy activities and can counteract negative emotions that lead to lack of motivation" (NCTE, 2004)

With my 11th grade students, putting involved listening to their vocal, passionate complaints about my announcement of the beginning of our poetry unit. Their reaction stunned me; since we were well into the school year, I had been certain that they trusted me not to use literature —even poetry—as a form of academic torture. However, their reactions were so spontaneous and candid that I caught a glimpse of the 6-year-olds who had become 16, 17, and even—in a few cases—18. They whined, slumped, and moaned. They grumbled, squirmed, and complained. Like small children, their responses were immediate and genuine, their revulsion displayed both physically and verbally. "I *hate* it. I never *get* it. Why do we have to *read* that stuff?"

Like many teachers who spend considerable amounts of time and energy planning instruction that is intended to be engaging for students, my first reaction to their protests was defensive. But my interest in student resistance allowed me to consider their reactions as an invitation to begin a dialogue. So we talked. I asked about their previous experiences with poetry, in school and out of school. Even the few students who quietly acknowledged their enjoyment of writing or reading poetry outside of school admitted no connection between this activity and the analysis of poems in English classes. If *these* students weren't excited about a poetry unit, who in this school would be?

My reaction to resistance was significant. Teachers experience pressure from numerous fronts, and a teacher's initial reaction to student resistance is likely to be defensive and angry. Good teachers are highly devoted to their content and methods. Excellent teachers spend time and energy investing imagination and passion into their lessons. Furthermore, effective teachers care about whether students learn relevant content.

When students respond with resistance, it is natural for teachers to feel disappointed, unappreciated, and upset. They may also be anxious about how students' resistance may affect their ability to earn high school credentials, since demonstration of content knowledge is critical to passing mandatory assessments. Despite these very real concerns, it is essential for teachers to reflect on classroom reactions and, even more importantly, those of our students.

It is in the spaces of struggle that structure and agency are destabilized and we can see our educational and social contexts as in flux (Weis, 2004). This does not, of course, imply that when students complain, teachers ought to capitulate. We must neither ignore nor romanticize resistance; however, we must recognize and respect it (Graf, 1999).

As a teacher, I could my value students' sociocultural norms without neglecting their need for exposure to mine. I recognized that, in this situation, developing a positive disposition toward poetry was more important than understanding literary terminology. If I could help my students develop a disposition to appreciate poetry, I could build a bridge toward cultural capital—a bridge that would not invalidate their own language experiences.

A traditional poetry unit in which we studied characteristics of poems, read about authors, and explored literary eras, might have reinforced the students' ability to analyze poetry according to an academic rubric. However, such instruction would fail to promote critical thought or to engage student resistance. I considered the possibility that, instead, students might engage with poetry in a personal way, to read poems that they enjoyed, to attain power through and experience pleasure in the very genre of poetry.

I imagined students learning to see themselves as readers and writers of poetry. An internet search with this possibility in mind led me to the *Favorite Poem Project* (Pinsky, 1997). I spent the first day of this unit reading aloud to the class, sharing poems that I loved, and poems that I did NOT love. I intentionally sought to provide a subjective space for them to dislike poetry, hoping that that might open a space for appreciation as well. Agency, it seemed to me, ought to flow in both directions.

By the end of the third class period, every student had selected and orally interpreted a "favorite poem" for the class. Selections ranged from Silverstein's nonsense verses to war protest poetry. The rest of the unit was equally rewarding. Students wrote their own poems and read them to the class. They responded to one another's work, sharing critiques and compliments. But the highlight of the unit was when an entry from a male student (who was a captain of the school's wrestling team) won second place in the school's poetry contest. When Vern's name was announced at a school-wide assembly, a series of emotions crossed his face: shock, dismay, and then—most amazingly—pride. By the end of class that day, this student was signing copies of the school literary magazine in which his poem appeared. He had, publicly, become a poet!

I was pleased at the outcome of the Favorite Poetry Project; after meeting the unit objectives, students no longer held an uncritical perspective of poetry. They had established personal connections with at least one work of poetry and provided public explanations for their choices—empowering activities that do not typify educational norms of working-class schools (Gos, 1995). Their resistance had not blocked effective learning; it had become a lever that enhanced the curriculum.

CONCLUSION

Through explication and empathy, we had used dialogue transform their experience of the literacy, allowing our working class students the opportunity to think of themselves as classmates with people outside of their own cultural norms.

Both "The Sniper" and the poetry unit began with an academic, middle-class assumption: that what was being taught was, in fact, obviously worth learning. As a teacher, I believe in the value of literary analysis. However, the content of my class was altered by the students' reactions—their candid resistance. They were resisting; I had to listen.

In conclusion, schools, as social institutions are necessarily infused with exercises of power. These exercises of power naturally result in student resistance, which can inhibit literacy learning. Two ways of addressing the negative effects of such resistance include expanding student choice and tapping into student resistance. If educators can provide spaces for resistance to become constructive, spaces where students have a choice and a voice, spaces where their native literacies are invited into schools, we can engage reluctant readers and writers in ways that will enable them to be successful students and, more importantly, successful and literate makers of meaning in society.

REFERENCES

Bizzell, P., Cooper, M., Okawa, G., Malinowitz, H., & Cushman, E. (1998, April 2). *Teaching writing for social change.* Paper presented at the Conference on College Composition and Communication, Chicago, IL.

Christopher, R., & Whitson, C. (1999, Spring). Toward a theory of working class literature. *Thought and action: The NEA Higher Education Journal,* 71-81.

Collins, J. (1993). Determination and contradiction: An appreciation and critique of the work of Pierre Bourdieu on language and education. In C. Calhoun (Ed.), *Bourdieu: Critical perspectives* (pp. 116-138). Chicago, IL: University of Chicago Press.

Finn. P. (1999). *Literacy with attitude: Educating working-class children in their own self-interest.* Albany, NY: State University of New York Press.

Foucault, M. (1975). *Discipline and punish: The birth of the prison* (A. Sheridan, Trans. 2nd ed.). New York: Vintage.

Foucault, M. (1983). The subject and power. In H. L. Dreyfus & P. Rabinow (Eds.), *Michel Foucault: Beyond structuralism and hermeneutics.* Chicago, IL: University of Chicago

Foucault, M. (1993). Power as knowledge. In C. Lemert (Ed.), *Social theory: The multicultural and classic readings.* Toronto Canada: Canada HarperCollins.

Freire, P. (2007). *Pedagogy of the oppressed.* New York, NY: Continuum. (Original work published 1968

Gos, M. (1995). Overcoming social class markers: Preparing working class students for college. *The WAC Clearing House 2005*(Special Issue: Panoramas and Vistas: New Direction in Writing Instruction).

Graf, G. (1999). The academic language gap. *The Academic Clearing House ,* 72(3), 140-142.

Grimm, N. M. (1998, April). *Redesigning academic identity kits.* Paper presented at the Conference on College Composition and Communication, Chicago, IL.

Livingstone, D. W., & Sawchuck, P. (2000). Beyond cultural capital theory: Hidden dimensions of working class learning. *Review of Education, Pedagogy and Cultural Studies,* 22(2), 121-146.

MacKenzie, L. (1998). A pedagogy of respect: Teaching as an ally of working-class college students. In A. Shepard, J. McMillan, & G. Tate (Eds.), *Coming to class: Pedagogy and the social class of teachers* (pp. 94-116). Portsmouth, England: Boynton/Cook.

MacLeod, J. (1995). *Ain't no makin' it: Aspirations and attainment in a low-income neighborhood.* Boulder, CO: Westview Press.

McNay, L. (2000). *Gender and Agency: Reconfiguring the subject in feminist and social theory.* Oxford, England: Polity Press.

Mitchell, J. P. (1994). *Money, class, and curriculum: A freshman composition reading unit.* Unpublished Journal Article accepted to *Writing on the Edge*, University of Mississippi.

National Council of Teachers of English Commission on Reading. (2004). *Adolescent literacy: A policy research brief.* Urbana, IL: Author.

O'Flaherty, L. (1923, January 12). The sniper. *The New Leader.*

Pinsky, R. (1997). *Favorite poem project.* Retrieved from http://www.favoritepoem.org

Sleeter, C. E. (1996, Autumn). Multicultural education as a social movement. *Theory into Practice, 35*, 239-247.

Van Galen, J. A., & Noblit, G. W. (Eds.). (2007). *Late to class: Social class and schooling in the new economy.* Albany, NY: State University of New York Press.

Weis, L. (2004). *Class reunion.* New York, NY: Routledge.

Willis, P. (1977). *Learning to labor: How working class kids get working class jobs.* New York, NY: Columbia University Press.

CHAPTER 10

LOOKING FORWARD

Empowerment, Social Justice, and Collective Agency

CONSTRUCTING CONVERSATIONS

High-stakes tests are reinforcing redefinitions of knowledge (empirical, not constructivist, and situated in the authority of the state), re-socialization of teachers, and the construction of identities that reproduce working-class conceptions of knowledge but middle-class neoliberal norms of meritocracy and individualism. Privileging an individualistic conception of learning and literacy limits the possibilities for collective action rooted in the (shifting reformations of the) working class—collective action that might result in the realization of resistance and political reform consistent with social justice.

Success in the new capitalism requires more than the types of literacy promoted in school. However, teachers in this working-class school enact pedagogical and literate identities that are consistent with the old capitalism. Their approach to learning and literacy is non-dialogic and they unwittingly promote a conception of writing and thinking that is domesticating and noncritical. Acting as agents of the state and in the shadow of high-stakes assessments, teachers in this school are preparing students

Power, Resistance, and Literacy: Writing for Social Justice, pp. 211–219
Copyright © 2011 by Information Age Publishing

to fill service occupations at the low end of the economic spectrum. Despite reform rhetoric of "high standards" and "critical thinking," these students are likely to construct working-class identities in the new capitalism, where they will learn that "the need for higher academic standards is disconnected from labor market data that predict that most students will face low-wage work involving only minimum cognitive skills" (Van Galen & Noblit, 2007, p. 11). Neoliberalism and the new capitalism have all but silenced the collective discourse of the White working class with respect to labor power. Young people today must reconstruct their identities in a society saturated by the rhetoric of equality but filled with institutions that reproduce inequality. Moreover, the generation Gee refers to as "Millennials" has only experienced life within the new capitalism. Van Galen states that

> Students who once might have grown up understanding the inherently contradictory interests of bosses and workers from the artifacts of their parents' union involvement, now have little or no access to discourse about worker interests. (p. 11)

Teachers in this working-class school count on their unions to negotiate salaries and benefits commensurate with their education and experience. (In this particular community, public school teacher salaries are far higher than the median income of most residents.) Although state reform initiatives are forcing teacher re-socialization toward working-class aspects of their occupation, teachers seem unaware of the potential connections with their working-class students and families. Current economic, political, and cultural conditions suggest two possible reasons for this. First, most of the teachers in this school were educated in working-class communities and may not themselves have experience with sociocultural approaches to learning, empowering literacies, or meaningful challenges to authorities. Second, as relatively new members of the professional managerial class in an economic environment where security is precarious (and in a political climate where they are being deprofessionalized), teachers may feel the need to maintain their social status in part by constructing identities *against* working-class Others. Regardless of the root causes, the regulatory nature of the testing regime reinstantiates the hegemonic relationships between teachers and students. Teachers are being judged by their students' performance on high-stakes state assessments yet, although there are glimpses of shared frustration (e.g., teachers who admit to students that test-based writing is inauthentic), significant protestations are nonexistent. Occasional discursive resistance notwithstanding, all teachers comply with state regulations. Students comply as participants in the testing regime as well; even the most resistant students take the examinations. Student resistance manifests at the classroom level, so students who resist are perceived (by themselves and by others) to fail as a result of their own poor choices.

The high-stakes testing-based accountability reform movement has had negative effects on students' experiences of schooling where the rhetoric of "no child left behind" purports to serve the needs of those most likely to be harmed by high-stakes tests. The discursive power of this message and its underlying neoliberal agenda causes working-class students to blame themselves for their inability to excel at performing academic literacies. Brantlinger (2007) describes how the cycle of blame is perpetuated through hegemonic discourse:

> In contrast to the invisibility of structural discrimination for affluent people, low-income parents and adolescents see and resent class-based practices. At the same time, illustrating the power of hegemonic discourse, to some extent low-income people share the dominant class perspective that their class is less smart, worthy, and respectable. Clearly, they internalize the distorted messages produced and circulated by dominant classes. Hence, they vacillate between blaming the system and blaming themselves. Self-blame results in their not protesting entitlements given to higher classes. (p. 242)

Whether cognizant or ignorant of the institutional, structural factors that affect their achievement, including the displacement of resources that served to enable earlier generations to survive working-class jobs, working-class Millennials are likely to accept their fate as their fault (Gee, 2004; Van Galen & Noblit, 2007).

Discourse acquisition, which includes practices of literacy such as writing, is coupled with identity construction. Identity construction constitutes and occurs within social institutions like schools. The possibilities students imagine are shaped, in part, by their interactions with teachers. Teachers, then, are often perceived as the key to social justice. While this prospect is promising, obstacles exist, particularly in the area of empowering literacy. Teachers have been socialized and acculturated into a form of academic literacy which Gee (2004) notes is relevant but currently insufficient for success in the new economy. Gee states that

> Just as we educators are beginning to get a handle on the issues connected to poor and minority children acquiring the languages and identities connected to schooling, our new capitalist, high-tech, global world is changing the nature of identities at play in the world and their connections to literacies and knowledge. (p. 94)

Clearly, the rules for success in the workforce have changed. However, teachers working in schools charged to prepare students for the new capitalism are themselves unprepared. In general, teachers in this study do not signify fluency with new literacies. Acquisition would require them to participate in another (perhaps more socially critical) identity. In fact, data analysis indicates that teachers in this working-class school are reconstructing their identities, reconciling middle-class aspirations with professional roles that are being reformed toward working-class norms. Neoliberal political philosophies and standards-based reform initiatives have had powerful effects on the roles of teachers. The state has reinstantiated the autonomy of literacy practices in examinations and teachers have appropriated the features of the examinations to guide their classroom literacy practices. Compulsory examinations foster a culture of compliance; resistance is perceived as hazardous and futile. Data in this study indicate that teachers' identities are being re-socialized toward application of pedagogies that promote literacies of exclusion and domestication, not empowerment. Current political realities provide an image of contradiction as schooling is promoted as a route to empowerment even as its everyday dynamics foster social reproduction.

Many scholars have looked to teacher resistance as a route to social justice. A few teachers in this study narrate resistance on a philosophical level even as they enact test-based instruction that they acknowledge as deficient. Some teachers and students indicate a grasp of the possibilities that writing can offer in terms of critical thinking. However, there is little evidence that such possibilities are being acted upon, at least within the school setting. And as teachers continue to experience the effects of re-socialization in the new global economy (where unions which now offer some stability have all but disappeared), it is likely that their power to enact change will diminish.

Student resistance offers another possibility for social justice; however, the extent to which knowledge and thought is reduced to a state-sanctioned hegemonic canon of facts and skills makes it difficult for working-class students to muster the means to resist. Their teachers and parents model acceptance of an individual, meritocratic social structure. Unlike students whose families have the resources to provide alternative forms of education, students in public schools have no choice but to pass state examinations to earn a high-school diploma. Students who resist the alienating curricula and parroting of texts that these exams require face dire consequences. Such students will enter the workforce without the basic high school credential; some will also lack the "basic" academic literacies to perform low-level service jobs. They also lack the confidence necessary to think of themselves as "smart and creative people" (Gee, 2004, p.13).

Although neoliberal policies supporting high-stakes tests can serve to limit students' possibilities by redefining what it means to be educated, there is room for optimism. Writing is a way of reimagining the possibilities for the future. Writing is a means of helping students imagine how to enact the agency within their resistance.

> Fundamentally, … the purpose of composition is ideological. Lacking the physical presence of an author, writing is potentially subversive of fixed subject-positions. Its significance is elusive, plural and variable. Writing comes to function, for Derrida, as the repressed Other of philosophical objectivity. As such, writing has been lionized and exalted by postmodern theorists as alterior, oppositional, and even feminine. Derridean terminology, which describes writing as embodying the freeplay of representation, carries a powerful rhetorical impact which allies the concept of writing with that of liberation, of libidinal freedom from repressive reason. (Hawkes, 1999, para. 10)

Since literacy practices are ideological, interrupting existing practices of literacy can open spaces for interrupting the ideology that (re)produces hegemonic power relations. Enacting critical literacy through writing offers the possibility to name class stratification without reproducing it (Van Galen & Noblit, 2007). As The New Literacy maintains, it is important to examine the sociocultural assumptions that underlie what it means to be literate, educated, and worthy of respect in our society. The dominant discourse today has appropriated what ought to be a dialogue about this issue, substituting slogans whose appeal hides their actual effects (e.g., No Child Left Behind legislation, in reality, increases the likelihood that the most vulnerable students will suffer dreadful academic and economic consequences). Powerful discourse is not easily interrupted; however it can be done.

Because direct resistance to high-stakes assessments will most certainly result in exclusion (for students, from credentials; for teachers, from employment), other measures must be considered. Consistent with the norms of the working-class identity, teachers and students in working-class settings can work together to challenge the status quo. Collective action, constituted from and through a sociocultural epistemology, provides a possibility for reform. Communities of practice wherein new literacies are explored and "ground rules" for academic literacies are made explicit suggest a space for change. Students situated in working-class schools need not "check their skills at the door" (Miller & Borowicz, 2005) as long as their teachers are prepared and willing to engage in dialogue. Newell (2005) reveals the possibilities of such an approach:

> as we consider what culturally significant ideas will be part of the curricular conversation, we must also know whom we are teaching. We will need to work top-down from a curricular perspective and bottom-up from our

understanding of classroom life and the teachers and students who live there both materially and socially. (p. 246)

The individualistic, meritocratic ideology of capitalism which permeates schooling makes it difficult to collect the resistance that always exists within relations of power (Foucault, 1993). Like knowledge, "writing is not value-neutral" (Newell, 2005, p. 217). Practices of writing (like other aspects of literacies) shape and are shaped by cultures and interrelations of power. Newell contends that writing plays a role in

> challenging or perpetuating social positions and injustices of members of various groups (Bell, 1997). The emergence of culturally responsive pedagogy, and the role that writing might play in these different ways of teaching and knowing, will help to elucidate how writing is used in communities to advance individual and communal goals in recursive cycles of activity. (p. 217)

The fragility of the working-class identity in the new economy, coupled with the anxieties associated with high-stakes testing, exacerbates the concern with which these young people face their futures. Writing instruction that is based on high-stakes testing advances neither the individual goals of these students nor the communal goals of their (social) classmates. A sociocultural approach to literacy and writing offers the possibility to engage students and teachers in ways that can empower both groups.

The alienating, commodifying, socially reproductive aspects of capitalism cannot be ameliorated by unidirectional resistance. To move toward social justice, resistance must emerge from both the scholarly community (which might include the teaching profession) and the working-class students whose needs are not being served by the current educational system. Because teachers straddle the class divide, embodying aspects of working-class and middle-class portfolios of experience, they too stand to benefit from reforms that enhance opportunities for the working class.

EXTENDING THE DIALOGUE

My work brings together scholarship connected to two subfields of education: sociology of education and pedagogies of education. Sociology of education tends to focus on how schools as social institutions function with respect to socioeconomic and political factors and how hegemonic forces affect and are affected by schooling. Scholars specializing in pedagogical aspects of education tend to look at how experiences of teaching and learning can interrupt existing power relations. Both subfields, however, converge on the purpose of fostering social justice.

The current reform movement claims to have raised standards (including those for literacy and writing) for student achievement, particularly for students who would have been "left behind" otherwise. But data in this study indicate that structuralist epistemologies have been reinforced by the implementation of high-stakes assessments. These epistemologies result in pedagogies that lead to domesticating writing, in which the authorial possibilities of students are reduced to parroting ideas of authorities in which power is already instantiated. These conditions reproduce the status quo.

Writing instruction is an essential aspect of education because language is a vehicle for thinking and discourse is a key constituent of identity. The way a person imagines herself in the world is affected by her language experiences, and the language experiences of students in this school (in particular with respect to writing) do not liberate possibilities for imagining oneself. Instead, they limit discursive possibilities. Students do not learn to imagine themselves as authentic writers who use written language to hone, explore and express their thoughts. Instead, they learn that knowledge and, therefore, thinking are instantiated in authorities and that learning is measured by performance on state assessments. Neither compliance nor resistance is effective in challenging the reproduction of social class identities that these conditions reinforce. Their middle-class and upper-class counterparts are likely to develop skills in academic writing and thinking that these students lack. Although a few Pontiac High students may, through experiences that occur beyond the walls of this inner-ring suburban public school, develop discursive identities that facilitate greater possibilities, most of them will not. Their ability to become shape-shifting portfolio people who envision themselves as intelligent and creative is restricted by their experiences of schooling.

Teachers in this school are experiencing deprofessionalization and, as they lose control and become alienated from their labor, are being resocialized toward norms of working-class identity. While this may result in replication of power relations historically prevalent in working-class schools, it also offers the possibility for seeking solidarity. If teachers can seek to learn about and *from* the culture of their working-class students (with the intent of developing connections that foster a space for constructive resistance to destructive neoliberal reform), pedagogical and social progress might occur. The collective power of working-class resistance is latent in this new economy and the reconstruction of a White working-class identity that includes teachers and students as partners rather than adversaries is an exciting prospect.

Multicultural, critical pedagogies incorporate a sociocultural perspective that facilitates student and teacher (as well as the synergy of student-and-teacher) agency in the pursuit of social justice. White working-class students are not typically considered in relation to multicultural initiatives, so it may not be immediately apparent that they can be disadvantaged by a structuralist rather than a sociocultural pedagogical approach. Because students at Pontiac High are White and suburban, and many have the accoutrements associated with "success" in the youth culture (i.e., cell phones, cars, computers, etc.), the need to access, understand and value their culture can be overlooked. In fact, White suburban working-class students would benefit from experiences of schooling that build on, rather than negate or reject, their cultural and discursive experiences. Multicultural initiatives grounded in sociocultural epistemologies might provide a means for these students to imagine possibilities beyond their inner-ring suburban neighborhood.

The standards-based reform movement has intensified the pressures on students and teachers in working-class schools. Increased economic disparities have resulted in increased social stratification, a condition which affects the experiences of students as they acquire literacies and ne-gotiate schooling. Shifting social relations complicate teachers' decisions with respect to pedagogical activities and curricular decisions. Students enact performances of compliance and resistance, and relational expecta-tions are constructed and reconstructed in these institutional dynamics. For the most part, students' constructions of social class are reproduced inside the walls of this working-class public high school.

Narrations of some students and teachers, however, reveal cracks in the walls of traditional schooling. In addition, research indicates that admin-istrators and teachers do not need to adopt test-preparatory pedagogies in order to help students succeed on examinations. Possibilities abound for pedagogical practices that serve dual purposes, providing transforma-tive educational and literacy experiences while simultaneously helping students develop the skills they need to pass high-stakes tests (Englert, Mariage, & Dunsmore, 2005; Miller & Borowicz, 2005; Newell, 2005). The New Literacy Studies and the movement toward employing formative assessments (Dorn, 2007) represent opportunities to combat the effects of high-stakes assessments on students and teachers. Despite the glimmers of hope that exist, the deep grammar of working-class schooling perme-ates this working-class school. To effect reform, all participants in the pro-cess of education must seek to widen the cracks in the walls. We have the tools: scholars have research, teachers provide authority and access, and students offer facility with new literacies. Collective resistance can reveal fractures in the walls of schooling and shed light on possibilities for social justice. Collective resistance can lead to transformation.

REFERENCES

Bell, L. A. (1997). Theoretical foundations for social justice in education. In M. Adams, L. A. Bell & P. Griffin (Eds.), *Teaching for diversity and social justice: A sourcebook* (pp. 3-15). New York, NY: Routledge.

Brantlinger, E. (2007). (Re)Turning to Marx to understand. In J. Van Galen & G. W. Noblit (Eds.), *Late to class: Social class and schooling in the new economy* (pp. 235-268). Albany, NY: State University of New York Press.

Dorn, S. (2007). *Accountability Frankenstein: Understanding and taming the monster*. Charlotte, NC: Information Age.

Englert, C. S., Mariage, T. V., & Dunsmore, K. (2005). Tenets of sociocultural theory in writing instruction research. In C. A. MacArthur, S. Graham & J. Fitzgerald (Eds.), *Handbook of Writing Research* (pp. 208-221). New York, NY: The Guilford Press.

Foucault, M. (1993). Power as knowledge. In C. Lemert (Ed.), *Social theory: The multicultural and classic readings*. Toronto Canada: Canada HarperCollins.

Gee, J. P. (2004). *Situated language and learning: A critique of traditional schooling*. New York, NY: Routledge.

Hawkes, D. (1999). Composition, capitalism and the new technology [Electronic Version]. *Bad Subjects*, 44. Retrieved from http://bad.eserver.org/issues/1999/44/hawkes.html

Miller, S., & Borowicz, S. (2005). *Why multimodal literacies? Designing digital bridges to 21st century teaching and learning*. Buffalo, NY: State University of New York Press.

Newell, G. E. (2005). Writing to learn: How alternative theories of school writing account for student performance. In C. A. MacArthur, S. Graham, & J. Fitzgerald (Eds.) *Handbook of Writing Research*. New York, NY: Guilford Press.

Van Galen, J. A., & Noblit, G. W. (Eds.). (2007). *Late to class: Social class and schooling in the new economy*. Albany, NY: State University of New York Press.

APPENDIXES

APPENDIX A

Interview Questions: STUDENTS

I. Background Questions

1. How long have you attended this school?
2. What grade/classes are you in now?
3. How would you describe yourself as a student?
4. How would your teachers describe you as a student?

II. Learning Literacy

1. Where did your parents go to school? What grade/level of did they finish?
2. Tell me about a negative writing experience.
3. What kinds of writing have you learned in school?
4. What kinds of writing do you do outside school?

III. Experiences as a Writer

1. How would you describe yourself as a writer?
2. What kinds of writing do you do in your classes (form and function)? For what purposes? How often?
3. What kinds of writing do you like to do? Why?
4. Tell me about a time when you loved to write.
5. Tell me about a time when you hated to write.
6. What kinds of writing do you dislike? Why?

7. Can you describe the process your writing (in each case) takes?
    a. Amount and quality of prewriting, including planning
8. What kinds responses do you get from writing you do?
9. Do you have any difficulties/challenges with regard to writing? If so, can you identify specific times and circumstances when the difficult began?
10. Does your English class impact your writing? If so, how?
11. What does it takes to be a good writer? Do you think you are a good writer? Why or why not?
12. Tell me about a time when you wrote something very important to you.

IV. Writing Instruction

1. How would your teachers describe you as a writer?
2. How would you describe your teachers as writers?
3. What is your goal as a student writer?
    • How do you try to accomplish this goal?
4. What types of assignments do you get?
    • On what topics?
    • How are the topics and forms of writing determined?
5. What classroom activities are associated with writing?
6. How is your writing assessed/graded?
    • Does the assessment affect you as a writer? How?
7. How could your teachers help you become a better writer?
8. How could your teachers make you want to write?
9. How would you change your school to improve writing instruction?
10. What effect, if any, have NYS exams had on you as a writer

V. Wrap up

1. To you, what is the best thing about writing?
2. What is the biggest challenge?
3. What most needs to be changed to make writing in school better?
    a. Why?
4. Does this school's writing instruction fulfill its purpose for most students? Does it help you?
5. Is there anything else about you as a writer/student that you'd like to share?
6. Is there anything that you think I have missed or that you think I should have asked you?
7. Is there anything else you would like to tell me?

APPENDIX B

Interview Questions: TEACHERS

I. Background Questions

1. How long have you been a teacher?
2. How long have you taught at this school?
3. What subject/classes do you teach?

II. Family/Educational Background

1. What is the educational background of your parents?
2. Where did you attend high school?
3. If you have children, where do they attend school?

III. Experiences as a Writer

1. How would you describe yourself as a writer?
2. What kinds of writing do you do? For what purposes? How often?
3. How would you describe your processes of writing?
4. What kinds of feedback does your writing elicit?
5. Does your writing impact your teaching? How?
6. Does your teaching affect you as a writer? How?
7. What do you think it takes to be a good writer? Are you a good writer? Why or why not?

IV. Student-Teacher Interactions

1. How would your students describe you as a teacher?
2. What students perform best in your classes?
3. What types of students have the most difficulty?
4. How would you characterize the students in this school in terms of ability and performance?
5. Has your teaching changed in the time you've been here? How?
6. Would you send your children to this school? Why or why not?

V. Teaching Writing

1. Where does writing fit into your curriculum?
2. How do you and your students use writing in your classes? How often do students write in class? Outside class?
3. What classroom activities are associated with writing?
4. What kinds of writing are assigned? For what purposes?

5. How do you develop assignments?
6. How do you assess student writing?
7. What coursework/in-service have you had that addresses writing instruction? How would you characterize these experiences? How have they affected you as a writer? As a teacher?
8. What factors impact your ability to help students become better writers?
9. How do NYS exams influence your use of writing in your classes?
10. How do interactions with administrators/colleagues/students/parents influence your uses of writing in the classes?
11. Has your approach to writing instruction changed over time? How?

VI. Students as Writers

1. How would you describe your students as writers?
2. How would students describe themselves as writers?
3. How do students respond when you ask them to write/assign writing? (personal responses—how to they react to the request and product response—what kind of work is turned in)
4. What is the biggest challenge student writers face?
5. What factors help students improve their writing?

VII. Wrap up

1. What is the biggest challenge about writing instruction?
2. What most needs to be changed to make students better writers/writing instruction better?
3. Does this school's writing instruction fulfill its purpose for most students? Why or why not?
4. Is there anything else about you as a teacher or writer that you'd like to address?
5. Is there anything else you'd like to tell me?

ABOUT THE AUTHOR

Julie Gorlewski is assistant professor of secondary education program at the State University of New York at New Paltz. Her research interests include social class and schooling, assessment, education reform, writing, and writing instruction, and youth culture. She has a PhD from the State University of New York at Buffalo in the social foundations of education, as well as certifications in secondary English and elementary education. She has over 15 years experience teaching secondary English in an inner ring suburban school district, where she also served as department chair, technology coordinator and learning center director. She has published numerous articles and book chapters and is currently editor of the *Research for the Classroom* column for the *English Journal*.